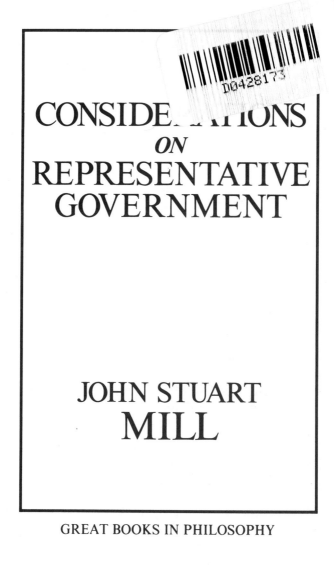

CONSIDERATIONS
ON
REPRESENTATIVE
GOVERNMENT

JOHN STUART
MILL

GREAT BOOKS IN PHILOSOPHY

Prometheus Books
Buffalo, New York

Published 1991 by Prometheus Books

Editorial offices located at 700 East Amherst Street, Buffalo,
New York 14215, and distribution facilities at 59 John Glenn
Drive, Amherst, New York 14228

Library of Congress Catalog Number: 90-63889
ISBN 0-87975-670-5

Printed on acid-free paper in the United States of America

Additional Volumes in Prometheus's Great Books in Philosophy Series

On God and Religion
by Bertrand Russell

On Liberty
by John Stuart Mill

Outlines of Pyrrhonism
by Sextus Empiricus

Paradoxes of Freedom
by Sidney Hook

The Philosophy of History
by Georg Wilhelm
    Friedrich Hegel

*Plato on Homosexuality:
Lysis, Phaedrus,*
and *Symposium*
by Plato

The Politics
by Aristotle

Pragmatism
by William James

The Prince
by Niccolo Machiavelli

Principia Ethica
by George Edward Moore

*The Principles of Morals
and Legislation*
by Jeremy Bentham

The Problems of Philosophy
by Bertrand Russell

*Reason, Social Myths,
and Democracy*
by Sidney Hook

*Reflections on the
Revolution in France*
by Edmund Burke

The Republic
by Plato

Rights of Man
by Thomas Paine

*Second Treatise on
Civil Government*
by John Locke

The Social Contract
by Jean-Jacques Rousseau

On Socialism
by John Stuart Mill

The Subjection of Women
by John Stuart Mill

*Three Dialogues Between
Hylas and Philonous*
by George Berkeley

Utilitarianism
by John Stuart Mill

*A Vindication of the
Rights of Women*
by Mary Wollstonecraft

JOHN STUART MILL was born in London on May 20, 1806, the son of noted Scottish economist and philosopher James Mill, who held an influential post in the powerful East India Company. Mill's natural talent and physical stamina were put to the test at a very young age when he undertook a highly structured and individualized upbringing orchestrated by his father, who believed that the mind was a passive receptacle for human experience. His education and training were so intese that he was reading Greek at the age of three and doing independent writing at six.

Mill's education broadened considerably after 1823 when he entered the East India Company to commence his life's career as his father had done before him. He traveled, became politically involved, and in so doing moved away from the narrower sectarian attitudes in which he had been raised. His ideas and imagination were ignited by the views of such diverse personalities as Wordsworth, Saint-Simon, Coleridge, Comte, and de Tocqueville. During his life, Mill wrote many influential works: *System of Logic* (1843); *Principles of Political Economy* (1848); *On Liberty* (1859); *The Subjection of Women* (1861); *Utilitarianism* (1863); *Examination of Sir William Hamilton's Philosophy* (1865); and *Autobiography* (1873). As a defender of individual freedom and human rights, John Stuart Mill lives on as a nineteenth-century champion of social reform. He died on May 7, 1873.

Contents

CONSIDERATIONS

ON

REPRESENTATIVE GOVERNMENT.

CHAPTER I.

TO WHAT EXTENT FORMS OF GOVERNMENT ARE A MATTER OF CHOICE.

ALL speculations concerning forms of government bear the impress, more or less exclusive, of two conflicting theories respecting political institutions; or, to speak more properly, conflicting conceptions of what political institutions are.

By some minds, government is conceived as strictly a practical art, giving rise to no questions but those of means and an end. Forms of government are assimilated to any other expedients for the attainment of human objects. They are regarded as wholly an affair of invention and contrivance. Being made by man, it is assumed that man has the choice either to make them or not, and how or on what pattern they shall be made. Government, according to this conception, is a problem, to be worked like any other question of business. The first step is to define the

purposes which governments are required to promote.
The next is to inquire what form of government is
best fitted to fulfill those purposes. Having satisfied
ourselves on these two points, and ascertained the
form of government which combines the greatest
amount of good with the least of evil, what further
remains is to obtain the concurrence of our countrymen, or those for whom the institutions are intended,
in the opinion which we have privately arrived at.
To find the best form of government; to persuade
others that it is the best; and, having done so, to stir
them up to insist on having it, is the order of ideas
in the minds of those who adopt this view of political
philosophy. They look upon a constitution in the
same light (difference of scale being allowed for) as
they would upon a steam plow or a threshing machine.

To these stand opposed another kind of political
reasoners, who are so far from assimilating a form of
government to a machine that they regard it as a sort
of spontaneous product, and the science of government as a branch (so to speak) of natural history.
According to them, forms of government are not a
matter of choice. We must take them, in the main,
as we find them. Governments can not be constructed by premeditated design. They "are not made,
but grow." Our business with them, as with the other facts of the universe, is to acquaint ourselves with
their natural properties, and adapt ourselves to them.
The fundamental political institutions of a people are
considered by this school as a sort of organic growth

from the nature and life of that people; a product of
their habits, instincts, and unconscious wants and desires, scarcely at all of their deliberate purposes.
Their will has had no part in the matter but that of
meeting the necessities of the moment by the contrivances of the moment, which contrivances, if in sufficient conformity to the national feelings and character, commonly last, and, by successive aggregation,
constitute a polity suited to the people who possess
it, but which it would be vain to attempt to superin-
duce upon any people whose nature and circumstances
had not spontaneously evolved it.

It is difficult to decide which of these doctrines
would be the most absurd, if we could suppose either
of them held as an exclusive theory. But the principles which men profess on any controverted subject
are usually a very imperfect exponent of the opinions
they really hold. No one believes that every people is capable of working every sort of institution.
Carry the analogy of mechanical contrivances as far
as we will, a man does not choose even an instrument
of timber and iron on the sole ground that it is in itself the best. He considers whether he possesses the
other requisites which must be combined with it to
render its employment advantageous, and, in particular, whether those by whom it will have to be worked possess the knowledge and skill necessary for its
management. On the other hand, neither are those
who speak of institutions as if they were a kind of
living organisms really the political fatalists they
give themselves out to be. They do not pretend that

mankind have absolutely no range of choice as to the government they will live under, or that a consideration of the consequences which flow from different forms of polity is no element at all in deciding which of them should be preferred. But, though each side greatly exaggerates its own theory, out of opposition to the other, and no one holds without modification to either, the two doctrines correspond to a deep-seated difference between two modes of thought; and though it is evident that neither of these is entirely in the right, yet it being equally evident that neither is wholly in the wrong, we must endeavor to get down to what is at the root of each, and avail ourselves of the amount of truth which exists in either.

Let us remember, then, in the first place, that political institutions (however the proposition may be at times ignored) are the work of men—owe their origin and their whole existence to human will. Men did not wake on a summer morning and find them sprung up. Neither do they resemble trees, which, once planted, "are aye growing" while men "are sleeping." In every stage of their existence they are made what they are by human voluntary agency. Like all things, therefore, which are made by men, they may be either well or ill made; judgment and skill may have been exercised in their production, or the reverse of these. And again, if a people have omitted, or from outward pressure have not had it in their power to give themselves a constitution by the tentative process of applying a corrective to each evil as it arose, or as the sufferers gained strength to resist it,

this retardation of political progress is no doubt a
great disadvantage to them, but it does not prove that
what has been found good for others would not have
been good also for them, and will not be so still when
they think fit to adopt it.

On the other hand, it is also to be borne in mind
that political machinery does not act of itself. As it
is first made, so it has to be worked, by men, and
even by ordinary men. It needs, not their simple acquiescence, but their active participation, and must be
adjusted to the capacities and qualities of such men
as are available. This implies three conditions. The
people for whom the form of government is intended
must be willing to accept it, or, at least, not so unwilling as to oppose an insurmountable obstacle to its
establishment. They must be willing and able to do
what is necessary to keep it standing. And they
must be willing and able to do what it requires of
them to enable it to fulfill its purposes. The word
"do" must be understood as including forbearances as
well as acts. They must be capable of fulfilling the
conditions of action and the conditions of self-restraint,
which are necessary either for keeping the established polity in existence, or for enabling it to achieve
the ends, its conduciveness to which forms its recom-
mendation.

The failure of any of these conditions renders a
form of government, whatever favorable promise it
may otherwise hold out, unsuitable to the particular
case.

The first obstacle, the repugnance of the people to

the particular form of government, needs little illustration, because it never can in theory have been overlooked. The case is of perpetual occurrence. Nothing but foreign force would induce a tribe of North
American Indians to submit to the restraints of a regular and civilized government. The same might have
been said, though somewhat less absolutely, of the
barbarians who overran the Roman Empire. It required centuries of time and an entire change of circumstances to discipline them into regular obedience
even to their own leaders, when not actually serving
under their banner. There are nations who will not
voluntarily submit to any government but that of certain families, which have from time immemorial had
the privilege of supplying them with chiefs. Some
nations could not, except by foreign conquest, be made
to endure a monarchy; others are equally averse to a
republic. The hinderance often amounts, for the time
being, to impracticability.

But there are also cases in which, though not averse
to a form of government—possibly even desiring it—
a people may be unwilling or unable to fulfill its conditions. They may be incapable of fulfilling such of
them as are necessary to keep the government even
in nominal existence. Thus a people may prefer a
free government; but if, from indolence, or careless-
ness, or cowardice, or want of public spirit, they are
unequal to the exertions necessary for preserving it;
if they will not fight for it when it is directly attack-
ed; if they can be deluded by the artifices used to
cheat them out of it; if, by momentary discourage-

ment, or temporary panic, or a fit of enthusiasm for an individual, they can be induced to lay their liberties at the feet even of a great man, or trust him with powers which enable him to subvert their institutions —in all these cases they are more or less unfit for liberty; and though it may be for their good to have had it even for a short time, they are unlikely long to enjoy it. Again, a people may be unwilling or unable to fulfill the duties which a particular form of government requires of them. A rude people, though in some degree alive to the benefits of civilized society, may be unable to practice the forbearances which it demands; their passions may be too violent, or their personal pride too exacting, to forego private conflict, and leave to the laws the avenging of their real or supposed wrongs. In such a case, a civilized government, to be really advantageous to them, will require to be in a considerable degree despotic; one over which they do not themselves exercise control, and which imposes a great amount of forcible restraint upon their actions. Again, a people must be considered unfit for more than a limited and qualified freedom who will not co-operate actively with the law and the public authorities in the repression of evil-doers. A people who are more disposed to shelter a criminal than to apprehend him; who, like the Hindoos, will perjure themselves to screen the man who has robbed them, rather than take trouble or expose themselves to vindictiveness by giving evidence against him; who, like some nations of Europe down to a recent date, if a man poniards another in the public street, pass by on the other side, because it is the business of the police to look to the matter, and it is safer not to interfere in what does not concern them; a people who are revolted by an execution, but not shocked at an assassination, require that the public authorities should be armed with much sterner powers of repression than elsewhere, since the first indispensable requisites of civilized life have nothing else to rest on. These deplorable states of feeling, in any people who have emerged from savage life, are, no doubt, usually the consequence of previous bad government, which has taught them to regard the law as made for other ends than their good, and its administrators as worse enemies than those who openly violate it. But, however little blame may be due to those in whom these mental habits have grown up, and however the habits may be ultimately conquerable by better government, yet, while they exist, a people so disposed can not be governed with as little power exercised over them as a people whose sympathies are on the side of the law, and who are willing to give active assistance in its enforcement. Again, representative institutions are of little value, and may be a mere instrument of tyranny or intrigue, when the generality of electors are not sufficiently interested in their own government to give their vote, or, if they vote at all, do not bestow their suffrages on public grounds, but sell them for money, or vote at the beck of some one who has control over them, or whom, for private reasons, they desire to propitiate. Popular election thus practised, instead of a security against

misgovernment, is but an additional wheel in its machinery. Besides these moral hinderances, mechanical difficulties are often an insuperable impediment to
forms of government. In the ancient world, though
there might be, and often was, great individual independence, there could be nothing like a regulated popular government beyond the bounds of a single city
community, because there did not exist the physical
conditions for the formation and propagation of a
public opinion except among those who could be
brought together to discuss public matters in the same
agora. This obstacle is generally thought to have
ceased by the adoption of the representative system.
But to surmount it completely required the press, and
even the newspaper press, the real equivalent, though
not, in all respects, an adequate one, of the Pnyx and
the Forum. There have been states of society in
which even a monarchy of any great territorial extent
could not subsist, but unavoidably broke up into petty principalities, either mutually independent, or held
together by a loose tie like the feudal, because the
machinery of authority was not perfect enough to
carry orders into effect at a great distance from the
person of the ruler. He depended mainly upon voluntary fidelity for the obedience even of his army,
nor did there exist the means of making the people
pay an amount of taxes sufficient for keeping up the
force necessary to compel obedience throughout a
large territory. In these and all similar cases, it must
be understood that the amount of the hinderance may
be either greater or less. It may be so great as to

make the form of government work very ill, without absolutely precluding its existence, or hindering it from being practically preferable to any other which can be had. This last question mainly depends upon a consideration which we have not yet arrived at — the tendencies of different forms of government to promote Progress.

We have now examined the three fundamental conditions of the adaptation of forms of government to the people who are to be governed by them. If the supporters of what may be termed the naturalistic theory of politics mean but to insist on the necessity of these three conditions; if they only mean that no government can permanently exist which does not fulfill the first and second conditions, and, in some considerable measure, the third, their doctrine, thus limited, is incontestable. Whatever they mean more than this appears to me altogether untenable. All that we are told about the necessity of an historical basis for institutions, of their being in harmony with the national usages and character, and the like, means either this, or nothing to the purpose. There is a great quantity of mere sentimentality connected with these and similar phrases, over and above the amount of rational meaning contained in them. But, considered practically, these alleged requisites of political institutions are merely so many facilities for realizing the three conditions. When an institution, or set of institutions, has the way prepared for it by the opinions, tastes, and habits of the people, they are not only more easily induced to accept it, but will more easily learn, and will be, from the beginning, better disposed to do what is required of them both for the preservation of the institutions, and for bringing them into such action as enables them to produce their best results. It would be a great mistake in any legislator not to shape his measures so as to take advantage of such pre-existing habits and feelings, when available. On the other hand, it is an exaggeration to elevate these mere aids and facilities into necessary conditions. People are more easily induced to do, and do more easily, what they are already used to; but people also learn to do things new to them. Familiarity is a great help; but much dwelling on an idea will make it familiar, even when strange at first. There are abundant instances in which a whole people have been eager for untried things. The amount of capacity which a people possess for doing new things, and adapting themselves to new circumstances, is itself one of the elements of the question. It is a quality in which different nations and different stages of civilization differ much from one another. The capability of any given people for fulfilling the conditions of a given form of government can not be pronounced on by any sweeping rule. Knowledge of the particular people, and general practical judgment and sagacity, must be the guides. There is also another consideration not to be lost sight of. A people may be unprepared for good institutions; but to kindle a desire for them is a necessary part of the preparation. To recommend and advocate a particular institution or form of government, and set its advantages in the strongest light, is one of the modes, often the only mode within reach, of educating the mind of the nation, not only for accepting or claiming, but also for working the institution. What means had Italian patriots, during the last and present generation, of preparing the Italian people for freedom in unity, but by inciting them to demand it? Those, however, who undertake such a task, need to be duly impressed, not solely with the benefits of the institution or polity which they recommend, but also with the capacities, moral, intellectual, and active, required for working it, that they may avoid, if possible, stirring up a desire too much in advance of the capacity.

The result of what has been said is that, within the limits set by the three conditions so often adverted to, institutions and forms of government *are* a matter of choice. To inquire into the best form of government in the abstract (as it is called) is not a chimerical, but a highly practical employment of scientific intellect; and to introduce into any country the best institutions which, in the existing state of that country, are capable of, in any tolerable degree, fulfilling the conditions, is one of the most rational objects to which practical effort can address itself. Every thing which can be said by way of disparaging the efficacy of human will and purpose in matters of government might be said of it in every other of its applications. In all things there are very strict limits to human power. It can only act by wielding some one or more of the forces of nature. Forces, therefore, that can be applied to the desired use, must exist, and will only act according to their own laws. We can not make the river run backward, but we do not therefore say that water-mills "are not made, but grow." In politics as in mechanics, the power which is to keep the engine going must be sought for *outside* the machinery; and if it is not forthcoming, or is insufficient to surmount the obstacles which may reasonably be expected, the contrivance will fail. This is no peculiarity of the political art, and amounts only to saying that it is subject to the same limitations and conditions as all other arts.

At this point we are met by another objection, or the same objection in a different form. The forces, it is contended, on which the greater political phenomena depend, are not amenable to the direction of politicians or philosophers. The government of a country, it is affirmed, is, in all substantial respects, fixed and determined beforehand by the state of the country in regard to the distribution of the elements of social power. Whatever is the strongest power in society will obtain the governing authority; and a change in the political constitution can not be durable unless preceded or accompanied by an altered distribution of power in society itself. A nation, therefore, can not choose its form of government. The mere details and practical organization it may choose, but the essence of the whole, the seat of the supreme power, is determined for it by social circumstances.

That there is a portion of truth in this doctrine I at once admit, but, to make it of any use, it must be reduced to a distinct expression and proper limits.

When it is said that the strongest power in society will make itself strongest in the government, what is meant by power? Not thews and sinews; otherwise pure democracy would be the only form of polity that could exist. To mere muscular strength add two other elements, property and intelligence, and we are nearer the truth, but far from having yet reached it. Not only is a greater number often kept down by a less, but the greater number may have a preponderance in property, and individually in intelligence, and may yet be held in subjection, forcible or otherwise, by a minority in both respects inferior to it. To make these various elements of power politically influential, they must be organized; and the advantage in organization is necessarily with those who are in possession of the government. A much weaker party in all other elements of power may greatly preponderate when the powers of government are thrown into the scale, and may long retain its predominance through this alone; though, no doubt, a government so situated is in the condition called in mechanics unstable equilibrium, like a thing balanced on its smaller end, which, if once disturbed, tends more and more to depart from, instead of reverting to, its previous state.

But there are still stronger objections to this theory of government in the terms in which it is usually stated. The power in society which has any tendency to convert itself into political power is not power quiescent, power merely passive, but active power; in other words, power actually exerted; that is to say, a very small portion of all the power in existence. Po-

litically speaking, a great part of all power consists in
will. How is it possible, then, to compute the elements of political power, while we omit from the com-
putation any thing which acts on the will? To think
that, because those who wield the power in society
wield in the end that of government, therefore it is of
no use to attempt to influence the constitution of the
government by acting on opinion, is to forget that
opinion is itself one of the greatest active social forces.
One person with a belief is a social power equal to
ninety-nine who have only interests. They who can
succeed in creating a general persuasion that a certain
form of government, or social fact of any kind, deserves to be preferred, have made nearly the most important step which can possibly be taken toward rang-
ing the powers of society on its side. On the day
when the protomartyr was stoned to death at Jerusa-
lem, while he who was to be the Apostle of the Gen-
tiles stood by "consenting unto his death," would any
one have supposed that the party of that stoned man
were then and there the strongest power in society?
And has not the event proved that they were so?
Because theirs was the most powerful of then existing
beliefs. The same element made a monk of Witten-
berg, at the meeting of the Diet of Worms, a more
powerful social force than the Emperor Charles the
Fifth, and all the princes there assembled. But these,
it may be said, are cases in which religion was concerned, and religious convictions are something peculiar in their strength. Then let us take a case purely
political, where religion, if concerned at all, was chief-

ly on the losing side. If any one requires to be convinced that speculative thought is one of the chief elements of social power, let him bethink himself of the
age in which there was scarcely a throne in Europe
which was not filled by a liberal and reforming king,
a liberal and reforming emperor, or, strangest of all, a
liberal and reforming pope; the age of Frederick the
Great, of Catharine the Second, of Joseph the Second,
of Peter Leopold, of Benedict XIV., of Ganganelli, of
Pombal, of D'Aranda; when the very Bourbons of
Naples were liberals and reformers, and all the active
minds among the noblesse of France were filled with
the ideas which were soon after to cost them so dear.
Surely a conclusive example how far mere physical
and economic power is from being the whole of social
power. It was not by any change in the distribution
of material interests, but by the spread of moral convictions, that negro slavery has been put an end to in
the British Empire and elsewhere. The serfs in Russia will owe their emancipation, if not to a sentiment
of duty, at least to the growth of a more enlightened
opinion respecting the true interest of the state. It is
what men think that determines how they act; and
though the persuasions and convictions of average
men are in a much greater degree determined by their
personal position than by reason, no little power is
exercised over them by the persuasions and convictions of those whose personal position is different, and
by the united authority of the instructed. When,
therefore, the instructed in general can be brought to
recognize one social arrangement, or political or other

institution, as good, and another as bad—one as desirable, another as condemnable, very much has been done toward giving to the one, or withdrawing from the other, that preponderance of social force which enables it to subsist. And the maxim that the government of a country is what the social forces in existence compel it to be, is true only in the sense in which it favors, instead of discouraging, the attempt to exercise, among all forms of government practicable in the existing condition of society, a rational choice.

CHAPTER II.

THE CRITERION OF A GOOD FORM OF GOVERNMENT.

THE form of government for any given country
being (within certain definite conditions) amenable to
choice, it is now to be considered by what test the
choice should be directed; what are the distinctive
characteristics of the form of government best fitted
to promote the interests of any given society.

Before entering into this inquiry, it may seem necessary to decide what are the proper functions of government; for, government altogether being only a
means, the eligibility of the means must depend on
their adaptation to the end. But this mode of stating
the problem gives less aid to its investigation than
might be supposed, and does not even bring the whole
of the question into view. For, in the first place, the
proper functions of a government are not a fixed
thing, but different in different states of society; much
more extensive in a backward than in an advanced
state. And, secondly, the character of a government
or set of political institutions can not be sufficiently
estimated while we confine our attention to the legitimate sphere of governmental functions; for, though
the goodness of a government is necessarily circumscribed within that sphere, its badness unhappily is
not. Every kind and degree of evil of which man-

kind are susceptible may be inflicted on them by their government, and none of the good which social existence is capable of can be any farther realized than as the constitution of the government is compatible with, and allows scope for, its attainment. Not to speak of indirect effects, the direct meddling of the public authorities has no necessary limits but those of human life, and the influence of government on the well-being of society can be considered or estimated in reference to nothing less than the whole of the interests of humanity.

Being thus obliged to place before ourselves, as the test of good and bad government, so complex an object as the aggregate interests of society, we would willingly attempt some kind of classification of those interests which, bringing them before the mind in definite groups, might give indication of the qualities by which a form of government is fitted to promote those various interests respectively. It would be a great facility if we could say the good of society consists of such and such elements; one of these elements requires such conditions, another such others; the government, then, which unites in the greatest degree all these conditions, must be the best. The theory of government would thus be built up from the separate theorems of the elements which compose a good state of society.

Unfortunately, to enumerate and classify the constituents of social well-being so as to admit of the formation of such theorems is no easy task. Most of those who, in the last or present generation, have applied themselves to the philosophy of politics in any comprehensive spirit, have felt the importance of such a classification, but the attempts which have been made toward it are as yet limited, so far as I am aware, to a single step. The classification begins and ends with a partition of the exigencies of society between the two heads of Order and Progress (in the phraseology of French thinkers); Permanence and Progression, in the words of Coleridge. This division is plausible and seductive, from the apparently clean-cut opposition between its two members, and the remarkable difference between the sentiments to which they appeal. But I apprehend that (however admissible for purposes of popular discourse) the distinction between Order, or Permanence and Progress, employed to define the qualities necessary in a government, is unscientific and incorrect.

For, first, what are Order and Progress? Concerning Progress there is no difficulty, or none which is apparent at first sight. When Progress is spoken of as one of the wants of human society, it may be supposed to mean Improvement. That is a tolerably distinct idea. But what is Order? Sometimes it means more, sometimes less, but hardly ever the whole of what human society needs except improvement.

In its narrowest acceptation, Order means Obedience. A government is said to preserve order if it succeeds in getting itself obeyed. But there are different degrees of obedience, and it is not every degree that is commendable. Only an unmitigated despotism demands that the individual citizen shall obey

unconditionally every mandate of persons in authority. We must at least limit the definition to such
mandates as are general, and issued in the deliberate
form of laws. Order, thus understood, expresses,
doubtless, an indispensable attribute of government.
Those who are unable to make their ordinances obeyed can not be said to govern. But, though a necessary condition, this is not the object of government.
That it should make itself obeyed is requisite, in order that it may accomplish some other purpose. We
are still to seek what is this other purpose which government ought to fulfill abstractedly from the idea of
improvement, and which has to be fulfilled in every
society, whether stationary or progressive.

In a sense somewhat more enlarged, Order means
the preservation of peace by the cessation of private
violence. Order is said to exist where the people of
the country have, as a general rule, ceased to prose-
cute their quarrels by private force, and acquired the
habit of referring the decision of their disputes and
the redress of their injuries to the public authorities.
But in this larger use of the term, as well as in the
former narrow one, Order expresses rather one of the
conditions of government than either its purpose or
the criterion of its excellence; for the habit may be
well established of submitting to the government, and
referring all disputed matters to its authority, and yet
the manner in which the government deals with those
disputed matters, and with the other things about
which it concerns itself, may differ by the whole interval which divides the best from the worst possible.

If we intend to comprise in the idea of Order all that society requires from its government which is not included in the idea of Progress, we must define Order as the preservation of all kinds and amounts of good which already exist, and Progress as consisting in the increase of them. This distinction does comprehend in one or the other section every thing which a government can be required to promote. But, thus understood, it affords no basis for a philosophy of government. We can not say that, in constituting a polity, certain provisions ought to be made for Order and certain others for Progress, since the conditions of Order, in the sense now indicated, and those of Progress, are not opposite, but the same. The agencies which tend to preserve the social good which already exists are the very same which promote the increase of it, and *vice versâ*, the sole difference being that a greater degree of those agencies is required for the latter purpose than for the former.

What, for example, are the qualities in the citizens individually, which conduce most to keep up the amount of good conduct, of good management, of success and prosperity, which already exist in society? Every body will agree that those qualities are industry, integrity, justice, and prudence. But are not these, of all qualities, the most conducive to improvement? and is not any growth of these virtues in the community in itself the greatest of improvements? If so, whatever qualities in the government are promotive of industry, integrity, justice, and prudence, conduce alike to permanence and to progression, only there is needed more of those qualities to make the society decidedly progressive than merely to keep it permanent. What, again, are the particular attributes in human beings which seem to have a more especial reference to Progress, and do not so directly suggest the ideas of Order and Preservation? They are chiefly the qualities of mental activity, enterprise, and courage. But are not all these qualities fully as much required for preserving the good we have as for adding to it? If there is any thing certain in human affairs, it is that valuable acquisitions are only to be retained by the continuation of the same energies which gained them. Things left to take care of themselves inevitably decay. Those whom success induces to relax their habits of care and thoughtfulness, and their willingness to encounter disagreeables, seldom long retain their good fortune at its height. The mental attribute which seems exclusively dedicated to Progress, and is the culmination of the tendencies to it, is Originality, or Invention. Yet this is no less necessary for Permanence, since, in the inevitable changes of human affairs, new inconveniences and dangers continually grow up, which must be encountered by new resources and contrivances, in order to keep things going on even only as well as they did before. Whatever qualities, therefore, in a government tend to encourage activity, energy, courage, originality, are requisites of Permanence as well as of Progress, only a somewhat less degree of them will, on the average, suffice for the former purpose than for the latter.

To pass now from the mental to the outward and

objective requisites of society : it is impossible to point out any contrivance in politics, or arrangement of social affairs, which conduces to Order only, or to Progress only; whatever tends to either promotes both. Take, for instance, the common institution of a police. Order is the object which seems most immediately interested in the efficiency of this part of the social organization. Yet, if it is effectual to promote Order, that is, if it represses crime, and enables every one to feel his person and property secure, can any state of things be more conducive to Progress? The greater security of property is one of the main conditions and causes of greater production, which is Progress in its most familiar and vulgarest aspect. The better repression of crime represses the dispositions which tend to crime, and this is Progress in a somewhat higher sense. The release of the individual from the cares and anxieties of a state of imperfect protection sets his faculties free to be employed in any new effort for improving his own state and that of others, while the same cause, by attaching him to social existence, and making him no longer see present or prospective enemies in his fellow-creatures, fosters all those feelings of kindness and fellowship toward others, and interest in the general well-being of the community, which are such important parts of social improvement.

Take, again, such a familiar case as that of a good system of taxation and finance. This would generally be classed as belonging to the province of Order. Yet what can be more conducive to Progress? A financial system which promotes the one, conduces, by the very same excellences, to the other. Economy, for example, equally preserves the existing stock of national wealth, and favors the creation of more. A just distribution of burdens, by holding up to every citizen an example of morality and good conscience applied to difficult adjustments, and an evidence of the value which the highest authorities attach to them, tends in an eminent degree to educate the moral sentiments of the community, both in respect of strength and of discrimination. Such a mode of levying the taxes as does not impede the industry, or unnecessarily interfere with the liberty of the citizen, promotes, not the preservation only, but the increase of the national wealth, and encourages a more active use of the individual faculties; and *vice versâ*, all errors in finance and taxation which obstruct the improvement of the people in wealth and morals, tend also, if of sufficiently serious amount, positively to impoverish and demoralize them. It holds, in short, universally, that when Order and Permanence are taken in their widest sense for the stability of existing advantages, the requisites of Progress are but the requisites of Order in a greater degree; those of Permanence merely those of Progress in a somewhat smaller measure.

In support of the position that Order is intrinsically different from Progress, and that preservation of existing and acquisition of additional good are sufficiently distinct to afford the basis of a fundamental classification, we shall perhaps be reminded that Progress may be at the expense of Order; that while we are acquiring, or striving to acquire, good of one kind, we

may be losing ground in respect to others; thus there
may be progress in wealth while there is deterioration
in virtue. Granting this, what it proves is, not that
Progress is generically a different thing from Permanence, but that wealth is a different thing from virtue.
Progress is Permanence and something more; and it
is no answer to this to say that Progress in one thing
does not imply Permanence in every thi∩g. No more
does Progress in one thing imply Progress in every
thing. Progress of any kind includes Permanence in
that same kind : whenever Permanence is sacrificed
to some particular kind of Progress, other Progress is
still more sacrificed to it; and if it be not worth the
sacrifice, not the interest of Permanence alone has been
disregarded, but the general interest of Progress has
been mistaken.

If these improperly contrasted ideas are to be used
at all in the attempt to give a first commencement of
scientific precision to the notion of good government,
it would be more philosophically correct to leave out
of the definition the word Order, and to say that the
best government is that which is most conducive to
Progress. For Progress includes Order, but Order
does not include Progress. Progress is á greater degree of that of which Order is a less. Order, in any
other sense, stands only for a part of the prerequisites
of good government, not for its idea and essence.
Order would find a more suitable place among the
conditions of Progress, since, if we would increase
our sum of good, nothing is more indispensable than
to take due care of what we already have. If we are

endeavoring after more riches, our very first rule should be, not to squander uselessly our existing means. Order, thus considered, is not an additional end to be reconciled with Progress, but a part and means of Progress itself. If a gain in one respect is purchased by a more than equivalent loss in the same or in any other, there is not Progress. Conduciveness to Progress, thus understood, includes the whole excellence of a government.

But, though metaphysically defensible, this definition of the criterion of good government is not appropriate, because, though it contains the whole of the truth, it recalls only a part. What is suggested by the term Progress is the idea of moving onward, whereas the meaning of it here is quite as much the prevention of falling back. The very same social causes — the same beliefs, feelings, institutions, and practices — are as much required to prevent society from retrograding as to produce a farther advance. Were there no improvement to be hoped for, life would be not the less an unceasing struggle against causes of deterioration, as it even now is. Politics, as conceived by the ancients, consisted wholly in this. The natural tendency of men and their works was to degenerate, which tendency, however, by good institutions virtuously administered, it might be possible for an indefinite length of time to counteract. Though we no longer hold this opinion; though most men in the present age profess the contrary creed, believing that the tendency of things, on the whole, is toward improvement, we ought not to forget that there is an incessant and ever-flowing current of human affairs toward the worse, consisting of all the follies, all the vices, all the negligences, indolences, and supinenesses of mankind, which is only controlled, and kept from sweeping all before it, by the exertions which some persons constantly, and others by fits, put forth in the direction of good and worthy objects. It gives a very insufficient idea of the importance of the strivings which take place to improve and elevate human nature and life to suppose that their chief value consists in the amount of actual improvement realized by their means, and that the consequence of their cessation would merely be that we should remain as we are. A very small diminution of those exertions would not only put a stop to improvement, but would turn the general tendency of things toward deterioration, which, once begun, would proceed with increasing rapidity, and become more and more difficult to check, until it reached a state often seen in history, and in which many large portions of mankind even now grovel; when hardly any thing short of superhuman power seems sufficient to turn the tide, and give a fresh commencement to the upward movement.

These reasons make the word Progress as unapt as the terms Order and Permanence to become the basis for a classification of the requisites of a form of government. The fundamental antithesis which these words express does not lie in the things themselves, so much as in the types of human character which answer to them. There are, we know, some minds in which caution, and others in which boldness, predominates; in some, the desire to avoid imperiling what is already possessed is a stronger sentiment than that which prompts to improve the old and acquire new advantages; while there are others who lean the contrary way, and are more eager for future than careful of present good. The road to the ends of both is the same, but they are liable to wander from it in opposite directions. This consideration is of importance in composing the *personnel* of any political body: persons of both types ought to be included in it, that the tendencies of each may be tempered, in so far as they are excessive, by a due proportion of the other. There needs no express provision to insure this object, provided care is taken to admit nothing inconsistent with it. The natural and spontaneous admixture of the old and the young, of those whose position and reputation are made, and those who have them still to make, will in general sufficiently answer the purpose, if only this natural balance is not disturbed by artificial regulation.

Since the distinction most commonly adopted for the classification of social exigencies does not possess the properties needful for that use, we have to seek for some other leading distinction better adapted to the purpose. Such a distinction would seem to be indicated by the considerations to which I now proceed.

If we ask ourselves on what causes and conditions good government in all its senses, from the humblest to the most exalted, depends, we find that the princi-

pal of them, the one which transcends all others, is the
qualities of the human beings composing the society
over which the government is exercised.

We may take, as a first instance, the administration
of justice; with the more propriety, since there is no
part of public business in which the mere machinery,
the rules and contrivances for conducting the details
of the operation, are of such vital consequence. Yet
even these yield in importance to the qualities of the
human agents employed. Of what efficacy are rules
of procedure in securing the ends of justice if the
moral condition of the people is such that the witnesses generally lie, and the judges and their subordinates take bribes? Again, how can institutions
provide a good municipal administration if there exists such indifference to the subject that those who
would administer honestly and capably can not be
induced to serve, and the duties are left to those who
undertake them because they have some private interest to be promoted? Of what avail is the most
broadly popular representative system if the electors
do not care to choose the best member of Parliament,
but choose him who will spend most money to be
elected? How can a representative assembly work
for good if its members can be bought, or if their ex-
citability of temperament, uncorrected by public discipline or private self-control, makes them incapable
of calm deliberation, and they resort to manual violence on the floor of the House, or shoot at one another with rifles? How, again, can government, or
any joint concern, be carried on in a tolerable manner

by a people so envious, that if one among them seems
likely to succeed in any thing, those who ought to co-
operate with him form a tacit combination to make
him fail? Whenever the general disposition of the
people is such that each individual regards those only
of his interests which are selfish, and does not dwell
on, or concern himself for, his share of the general
interest, in such a state of things good government is
impossible. The influence of defects of intelligence
in obstructing all the elements of good government
requires no illustration. Government consists of acts
done by human beings; and if the agents, or those
who choose the agents, or those to whom the agents
are responsible, or the lookers-on whose opinion ought
to influence and check all these, are mere masses of
ignorance, stupidity, and baleful prejudice, every operation of government will go wrong; while, in proportion as the men rise above this standard, so will
the government improve in quality up to the point
of excellence, attainable but nowhere attained, where
the officers of government, themselves persons of superior virtue and intellect, are surrounded by the atmosphere of a virtuous and enlightened public opinion.

The first element of good government, therefore,
being the virtue and intelligence of the human beings
composing the community, the most important point
of excellence which any form of government can possess is to promote the virtue and intelligence of the
people themselves. The first question in respect to
any political institutions is how far they tend to foster
in the members of the community the various desira-

ble qualities, moral or intellectual, or rather (following Bentham's more complete classification) moral,
intellectual, and active. The government which does
this the best has every likelihood of being the best in
all other respects, since it is on these qualities, so far
as they exist in the people, that all possibility of
goodness in the practical operations of the government depends.

We may consider, then, as one criterion of the
goodness of a government, the degree in which it
tends to increase the sum of good qualities in the
governed, collectively and individually, since, besides
that their well-being is the sole object of government,
their good qualities supply the moving force which
works the machinery. This leaves, as the other con-
stituent element of the merit of a government, the
quality of the machinery itself; that is, the degree in
which it is adapted to take advantage of the amount
of good qualities which may at any time exist, and
make them instrumental to the right purposes. Let
us again take the subject of judicature as an example
and illustration. The judicial system being given,
the goodness of the administration of justice is in the
compound ratio of the worth of the men composing
the tribunals, and the worth of the public opinion
which influences or controls them. But all the difference between a good and a bad system of judicature
lies in the contrivances adopted for bringing whatever
moral and intellectual worth exists in the community
to bear upon the administration of justice, and making
it duly operative on the result. The arrangements

for rendering the choice of the judges such as to obtain the highest average of virtue and intelligence; the salutary forms of procedure; the publicity which allows observation and criticism of whatever is amiss; the liberty of discussion and censure through the press; the mode of taking evidence, according as it is well or ill adapted to elicit truth; the facilities, whatever be their amount, for obtaining access to the tribunals; the arrangements for detecting crimes and apprehending offenders—all these things are not the power, but the machinery for bringing the power into contact with the obstacle; and the machinery has no action of itself, but without it the power, let it be ever so ample, would be wasted and of no effect. A similar distinction exists in regard to the constitution of the executive departments of administration. Their machinery is good when the proper tests are prescribed for the qualifications of officers, the proper rules for their promotion; when the business is conveniently distributed among those who are to transact it, a convenient and methodical order established for its transaction, a correct and intelligible record kept of it after being transacted; when each individual knows for what he is responsible, and is known to others as responsible for it; when the best-contrived checks are provided against negligence, favoritism, or jobbery in any of the acts of the department. But political checks will no more act of themselves than a bridle will direct a horse without a rider. If the checking functionaries are as corrupt or as negligent as those whom they ought to check, and if the public, the

mainspring of the whole checking machinery, are too
ignorant, too passive, or too careless and inattentive
to do their part, little benefit will be derived from the
best administrative apparatus. Yet a good apparatus
is always preferable to a bad. It enables such insufficient moving or checking power as exists to act at
the greatest advantage; and without it, no amount
of moving or checking power would be sufficient.
Publicity, for instance, is no impediment to evil, nor
stimulus to good, if the public will not look at what
is done; but without publicity, how could they either
check or encourage what they were not permitted to
see? The ideally perfect constitution of a public office is that in which the interest of the functionary is
entirely coincident with his duty. No mere system
will make it so, but still less can it be made so without a system, aptly devised for the purpose.

What we have said of the arrangements for the detailed administration of the government is still more
evidently true of its general constitution. All government which aims at being good is an organization
of some part of the good qualities existing in the individual members of the community for the conduct
of its collective affairs. A representative constitution
is a means of bringing the general standard of intelligence and honesty existing in the community, and the
individual intellect and virtue of its wisest members,
more directly to bear upon the government, and in-
vesting them with greater influence in it than they
would have under any other mode of organization;
though, under any, such influence as they do have is

FORM OF GOVERNMENT. 43

the source of all good that there is in the government,
and the hinderance of every evil that there is not.
The greater the amount of these good qualities which
the institutions of a country succeed in organizing,
and the better the mode of organization, the better
will be the government.

We have now, therefore, obtained a foundation for
a twofold division of the merit which any set of political institutions can possess. It consists partly of
the degree in which they promote the general mental
advancement of the community, including under that
phrase advancement in intellect, in virtue, and in practical activity and efficiency, and partly of the degree
of perfection with which they organize the moral, intellectual, and active worth already existing, so as to
operate with the greatest effect on public affairs. A
government is to be judged by its action upon men
and by its action upon things; by what it makes of
the citizens and what it does with them; its tendency
to improve or deteriorate the people themselves, and
the goodness or badness of the work it performs for
them, and by means of them. Government is at once
a great influence acting on the human mind, and a set
of organized arrangements for public business: in the
first capacity its beneficial action is chiefly indirect,
but not therefore less vital, while its mischievous action may be direct.

The difference between these two functions of a
government is not, like that between Order and Progress, a difference merely in degree, but in kind. We
must not, however, suppose that they have no intimate

connection with one another. The institutions which
insure the best management of public affairs practicable in the existing state of cultivation, tend by this
alone to the farther improvement of that state. A
people which had the most just laws, the purest and
most efficient judicature, the most enlightened administration, the most equitable and least onerous system
of finance, compatible with the stage it had attained
in moral and intellectual advancement, would be in a
fair way to pass rapidly into a higher stage. Nor is
there any mode in which political institutions can
contribute more effectually to the improvement of the
people than by doing their more direct work well.
And reversely, if their machinery is so badly constructed that they do their own particular business
ill, the effect is felt in a thousand ways in lowering
the morality and deadening the intelligence and activity of the people. But the distinction is nevertheless real, because this is only one of the means by
which political institutions improve or deteriorate the
human mind, and the causes and modes of that beneficial or injurious influence remain a distinct and
much wider subject of study.

Of the two modes of operation by which a form of
government or set of political institutions affects the
welfare of the community—its operation as an agency
of national education, and its arrangements for conducting the collective affairs of the community in the
state of education in which they already are, the last
evidently varies much less, from difference of country
and state of civilization, than the first. It has also

FORM OF GOVERNMENT.   45

much less to do with the fundamental constitution of
the government. The mode of conducting the practical business of government, which is best under a
free constitution, would generally be best also in an
absolute monarchy, only an absolute monarchy is not
so likely to practice it. The laws of property, for example; the principles of evidence and judicial procedure; the system of taxation and of financial administration, need not necessarily be different in different forms of government. Each of these matters
has principles and rules of its own, which are a subject of separate study. General jurisprudence, civil
and penal legislation, financial and commercial policy,
are sciences in themselves, or, rather, separate members of the comprehensive science or art of government; and the most enlightened doctrines on all these
subjects, though not equally likely to be understood
and acted on under all forms of government, yet, if
understood and acted on, would in general be equally
beneficial under them all. It is true that these doctrines could not be applied without some modifications
to all states of society and of the human mind; nevertheless, by far the greater number of them would
require modifications solely of detail to adapt them
to any state of society sufficiently advanced to possess
rulers capable of understanding them. A government to which they would be wholly unsuitable must
be one so bad in itself, or so opposed to public feeling, as to be unable to maintain itself in existence by
honest means.

It is otherwise with that portion of the interests of

the community which relate to the better or worse
training of the people themselves. Considered as instrumental to this, institutions need to be radically different, according to the stage of advancement already
reached. The recognition of this truth, though for the
most part empirically rather than philosophically, may
be regarded as the main point of superiority in the
political theories of the present above those of the last
age, in which it was customary to claim representative
democracy for England or France by arguments which
would equally have proved it the only fit form of government for Bedouins or Malays. The state of different communities, in point of culture and development, ranges downward to a condition very little above
the highest of the beasts. The upward range, too, is
considerable, and the future possible extension vastly
greater. A community can only be developed out of
one of these states into a higher by a concourse of influences, among the principal of which is the government to which they are subject. In all states of human improvement ever yet attained, the nature and
degree of authority exercised over individuals, the distribution of power, and the conditions of command
and obedience, are the most powerful of the influences,
except their religious belief, which make them what
they are, and enable them to become what they can
be. They may be stopped short at any point in their
progress by defective adaptation of their government
to their particular stage of advancement. And the
one indispensable merit of a government, in favor of
which it may be forgiven almost any amount of other

demerit compatible with progress, is that its operation
on the people is favorable, or not unfavorable, to the
next step which it is necessary for them to take in
order to raise themselves to a higher level.
Thus (to repeat a former example) a people in a
state of savage independence, in which every one lives
for himself, exempt, unless by fits, from any external
control, is practically incapable of making any progress in civilization until it has learned to obey. The
indispensable virtue, therefore, in a government which
establishes itself over a people of this sort is that it
make itself obeyed. To enable it to do this, the constitution of the government must be nearly, or quite
despotic. A constitution in any degree popular, dependent on the voluntary surrender by the different
members of the community of their individual freedom
of action, would fail to enforce the first lesson which
the pupils, in this stage of their progress, require. Accordingly, the civilization of such tribes, when not the
result of juxtaposition with others already civilized,
is almost always the work of an absolute ruler, deriving his power either from religion or military prow-
ess—very often from foreign arms.

Again, uncivilized races, and the bravest and most
energetic still more than the rest, are averse to continuous labor of an unexciting kind. Yet all real civilization is at this price; without such labor, neither
can the mind be disciplined into the habits required
by civilized society, nor the material world prepared
to receive it. There needs a rare concurrence of circumstances, and for that reason often a vast length of

time, to reconcile such a people to industry, unless
they are for a while compelled to it.   Hence even personal slavery, by giving a commencement to industrial
life, and enforcing it as the exclusive occupation of
the most numerous portion of the community, may
accelerate the transition to a better freedom than that
of fighting and rapine.   It is almost needless to say
that this excuse for slavery is only available in a very
early state of society.   A civilized people have far
other means of imparting civilization to those under
their influence; and slavery is, in all its details, so repugnant to that government of law, which is the foundation of all modern life, and so corrupting to the mas-
ter-class when they have once come under civilized
influences, that its adoption under any circumstances
whatever in modern society is a relapse into worse
than barbarism.

   At some period, however, of their history, almost
every people, now civilized, have consisted, in majority, of slaves.   A people in that condition require to
raise them out of it a very different polity from a nation of savages.   If they are energetic by nature, and
especially if there be associated with them in the same
community an industrious class who are neither slaves
nor slave-owners (as was the case in Greece), they
need, probably, no more to insure their improvement
than to make them free: when freed, they may often
be fit, like Roman freedmen, to be admitted at once
into the full rights of citizenship.   This, however, is
not the normal condition of slavery, and is generally
a sign that it is becoming obsolete.   A slave, properly

so called, is a being who has not learned to help himself. He is, no doubt, one step in advance of a savage.
He has not the first lesson of political society still to
acquire. He has learned to obey. But what he obeys
is only a direct command. It is the characteristic of
born slaves to be incapable of conforming their conduct to a rule or law. They can only do what they
are ordered, and only when they are ordered to do it.
If a man whom they fear is standing over them and
threatening them with punishment, they obey; but
when his back is turned, the work remains undone.
The motive determining them must appeal, not to their
interests, but to their instincts; immediate hope or immediate terror. A despotism which may tame the
savage will, in so far as it is a despotism, only con-
firm the slaves in their incapacities. Yet a government under their own control would be entirely un-
manageable by them. Their improvement can not
come from themselves, but must be superinduced from
without. The step which they have to take, and their
only path to improvement, is to be raised from a government of will to one of law. They have to be
taught self-government, and this, in its initial stage,
means the capacity to act on general instructions.
What they require is not a government of force, but
one of guidance. Being, however, in too low a state
to yield to the guidance of any but those to whom
they look up as the possessors of force, the sort of
government fittest for them is one which possesses
force, but seldom uses it; a parental despotism or aristocracy, resembling the St. Simonian form of social-

ism; maintaining a general superintendence over all the operations of society, so as to keep before each the sense of a present force sufficient to compel his obedience to the rule laid down, but which, owing to the impossibility of descending to regulate all the minutiæ of industry and life, necessarily leaves and induces individuals to do much of themselves. This, which may be termed the government of leading-strings, seems to be the one required to carry such a people the most rapidly through the next necessary step in social progress. Such appears to have been the idea of the government of the Incas of Peru, and such was that of the Jesuits in Paraguay. I need scarcely remark that leading-strings are only admissible as a means of gradually training the people to walk alone.

It would be out of place to carry the illustration farther. To attempt to investigate what kind of government is suited to every known state of society would be to compose a treatise, not on representative government, but on political science at large. For our more limited purpose we borrow from political philosophy only its general principles. To determine the form of government most suited to any particular people, we must be able, among the defects and short-comings which belong to that people, to distinguish those that are the immediate impediment to progress —to discover what it is which (as it were) stops the way. The best government for them is the one which tends most to give them that for want of which they can not advance, or advance only in a lame and lopsided manner. We must not, however, forget the reservation necessary in all things which have for their object improvement or Progress, namely, that in seeking the good which is needed, no damage, or as little as possible, be done to that already possessed. A people of savages should be taught obedience, but not in such a manner as to convert them into a people of slaves. And (to give the observation a higher generality) the form of government which is most effectual for carrying a people through the next stage of progress will still be very improper for them if it does this in such a manner as to obstruct, or positively unfit them for, the step next beyond. Such cases are frequent, and are among the most melancholy facts in history. The Egyptian hierarchy, the paternal despotism of China, were very fit instruments for carrying those nations up to the point of civilization which they attained. But, having reached that point, they were brought to a permanent halt for want of mental liberty and individuality—requisites of improvement which the institutions that had carried them thus far entirely incapacitated them from acquiring—and as the institutions did not break down and give place to others, farther improvement stopped. In contrast with these nations, let us consider the example of an opposite character afforded by another and a comparatively insignificant Oriental people—the Jews. They, too, had an absolute monarchy and a hierarchy, and their organized institutions were as obviously of sacerdotal origin as those of the Hindoos. These did for them what was done for other Oriental races by their institutions—subdued them to industry and order, and gave them a national life. But neither their kings nor their priests ever obtained, as in those other countries, the exclusive moulding of their character. Their religion, which enabled persons of genius and a high religious tone to be regarded and to regard themselves as inspired from heaven, gave existence to an inestimably precious unorganized institution—the Order (if it may be so termed) of Prophets. Under the protection, generally though not always effectual, of their sacred character, the Prophets were a power in the nation, often more than a match for kings and priests, and kept up, in that little corner of the earth, the antagonism of influences which is the only real security for continued progress. Religion, consequently, was not there what it has been in so many other places— a consecration of all that was once established, and a barrier against farther improvement. The remark of a distinguished Hebrew, M. Salvador, that the Prophets were, in Church and State, the equivalent of the modern liberty of the press, gives a just but not an adequate conception of the part fulfilled in national and universal history by this great element of Jewish life; by means of which, the canon of inspiration never being complete, the persons most eminent in genius and moral feeling could not only denounce and reprobate, with the direct authority of the Almighty, whatever appeared to them deserving of such treatment, but could give forth better and higher interpretations of the national religion, which thenceforth became part of the religion. Accordingly, whoever

can divest himself of the habit of reading the Bible as
if it was one book, which until lately was equally inveterate in Christians and in unbelievers, sees with
admiration the vast interval between the morality and
religion of the Pentateuch, or even of the historical
books (the unmistakable work of Hebrew Conservatives of the sacerdotal order), and the morality and
religion of the prophecies—a distance as wide as between these last and the Gospels. Conditions more
favorable to Progress could not easily exist; accordingly, the Jews, instead of being stationary like other
Asiatics, were, next to the Greeks, the most progressive people of antiquity, and, jointly with them, have
been the starting-point and main propelling agency
of modern cultivation.

It is, then, impossible to understand the question of
the adaptation of forms of government to states of
society, without taking into account not only the next
step, but all the steps which society has yet to make;
both those which can be foreseen, and the far wider
indefinite range which is at present out of sight. It
follows, that to judge of the merits of forms of government, an ideal must be constructed of the form of
government most eligible in itself, that is, which, if
the necessary conditions existed for giving effect to
its beneficial tendencies, would, more than all others,
favor and promote, not some one improvement, but
all forms and degrees of it. This having been done,
we must consider what are the mental conditions of
all sorts necessary to enable this government to realize its tendencies, and what, therefore, are the various

defects by which a people is made incapable of reaping its benefits. It would then be possible to construct a theorem of the circumstances in which that form of government may wisely be introduced; and also to judge, in cases in which it had better not be introduced, what inferior forms of polity will best carry those communities through the intermediate stages which they must traverse before they can become fit for the best form of government.

Of these inquiries, the last does not concern us here, but the first is an essential part of our subject; for we may, without rashness, at once enunciate a proposition, the proofs and illustrations of which will present themselves in the ensuing pages, that this ideally best form of government will be found in some one or other variety of the Representative System.

CHAPTER III.

THAT THE IDEALLY BEST FORM OF GOVERNMENT IS
REPRESENTATIVE GOVERNMENT.

It has long (perhaps throughout the entire duration
of British freedom) been a common form of speech,
that if a good despot could be insured, despotic monarchy would be the best form of government. I look
upon this as a radical and most pernicious misconcep-
tion of what good government is, which, until it can
be got rid of, will fatally vitiate all our speculations
on government.

The supposition is, that absolute power, in the
hands of an eminent individual, would insure a virtuous and intelligent performance of all the duties of
government. Good laws would be established and
enforced, bad laws would be reformed; the best men
would be placed in all situations of trust; justice
would be as well administered, the public burdens
would be as light and as judiciously imposed, every
branch of administration would be as purely and as
intelligently conducted as the circumstances of the
country and its degree of intellectual and moral cultivation would admit. I am willing, for the sake of
the argument, to concede all this, but I must point
out how great the concession is, how much more is
needed to produce even an approximation to these

results than is conveyed in the simple expression, a
good despot. Their realization would in fact imply,
not merely a good monarch, but an all-seeing one.
He must be at all times informed correctly, in considerable detail, of the conduct and working of every
branch of administration, in every district of the
country, and must be able, in the twenty-four hours
per day, which are all that is granted to a king as to
the humblest laborer, to give an effective share of attention and superintendence to all parts of this vast
field ; or he must at least be capable of discerning
and choosing out, from among the mass of his subjects, not only a large abundance of honest and able
men, fit to conduct every branch of public administration under supervision and control, but also the small
number of men of eminent virtues and talents who
can be trusted not only to do without that supervision,
but to exercise it themselves over others. So extraordinary are the faculties and energies required for
performing this task in any supportable manner, that
the good despot whom we are supposing can hardly
be imagined as consenting to undertake it unless as a
refuge from intolerable evils, and a transitional preparation for something beyond. But the argument can
do without even this immense item in the account.
Suppose the difficulty vanquished. What should we
then have? One man of superhuman mental activity
managing the entire affairs of a mentally passive people. Their passivity is implied in the very idea of
absolute power. The nation as a whole, and every
individual composing it, are without any potential

voice in their own destiny. They exercise no will in
respect to their collective interests. All is decided
for them by a will not their own, which it is legally
a crime for them to disobey. What sort of human
beings can be formed under such a regimen? What
development can either their thinking or their active
faculties attain under it? On matters of pure theory
they might perhaps be allowed to speculate, so long
as their speculations either did not approach politics,
or had not the remotest connection with its practice.
On practical affairs they could at most be only suffered to suggest; and even under the most moderate
of despots, none but persons of already admitted or
reputed superiority could hope that their suggestions
would be known to, much less regarded by, those
who had the management of affairs. A person must
have a very unusual taste for intellectual exercise in
and for itself who will put himself to the trouble of
thought when it is to have no outward effect, or
qualify himself for functions which he has no chance
of being allowed to exercise. The only sufficient in-
citement to mental exertion, in any but a few minds
in a generation, is the prospect of some practical use
to be made of its results. It does not follow that the
nation will be wholly destitute of intellectual power.
The common business of life, which must necessarily
be performed by each individual or family for themselves, will call forth some amount of intelligence and
practical ability within a certain narrow range of
ideas. There may be a select class of *savants* who
cultivate science with a view to its physical uses or

for the pleasure of the pursuit. There will be a bureaucracy, and persons in training for the bureaucracy, who will be taught at least some empirical maxims of government and public administration. There may be, and often has been, a systematic organization of the best mental power in the country in some special direction (commonly military) to promote the grandeur of the despot. But the public at large remain without information and without interest on all the greater matters of practice; or, if they have any knowledge of them, it is but a *dilettante* knowledge, like that which people have of the mechanical arts who have never handled a tool. Nor is it only in their intelligence that they suffer. Their moral capacities are equally stunted. Wherever the sphere of action of human beings is artificially circumscribed, their sentiments are narrowed and dwarfed in the same proportion. The food of feeling is action; even domestic affection lives upon voluntary good offices. Let a person have nothing to do for his country, and he will not care for it. It has been said of old that in a despotism there is at most but one patriot, the despot himself; and the saying rests on a just appreciation of the effects of absolute subjection even to a good and wise master. Religion remains; and here, at least, it may be thought, is an agency that may be relied on for lifting men's eyes and minds above the dust at their feet. But religion, even supposing it to escape perversion for the purposes of despotism, ceases in these circumstances to be a social concern, and narrows into a personal affair between an individual and his Maker, in which the issue at stake is but his private salvation. Religion in this shape is quite consistent with the most selfish and contracted egoism, and identifies the votary as little in feeling with the rest of his kind as sensuality itself.

A good despotism means a government in which, so far as depends on the despot, there is no positive oppression by officers of state, but in which all the collective interests of the people are managed for them, all the thinking that has relation to collective interests done for them, and in which their minds are formed by, and consenting to, this abdication of their own energies. Leaving things to the government, like leaving them to Providence, is synonymous with caring nothing about them, and accepting their results, when disagreeable, as visitations of Nature. With the exception, therefore, of a few studious men who take an intellectual interest in speculation for its own sake, the intelligence and sentiments of the whole people are given up to the material interests, and when these are provided for, to the amusement and ornamentation of private life. But to say this is to say, if the whole testimony of history is worth any thing, that the era of national decline has arrived; that is, if the nation had ever attained any thing to decline from. If it has never risen above the condition of an Oriental people, in that condition it continues to stagnate; but if, like Greece or Rome, it had realized any thing higher, through the energy, patriotism, and enlargement of mind, which, as national qualities, are the fruits solely of freedom, it relapses in a few generations into the Oriental state. And that state does not mean stupid tranquillity, with security against change for the worse; it often means being overrun, conquered, and reduced to domestic slavery either by a stronger despot, or by the nearest barbarous people who retain along with their savage rudeness the energies of freedom.

Such are not merely the natural tendencies, but the inherent necessities of despotic government, from which there is no outlet, unless in so far as the despotism consents not to be despotism; in so far as the supposed good despot abstains from exercising his power, and, though holding it in reserve, allows the general business of government to go on as if the people really governed themselves. However little probable it may be, we may imagine a despot observing many of the rules and restraints of constitutional government. He might allow such freedom of the press and of discussion as would enable a public opinion to form and express itself on national affairs. He might suffer local interests to be managed, without the interference of authority, by the people themselves. He might even surround himself with a council or councils of government, freely chosen by the whole or some portion of the nation, retaining in his own hands the power of taxation, and the supreme legislative as well as executive authority. Were he to act thus, and so far abdicate as a despot, he would do away with a considerable part of the evils characteristic of despotism. Political activity and capacity for public affairs would no longer be prevented from growing up in the body of the nation, and a public opinion would form itself, not the mere echo of the government. But such improvement would be the beginning of new difficulties. This public opinion, independent of the monarch's dictation, must be either with him or against him; if not the one, it will be the other. All governments must displease many persons, and these having now regular organs, and being able to express their sentiments, opinions adverse to the measures of government would often be expressed. What is the monarch to do when these unfavorable opinions happen to be in the majority? Is he to alter his course? Is he to defer to the nation? If so, he is no longer a despot, but a constitutional king; an organ or first minister of the people, distinguished only by being irremovable. If not, he must either put down opposition by his despotic power, or there will arise a permanent antagonism between the people and one man, which can have but one possible ending. Not even a religious principle of passive obedience and "right divine" would long ward off the natural consequences of such a position. The monarch would have to succumb, and conform to the conditions of constitutional royalty, or give place to some one who would. The despotism, being thus chiefly nominal, would possess few of the advantages supposed to belong to absolute monarchy, while it would realize in a very imperfect degree those of a free government, since, however great an amount of liberty the citizens might practically enjoy, they could never forget that they held it on sufferance, and by a concession which, under the existing constitution of the state, might at any moment be resumed; that they were legally slaves, though of a prudent or indulgent master.

It is not much to be wondered at if impatient or disappointed reformers, groaning under the impediments opposed to the most salutary public improvements by the ignorance, the indifference, the untractableness, the perverse obstinacy of a people, and the corrupt combinations of selfish private interests, armed with the powerful weapons afforded by free institutions, should at times sigh for a strong hand to bear down all these obstacles, and compel a recalcitrant people to be better governed.   But (setting aside the fact that for one despot who now and then reforms an abuse, there are ninety-nine who do nothing but create them) those who look in any such direction for the realization of their hopes leave out of the idea of good government its principal element, the improvement of the people themselves.   One of the benefits of freedom is that under it the ruler can not pass by the people's minds, and amend their affairs for them without amending *them*.   If it were possible for a people to be well governed in spite of themselves, their good government would last no longer than the freedom of a people usually lasts who have been liberated by foreign arms without their own co-operation.   It is true, a despot may educate the people, and to do so really would be the best apology for his despotism.   But any education which aims at making human beings other than machines, in the long run makes them claim to have the control of their own actions.   The leaders of French philosophy in the eighteenth century had been educated by the Jesuits. Even Jesuit education, it seems, was sufficiently real to call forth the appetite for freedom. Whatever invigorates the faculties, in however small a measure, creates an increased desire for their more unimpeded exercise; and a popular education is a failure if it educates the people for any state but that which it will certainly induce them to desire, and most probably to demand.

I am far from condemning, in cases of extreme exigency, the assumption of absolute power in the form of a temporary dictatorship. Free nations have, in times of old, conferred such power by their own choice, as a necessary medicine for diseases of the body politic which could not be got rid of by less violent means. But its acceptance, even for a time strictly limited, can only be excused, if, like Solon or Pittacus, the dictator employs the whole power he assumes in removing the obstacles which debar the nation from the enjoyment of freedom. A good despotism is an altogether false ideal, which practically (except as a means to some temporary purpose) becomes the most senseless and dangerous of chimeras. Evil for evil, a good despotism, in a country at all advanced in civilization, is more noxious than a bad one, for it is far more relaxing and enervating to the thoughts, feelings, and energies of the people. The despotism of Augustus prepared the Romans for Tiberius. If the whole tone of their character had not first been prostrated by nearly two generations of that mild slavery, they would probably have had spirit enough left to rebel against the more odious one.

There is no difficulty in showing that the ideally
best form of government is that in which the sovereignty, or supreme controlling power in the last resort, is vested in the entire aggregate of the community, every citizen not only having a voice in the
exercise of that ultimate sovereignty, but being, at
least occasionally, called on to take an actual part in
the government by the personal discharge of some
public function, local or general.

To test this proposition, it has to be examined in
reference to the two branches into which, as pointed
out in the last chapter, the inquiry into the goodness
of a government conveniently divides itself, namely,
how far it promotes the good management of the
affairs of society by means of the existing faculties,
moral, intellectual, and active, of its various members,
and what is its effect in improving or deteriorating
those faculties.

The ideally best form of government, it is scarcely
necessary to say, does not mean one which is practicable or eligible in all states of civilization, but the
one which, in the circumstances in which it is practicable and eligible, is attended with the greatest
amount of beneficial consequences, immediate and
prospective. A completely popular government is
the only polity which can make out any claim to this
character. It is pre-eminent in both the departments
between which the excellence of a political Constitution is divided. It is both more favorable to present
good government, and promotes a better and higher
form of national character than any other polity what-
soever.

Its superiority in reference to present well-being rests upon two principles, of as universal truth and applicability as any general propositions which can be laid down respecting human affairs. The first is, that the rights and interests of every or any person are only secure from being disregarded when the person interested is himself able, and habitually disposed to stand up for them. The second is, that the general prosperity attains a greater height, and is more widely diffused, in proportion to the amount and variety of the personal energies enlisted in promoting it.

Putting these two propositions into a shape more special to their present application—human beings are only secure from evil at the hands of others in proportion as they have the power of being, and are self-*protecting*; and they only achieve a high degree of success in their struggle with Nature in proportion as they are self-*dependent*, relying on what they themselves can do, either separately or in concert, rather than on what others do for them.

The former proposition—that each is the only safe guardian of his own rights and interests—is one of those elementary maxims of prudence which every person capable of conducting his own affairs implicitly acts upon wherever he himself is interested. Many, indeed, have a great dislike to it as a political doctrine, and are fond of holding it up to obloquy as a doctrine of universal selfishness. To which we may answer, that whenever it ceases to be true that mankind, as a rule, prefer themselves to others, and those nearest to them to those more remote, from that moment Communism is not only practicable, but the only defensible form of society, and will, when that time arrives, be assuredly carried into effect. For my own part, not believing in universal selfishness, I have no difficulty in admitting that Communism would even now be practicable among the *élite* of mankind, and may become so among the rest. But as this opinion is any thing but popular with those defenders of existing institutions who find fault with the doctrine of the general predominance of self-interest, I am inclined to think they do in reality believe that most men consider themselves before other people. It is not, however, necessary to affirm even thus much in order to support the claim of all to participate in the sovereign power. We need not suppose that when power resides in an exclusive class, that class will knowingly and deliberately sacrifice the other classes to themselves: it suffices that, in the absence of its natural defenders, the interest of the excluded is always in danger of being overlooked; and, when looked at, is seen with very different eyes from those of the persons whom it directly concerns. In this country, for example, what are called the working-classes may be considered as excluded from all direct participation in the government. I do not believe that the classes who do participate in it have in general any intention of sacrificing the working classes to themselves. They once had that intention; witness the persevering attempts so long made to keep down wages by law. But in the present day, their ordinary disposition is the very opposite: they willingly make considerable

sacrifices, especially of their pecuniary interest, for the
benefit of the working classes, and err rather by too
lavish and indiscriminating beneficence; nor do I believe that any rulers in history have been actuated by
a more sincere desire to do their duty toward the
poorer portion of their countrymen. Yet does Parliament, or almost any of the members composing it,
ever for an instant look at any question with the eyes
of a working man? When a subject arises in which
the laborers as such have an interest, is it regarded
from any point of view but that of the employers of
labor? I do not say that the working men's view
of these questions is in general nearer to truth than
the other, but it is sometimes quite as near; and in
any case it ought to be respectfully listened to, instead
of being, as it is, not merely turned away from, but
ignored. On the question of strikes, for instance, it is
doubtful if there is so much as one among the leading
members of either House who is not firmly convinced
that the reason of the matter is unqualifiedly on the
side of the masters, and that the men's view of it is
simply absurd. Those who have studied the question know well how far this is from being the case,
and in how different, and how infinitely less superficial a manner the point would have to be argued if
the classes who strike were able to make themselves
heard in Parliament.

It is an inherent condition of human affairs that no
intention, however sincere, of protecting the interests
of others can make it safe or salutary to tie up their
own hands. Still more obviously true is it that by

their own hands only can any positive and durable improvement of their circumstances in life be worked out. Through the joint influence of these two princi- ples, all free communities have both been more exempt from social injustice and crime, and have attained more brilliant prosperity than any others, or than they themselves after they lost their freedom. Contrast the free states of the world, while their freedom lasted, with the contemporary subjects of monarchical or oli- garchical despotism: the Greek cities with the Per- sian satrapies; the Italian republics, and the free towns of Flanders and Germany, with the feudal monarchies of Europe; Switzerland, Holland, and England with Austria or ante-revolutionary France. Their superior prosperity was too obvious ever to have been gainsayed; while their superiority in good government and social relations is proved by the pros- perity, and is manifest besides in every page of his- tory. If we compare, not one age with another, but the different governments which coexisted in the same age, no amount of disorder which exaggeration itself can pretend to have existed amid the publicity of the free states can be compared for a moment with the contemptuous trampling upon the mass of the people which pervaded the whole life of the monarchical countries, or the disgusting individual tyranny which was of more than daily occurrence under the systems of plunder which they called fiscal arrangements, and in the secrecy of their frightful courts of justice.

It must be acknowledged that the benefits of free- dom, so far as they have hitherto been enjoyed, were

obtained by the evtension of its privileges to a part
only of the community, and that a government in
which they are extended impartially to all is a desid-
eratum still unrealized. But, though every approach
to this has an independent value, and in many cases
more than an approach could not, in the existing state
of general improvement, be made, the participation of
all in these benefits is the ideally perfect conception
of free government. In proportion as any, no matter
who, are excluded from it, the interests of the excluded are left without the guaranty accorded to the
rest, and they themselves have less scope and encouragement than they might otherwise have to that exertion of their energies for the good of themselves
and of the community to which the general prosperity is always proportioned.

Thus stands the case as regards present well-being
—the good management of the affairs of the existing
generation. If we now pass to the influence of the
form of government upon character, we shall find the
superiority of popular government over every other
to be, if possible, still more decided and indisputable.

This question really depends upon a still more fundamental one, viz., which of two common types of
character, for the general good of humanity, it is most
desirable should predominate—the active or the passive type; that which struggles against evils, or that
which endures them; that which bends to circumstances, or that which endeavors to bend circumstances to itself.

The commonplaces of moralists and the general

sympathies of mankind are in favor of the passive type. Energetic characters may be admired, but the acquiescent and submissive are those which most men personally prefer. The passiveness of our neighbors increases our own sense of security, and plays into the hands of our willfulness. Passive characters, if we do not happen to need their activity, seem an obstruction the less in our own path. A contented character is not a dangerous rival. Yet nothing is more certain than that improvement in human affairs is wholly the work of the uncontented characters; and, moreover, that it is much easier for an active mind to acquire the virtues of patience, than for a passive one to assume those of energy.

Of the three varieties of mental excellence, intellectual, practical, and moral, there never could be any doubt, in regard to the first two, which side had the advantage. All intellectual superiority is the fruit of active effort. Enterprise, the desire to keep moving, to be trying and accomplishing new things for our own benefit or that of others, is the parent even of speculative, and much more of practical talent. The intellectual culture compatible with the other type is of that feeble and vague description which belongs to a mind that stops at amusement or at simple contemplation. The test of real and vigorous thinking, the thinking which ascertains truths instead of dreaming dreams, is successful application to practice. Where that purpose does not exist, to give definiteness, precision, and an intelligible meaning to thought, it generates nothing better than the mystical metaphysics of the Pythagoreans or the Veds. With respect to practical improvement, the case is still more evident. The character which improves human life is that which struggles with natural powers and tendencies, not that which gives way to them. The self-benefiting qualities are all on the side of the active and energetic character, and the habits and conduct which promote the advantage of each individual member of the community must be at least a part of those which conduce most in the end to the advancement of the community as a whole.

But, on the point of moral preferability, there seems at first sight to be room for doubt. I am not referring to the religious feeling which has so generally existed in favor of the inactive character, as being more in harmony with the submission due to the divine will. Christianity, as well as other religions, has fostered this sentiment; but it is the prerogative of Christianity, as regards this and many other perversions, that it is able to throw them off. Abstractedly from religious considerations, a passive character, which yields to obstacles instead of striving to overcome them, may not indeed be very useful to others, no more than to itself, but it might be expected to be at least inoffensive. Contentment is always counted among the moral virtues. But it is a complete error to suppose that contentment is necessarily or naturally attendant on passivity of character: and unless it is, the moral consequences are mischievous. Where there exists a desire for advantages not possessed, the mind which does not potentially possess them by means of its own energies is apt to look with hatred and malice on those who do. The person bestirring himself with hopeful prospects to improve his circumstances is the one who feels good-will toward others engaged in, or who have succeeded in the same pursuit. And where the majority are so engaged, those who do not attain the object have had the tone given to their feelings by the general habit of the country, and ascribe their failure to want of effort or opportunity, or to their personal ill luck. But those who, while desiring what others possess, put no energy into striving for it, are either incessantly grumbling that fortune does not do for them what they do not attempt to do for themselves, or overflowing with envy and ill-will toward those who possess what they would like to have.

In proportion as success in life is seen or believed to be the fruit of fatality or accident and not of exertion, in that same ratio does envy develop itself as a point of national character. The most envious of all mankind are the Orientals. In Oriental moralists, in Oriental tales, the envious man is markedly prominent. In real life, he is the terror of all who possess any thing desirable, be it a palace, a handsome child, or even good health and spirits: the supposed effect of his mere look constitutes the all-pervading superstition of the evil eye. Next to Orientals in envy, as in inactivity, are some of the Southern Europeans. The Spaniards pursued all their great men with it, embittered their lives, and generally succeeded in putting an early stop to their successes.* With the French,

* I limit the expression to past time, because I would. say nothing

who are essentially a Southern people, the double education of despotism and Catholicism has, in spite of their impulsive temperament, made submission and endurance the common character of the people, and their most received notion of wisdom and excellence; and if envy of one another, and of all superiority, is not more rife among them than it is, the circumstance must be ascribed to the many valuable counteracting elements in the French character, and most of all to the great individual energy which, though less persistent and more intermittent than in the self-helping and struggling Anglo-Saxons, has nevertheless manifested itself among the French in nearly every direction in which the operation of their institutions has been favorable to it.

There are, no doubt, in all countries, really contented characters, who not merely do not seek, but do not desire what they do not already possess, and these naturally bear no ill-will toward such as have apparently a more favored lot. But the great mass of seeming contentment is real discontent, combined with indolence or self-indulgence, which, while taking no legitimate means of raising itself, delights in bringing others down to its own level. And if we look narrowly even at the cases of innocent contentment, we perceive that they only win our admiration when the

derogatory of a great, and now at last a free people, who are entering into the general movement of European progress with a vigor which bids fair to make up rapidly the ground they have lost. No one can doubt what Spanish intellect and energy are capable of; and their faults as a people are chiefly those for which freedom and industrial ardor are a real specific.

indifference is solely to improvement in outward circumstances, and there is a striving for perpetual advancement in spiritual worth, or at least a disinterested zeal to benefit others. The contented man, or the contented family, who have no ambition to make any one else happier, to promote the good of their country or their neighborhood, or to improve themselves in moral excellence, excite in us neither admiration nor approval. We rightly ascribe this sort of contentment to mere unmanliness and want of spirit. The content which we approve is an ability to do cheerfully without what can not be had, a just appreciation of the comparative value of different objects of desire, and a willing renunciation of the less when incompatible with the greater. These, however, are excellences more natural to the character, in proportion as it is actively engaged in the attempt to improve its own or some other lot. He who is continually measuring his energy against difficulties, learns what are the difficulties insuperable to him, and what are those which, though he might overcome, the success is not worth the cost. He whose thoughts and activities are all needed for, and habitually employed in, practicable and useful enterprises, is the person of all others least likely to let his mind dwell with brooding discontent upon things either not worth attaining, or which are not so to him. Thus the active, self-helping character is not only intrinsically the best, but is the likeliest to acquire all that is really excellent or desirable in the opposite type.

The striving, go-ahead character of England and

the United States is only a fit subject of disapproving
criticism on account of the very secondary objects on
which it commonly expends its strength. In itself it
is the foundation of the best hopes for the general improvement of mankind. It has been acutely remark-
ed, that whenever any thing goes amiss, the habitual
impulse of French people is to say, " Il faut de la patience;" and of English people, "What a shame!"
The people who think it a shame when any thing
goes wrong—who rush to the conclusion that the evil
could and ought to have been prevented, are those
who, in the long run, do most to make the world better. If the desires are low placed, if they extend to
little beyond physical comfort and the show of riches,
the immediate results of the energy will not be much
more than the continual extension of man's power
over material objects; but even this makes room, and
prepares the mechanical appliances for the greatest
intellectual and social achievements; and while the
energy is there, some persons will apply it, and it will
be applied more and more, to the perfecting, not of
outward circumstances alone, but of man's inward nature. Inactivity, unaspiringness, absence of desire, is
a more fatal hinderance to improvement than any misdirection of energy, and is that through which alone,
when existing in the mass, any very formidable misdirection by an energetic few becomes possible. It is
this, mainly, which retains in a savage or semi-savage
state the great majority of the human race.

Now there can be no kind of doubt that the passive
type of character is favored by the government of

one or a few, and the active self-helping type by that
of the many. Irresponsible rulers need the quiescence of the ruled more than they need any activity
but that which they can compel. Submissiveness to
the prescriptions of men as necessities of nature is the
lesson inculcated by all governments upon those who
are wholly without participation in them. The will
of superiors, and the law as the will of superiors, must
be passively yielded to. But no men are mere instruments or materials in the hands of their rulers
who have will, or spirit, or a spring of internal activity in the rest of their proceedings, and any manifestation of these qualities, instead of receiving encouragement from despots, has to get itself forgiven by
them. Even when irresponsible rulers are not sufficiently conscious of danger from the mental activity
of their subjects to be desirous of repressing it, the
position itself is a repression. Endeavor is even more
effectually restrained by the certainty of its impo-
tence than by any positive discouragement. Between
subjection to the will of others and the virtues of self-
help and self-government there is a natural incompatibility. This is more or less complete according as the
bondage is strained or relaxed. Rulers differ very
much in the length to which they carry the control
of the free agency of their subjects, or the suppression
of it by managing their business for them. But the
difference is in degree, not in principle; and the best
despots often go the greatest lengths in chaining up
the free agency of their subjects. A bad despot, when
his own personal indulgences have been provided for,

may sometimes be willing to let the people alone; but a good despot insists on doing them good by making them do their own business in a better way than they themselves know of. The regulations which restricted to fixed processes all the leading branches of French manufactures were the work of the great Colbert.

Very different is the state of the human faculties where a human being feels himself under no other external restraint than the necessities of nature, or mandates of society which he has his share in imposing, and which it is open to him, if he thinks them wrong, publicly to dissent from, and exert himself actively to get altered. No doubt, under a government partially popular, this freedom may be exercised even by those who are not partakers in the full privileges of citizenship; but it is a great additional stimulus to any one's self-help and self-reliance when he starts from an even ground, and has not to feel that his success depends on the impression he can make upon the sentiments and dispositions of a body of whom he is not one. It is a great discouragement to an individual, and a still greater one to a class, to be left out of the constitution; to be reduced to plead from outside the door to the arbiters of their destiny, not taken into the consultation within. The maximum of the invigorating effect of freedom upon the character is only obtained when the person acted on either is, or is looking forward to become, a citizen as fully privileged as any other. What is still more important than even this matter of feeling is the prac-

tical discipline which the character obtains from the
occasional demand made upon the citizens to exercise,
for a time and in their turn, some social function. It
is not sufficiently considered how little there is in
most men's ordinary life to give any largeness either
to their conceptions or to their sentiments. Their
work is a routine; not a labor of love, but of self-interest in the most elementary form, the satisfaction of
daily wants; neither the thing done, nor the process
of doing it, introduces the mind to thoughts or feelings extending beyond individuals; if instructive
books are within their reach, there is no stimulus to
read them; and, in most cases, the individual has no
access to any person of cultivation much superior to
his own. Giving him something to do for the public
supplies, in a measure, all these deficiencies. If circumstances allow the amount of public duty assigned
him to be considerable, it makes him an educated
man. Notwithstanding the defects of the social system and moral ideas of antiquity, the practice of the
dicastery and the ecclesia raised the intellectual standard of an average Athenian citizen far beyond any
thing of which there is yet an example in any other
mass of men, ancient or modern. The proofs of this
are apparent in every page of our great historian of
Greece; but we need scarcely look farther than to
the high quality of the addresses which their great
orators deemed best calculated to act with effect on
their understanding and will. A benefit of the same
kind, though far less in degree, is produced on Englishmen of the lower middle class by their liability

to be placed on juries and to serve parish offices,
which, though it does not occur to so many, nor is
so continuous, nor introduces them to so great a variety of elevated considerations as to admit of comparison with the public education which every citizen of
Athens obtained from her democratic institutions,
makes them nevertheless very different beings, in
range of ideas and development of faculties, from
those who have done nothing in their lives but drive
a quill, or sell goods over a counter. Still more salutary is the moral part of the instruction afforded by
the participation of the private citizen, if even rarely,
in public functions. He is called upon, while so engaged, to weigh interests not his own; to be guided,
in case of conflicting claims, by another rule than his
private partialities; to apply, at every turn, principles
and maxims which have for their reason of existence
the general good ; and he usually finds associated
with him in the same work minds more familiarized
than his own with these ideas and operations, whose
study it will be to supply reasons to his understanding, and stimulation to his feeling for the general
good. He is made to feel himself one of the public,
and whatever is their interest to be his interest.
Where this school of public spirit does not exist,
scarcely any sense is entertained that private persons,
in no eminent social situation, owe any duties to society except to obey the laws and submit to the government. There is no unselfish sentiment of identifi-
cation with the public. Every thought and feeling,
either of interest or of duty, is absorbed in the indi-

vidual and in the family. The man never thinks of any collective interest, of any objects to be pursued jointly with others, but only in competition with them, and in some measure at their expense. A neighbor, not being an ally or an associate, since he is never engaged in any common undertaking for the joint benefit, is therefore only a rival. Thus even private morality suffers, while public is actually extinct. Were this the universal and only possible state of things, the utmost aspirations of the lawgiver or the moralist could only stretch to making the bulk of the community a flock of sheep innocently nibbling the grass side by side.

From these accumulated considerations, it is evident that the only government which can fully satisfy all the exigencies of the social state is one in which the whole people participate; that any participation, even in the smallest public function, is useful; that the participation should every where be as great as the general degree of improvement of the community will allow; and that nothing less can be ultimately desirable than the admission of all to a share in the sovereign power of the state. But since all can not, in a community exceeding a single small town, participate personally in any but some very minor portions of the public business, it follows that the ideal type of a perfect government must be representative.

CHAPTER IV.

UNDER WHAT SOCIAL CONDITIONS REPRESENTATIVE GOVERNMENT IS INAPPLICABLE.

WE have recognized in representative government the ideal type of the most perfect polity for which, in consequence, any portion of mankind are better adapted in proportion to their degree of general improvement. As they range lower and lower in development, that form of government will be, generally speaking, less suitable to them, though this is not true universally; for the adaptation of a people to representative government does not depend so much upon the place they occupy in the general scale of humanity as upon the degree in which they possess certain special requisites; requisites, however, so closely connected with their degree of general advancement, that any variation between the two is rather the exception than the rule. Let us examine at what point in the descending series representative government ceases altogether to be admissible, either through its own unfitness or the superior fitness of some other regimen.

First, then, representative, like any other government, must be unsuitable in any case in which it can not permanently subsist—*i. e.*, in which it does not fulfill the three fundamental conditions enumerated in the first chapter. These were, 1. That the people should be willing to receive it. 2. That they should be willing and able to do what is necessary for its preservation. 3. That they should be willing and able to fulfill the duties and discharge the functions which it imposes on them.

The willingness of the people to accept representative government only becomes a practical question when an enlightened ruler, or a foreign nation or nations who have gained power over the country, are disposed to offer it the boon. To individual reformers the question is almost irrelevant, since, if no other objection can be made to their enterprise than that the opinion of the nation is not yet on their side, they have the ready and proper answer, that to bring it over to their side is the very end they aim at. When opinion is really adverse, its hostility is usually to the fact of change rather than to representative government in itself. The contrary case is not indeed unexampled; there has sometimes been a religious repugnance to any limitation of the power of a particular line of rulers; but, in general, the doctrine of passive obedience meant only submission to the will of the powers that be, whether monarchical or popular. In any case in which the attempt to introduce representative government is at all likely to be made, indifference to it, and inability to understand its processes and requirements, rather than positive opposition, are the obstacles to be expected. These, however, are as fatal, and may be as hard to be got rid of as actual aversion; it being easier, in most cases, to change the

direction of an active feeling than to create one in a
state previously passive. When a people have no
sufficient value for, and attachment to, a representative constitution, they have next to no chance of retaining it. In every country, the executive is the
branch of the government which wields the immediate
power, and is in direct contact with the public; to it,
principally, the hopes and fears of individuals are directed, and by it both the benefits, and the terrors, and
prestige of government are mainly represented to the
public eye. Unless, therefore, the authorities whose
office it is to check the executive are backed by an
effective opinion and feeling in the country, the executive has always the means of setting them aside
or compelling them to subservience, and is sure to be
well supported in doing so. Representative institutions necessarily depend for permanence upon the
readiness of the people to fight for them in case of
their being endangered. If too little valued for this,
they seldom obtain a footing at all, and if they do,
are almost sure to be overthrown as soon as the head
of the government, or any party leader who can muster force for a *coup de main*, is willing to run some
small risk for absolute power.

These considerations relate to the two first causes
of failure in a representative government. The third
is when the people want either the will or the capacity to fulfill the part which belongs to them in a representative constitution. When nobody, or only some
small fraction, feels the degree of interest in the general affairs of the state necessary to the formation of

a public opinion, the electors will seldom make any
use of the right of the suffrage but to serve their
private interest, or the interest of their locality, or of
some one with whom they are connected as adherents
or dependents. The small class who, in this state of
public feeling, gain the command of the representative body, for the most part use it solely as a means of
seeking their fortune. If the executive is weak, the
country is distracted by mere struggles for place; if
strong, it makes itself despotic, at the cheap price of
appeasing the representatives, or such of them as are
capable of giving trouble, by a share of the spoil; and
the only fruit produced by national representation is,
that in addition to those who really govern, there is
an assembly quartered on the public, and no abuse in
which a portion of the assembly are interested is at all
likely to be removed. When, however, the evil stops
here, the price may be worth paying for the publicity
and discussion which, though not an invariable, are a
natural accompaniment of any, even nominal, representation. In the modern kingdom of Greece, for example, it can hardly be doubted that the place-hunters who chiefly compose the representative assembly,
though they contribute little or nothing directly to
good government, nor even much temper the arbitrary
power of the executive, yet keep up the idea of popular rights, and conduce greatly to the real liberty of
the press which exists in that country. This benefit,
however, is entirely dependent on the coexistence
with the popular body of an hereditary king. If, instead of struggling for the favors of the chief ruler,

these selfish and sordid factions struggled for the chief place itself, they would certainly, as in Spanish America, keep the country in a state of chronic revolution and civil war. A despotism, not even legal, but of illegal violence, would be alternately exercised by a succession of political adventurers, and the name and forms of representation would have no effect but to prevent despotism from attaining the stability and security by which alone its evils can be mitigated or its few advantages realized.

The preceding are the cases in which representative government can not permanently exist. There are others in which it possibly might exist, but in which some other form of government would be preferable. These are principally when the people, in order to advance in civilization, have some lesson to learn, some habit not yet acquired, to the acquisition of which representative government is likely to be an impediment.

The most obvious of these cases is the one already considered, in which the people have still to learn the first lesson of civilization, that of obedience. A race who have been trained in energy and courage by struggles with Nature and their neighbors, but who have not yet settled down into permanent obedience to any common superior, would be little likely to acquire this habit under the collective government of their own body. A representative assembly drawn from among themselves would simply reflect their own turbulent insubordination. It would refuse its authority to all proceedings which would impose, on

their savage independence, any improving restraint.
The mode in which such tribes are usually brought
to submit to the primary conditions of civilized society is through the necessities of warfare, and the
despotic authority indispensable to military command.
A military leader is the only superior to whom they
will submit, except occasionally some prophet supposed to be inspired from above, or conjuror regarded
as possessing miraculous power. These may exercise
a temporary ascendency, but as it is merely personal,
it rarely effects any change in the general habits of
the people, unless the prophet, like Mohammed, is also
a military chief, and goes forth the armed apostle of
a new religion; or unless the military chiefs ally themselves with his influence, and turn it into a prop for
their own government.

A people are no less unfitted for representative
government by the contrary fault to that last speci-
fied—by extreme passiveness, and ready submission
to tyranny. If a people thus prostrated by character
and circumstances could obtain representative institutions, they would inevitably choose their tyrants as
their representatives, and the yoke would be made
heavier on them by the contrivance which *primâ facie*
might be expected to lighten it. On the contrary,
many a people has gradually emerged from this condition by the aid of a central authority, whose position has made it the rival, and has ended by making
it the master, of the local despots, and which, above
all, has been single. French history, from Hugh Ca-
pet to Richelieu and Louis XIV., is a continued ex-

ample of this course of things. Even when the king was scarcely so powerful as many of his chief feudatories, the great advantage which he derived from being but one has been recognized by French historians. To him the eyes of *all* the locally oppressed were turned; he was the object of hope and reliance throughout the kingdom, while each local potentate was only powerful within a more or less confined space. At his hands, refuge and protection were sought from every part of the country against first one, then another of the immediate oppressors. His progress to ascendency was slow, but it resulted from successively taking advantage of opportunities which offered themselves only to him. It was, therefore, sure; and, in proportion as it was accomplished, it abated, in the oppressed portion of the community, the habit of submitting to oppression. The king's interest lay in encouraging all partial attempts on the part of the serfs to emancipate themselves from their masters, and place themselves in immediate subordination to himself. Under his protection numerous communities were formed which knew no one above them but the king. Obedience to a distant monarch is liberty itself compared with the dominion of the lord of the neighboring castle; and the monarch was long compelled by necessities of position to exert his authority as the ally rather than the master of the classes whom he had aided in effecting their liberation. In this manner a central power, despotic in principle, though generally much restricted in practice, was mainly instrumental in carrying the people through a necessary stage of improvement, which representative government, if real, would most likely have prevented them from entering upon. There are parts of Europe where the same work is still to be done, and no prospect of its being done by any other means. Nothing short of despotic rule or a general massacre could effect the emancipation of the serfs in the Russian Empire.

The same passages of history forcibly illustrate another mode in which unlimited monarchy overcomes obstacles to the progress of civilization which representative government would have had a decided tendency to aggravate. One of the strongest hinderances to improvement, up to a rather advanced stage, is an inveterate spirit of locality. Portions of mankind, in many other respects capable of, and prepared for freedom, may be unqualified for amalgamating into even the smallest nation. Not only may jealousies and antipathies repel them from one another, and bar all possibility of voluntary union, but they may not yet have acquired any of the feelings or habits which would make the union real, supposing it to be nominally accomplished. They may, like the citizens of an ancient community, or those of an Asiatic village, have had considerable practice in exercising their faculties on village or town interests, and have even realized a tolerably effective popular government on that restricted scale, and may yet have but slender sympathies with any thing beyond, and no habit or capacity of dealing with interests common to many such communities. I am not aware that history furnishes any example in which a number of these po-

litical atoms or corpuscles have coalesced into a body,
and learned to feel themselves one people, except
through previous subjection to a central authority
common to all.* It is through the habit of deferring
to that authority, entering into its plans and subserv-
ing its purposes, that a people such as we have supposed receive into their minds the conception of large
interests common to a considerable geographical extent. Such interests, on the contrary, are necessarily
the predominant consideration in the mind of the central ruler; and through the relations, more or less
intimate, which he progressively establishes with the
localities, they become familiar to the general mind.
The most favorable concurrence of circumstances under which this step in improvement could be made
would be one which should raise up representative
institutions without representative government; a representative body or bodies, drawn from the localities,
making itself the auxiliary and instrument of the central power, but seldom attempting to thwart or control it. The people being thus taken, as it were, into
council, though not sharing the supreme power, the
political education given by the central authority is
carried home, much more effectually than it could
otherwise be, to the local chiefs and to the population
generally, while, at the same time, a tradition is kept

---

* Italy, which alone can be quoted as an exception, is only so in
regard to the final stage of its transformation. The more difficult
previous advance from the city isolation of Florence, Pisa, or Milan,
to the provincial unity of Tuscany or Lombardy, took place in the
usual manner.

up of government by general consent, or, at least, the
sanction of tradition is not given to government without it, which, when consecrated by custom, has so oft-
en put a bad end to a good beginning, and is one of
the most frequent cases of the sad fatality which in
most countries has stopped improvement in so early
a stage, because the work of some one period has been
so done as to bar the needful work of the ages following. Meanwhile, it may be laid down as a political
truth, that by irresponsible monarchy rather than by
representative government can a multitude of insignificant political units be welded into a people, with
common feelings of cohesion, power enough to protect
itself against conquest or foreign aggression, and affairs
sufficiently various and considerable of its own to occupy worthily and expand to fit proportions the social
and political intelligence of the population.

For these several reasons, kingly government, free
from the control (though perhaps strengthened by the
support) of representative institutions, is the most suitable form of polity for the earliest stages of any community, not excepting a city community like those of
ancient Greece ; where, accordingly, the government
of kings, under some real, but no ostensible or constitutional control by public opinion, did historically precede by an unknown and probably great duration all
free institutions, and gave place at last, during a considerable lapse of time, to oligarchies of a few families.

A hundred other infirmities or shortcomings in a
people might be pointed out which *pro tanto* disqualify them from making the best use of representative

government; but in regard to these it is not equally obvious that the government of One or a Few would have any tendency to cure or alleviate the evil. Strong prejudices of any kind; obstinate adherence to old habits; positive defects of national character, or mere ignorance, and deficiency of mental cultivation, if prevalent in a people, will be in general faithfully reflected in their representative assemblies; and should it happen that the executive administration, the direct management of public affairs, is in the hands of persons comparatively free from these defects, more good would frequently be done by them when not hampered by the necessity of carrying with them the voluntary assent of such bodies. But the mere position of the rulers does not in these, as it does in the other cases which we have examined, of itself invest them with interests and tendencies operating in the beneficial direction. From the general weaknesses of the people or of the state of civilization, the One and his counselors, or the Few, are not likely to be habitually exempt, except in the case of their being foreigners, belonging to a superior people or a more advanced state of society. Then, indeed, the rulers may be, to almost any extent, superior in civilization to those over whom they rule; and subjection to a foreign government of this description, notwithstanding its inevitable evils, is often of the greatest advantage to a people, carrying them rapidly through several stages of progress, and clearing away obstacles to improvement which might have lasted indefinitely if the subject population had been left unassisted to its native

tendencies and chances. In a country not under the
dominion of foreigners, the only cause adequate to producing similar benefits is the rare accident of a monarch of extraordinary genius. There have been in
history a few of these who, happily for humanity, have
reigned long enough to render some of their improvements permanent, by leaving them under the guard-
ianship of a generation which had grown up under
their influence. Charlemagne may be cited as one instance; Peter the Great is another. Such examples,
however, are so unfrequent that they can only be
classed with the happy accidents which have so often
decided at a critical moment whether some leading
portion of humanity should make a sudden start, or
sink back toward barbarism—chances like the existence of Themistocles at the time of the Persian invasion, or of the first or third William of Orange. It
would be absurd to construct institutions for the mere
purpose of taking advantage of such possibilities, especially as men of this calibre, in any distinguished
position, do not require despotic power to enable them
to exert great influence, as is evidenced by the three
last mentioned. The case most requiring consideration in reference to institutions is the not very uncommon one in which a small but leading portion of the
population, from difference of race, more civilized origin, or other peculiarities of circumstance, are markedly superior in civilization and general character to
the remainder. Under these conditions, government
by the representatives of the mass would stand a
chance of depriving them of much of the benefit they

might derive from the greater civilization of the superior ranks, while government by the representatives
of those ranks would probably rivet the degradation
of the multitude, and leave them no hope of decent
treatment except by ridding themselves of one of the
most valuable elements of future advancement. The
best prospect of improvement for a people thus composed lies in the existence of a constitutionally unlimited, or at least a practically preponderant authority
in the chief ruler of the dominant class. He alone has
by his position an interest in raising and improving
the mass, of whom he is not jealous, as a counterpoise
to his associates, of whom he is; and if fortunate circumstances place beside him, not as controllers, but
as subordinates, a body representative of the superior
caste, which, by its objections and questionings, and its
occasional outbreaks of spirit, keeps alive habits of collective resistance, and may admit of being, in time and
by degrees, expanded into a really national representation (which is in substance the history of the English
Parliament), the nation has then the most favorable
prospects of improvement which can well occur to a
community thus circumstanced and constituted.

Among the tendencies which, without absolutely
rendering a people unfit for representative government, seriously incapacitate them from reaping the full
benefit of it, one deserves particular notice. There
are two states of the inclinations, intrinsically very
different, but which have something in common, by
virtue of which they often coincide in the direction
they give to the efforts of individuals and of nations;

one is, the desire to exercise power over others; the other is disinclination to have power exercised over themselves. The difference between different portions of mankind in the relative strength of these two dispositions is one of the most important elements in their history. There are nations in whom the passion for governing others is so much stronger than the desire of personal independence, that for the mere shadow of the one they are found ready to sacrifice the whole of the other. Each one of their number is willing, like the private soldier in an army, to abdicate his personal freedom of action into the hands of his general, provided the army is triumphant and victorious, and he is able to flatter himself that he is one of a conquering host, though the notion that he has himself any share in the domination exercised over the conquered is an illusion. A government strictly limited in its powers and attributions, required to hold its hands from overmeddling, and to let most things go on without its assuming the part of guardian or director, is not to the taste of such a people; in their eyes the possessors of authority can hardly take too much upon themselves, provided the authority itself is open to general competition. An average individual among them prefers the chance, however distant or improbable, of wielding some share of power over his fellow-citizens, above the certainty, to himself and others, of having no unnecessary power exercised over them. These are the elements of a people of place-hunters, in whom the course of politics is mainly determined by place-hunting; where equality alone is

cared for, but not liberty; where the contests of political parties are but struggles to decide whether the
power of meddling in every thing shall belong to one
class or another, perhaps merely to one knot of public
men or another; where the idea entertained of democracy is merely that of opening offices to the competition of all instead of a few; where, the more popular the institutions, the more innumerable are the
places created, and the more monstrous the overgov-
ernment exercised by all over each, and by the executive over all. It would be as unjust as it would be
ungenerous to offer this, or any thing approaching to
it, as an unexaggerated picture of the French people;
yet the degree in which they do participate in this
type of character has caused representative government by a limited class to break down by excess of
corruption, and the attempt at representative government by the whole male population to end in giving
one man the power of consigning any number of the
rest, without trial, to Lambessa or Cayenne, provided
he allows all of them to think themselves not excluded from the possibility of sharing his favors.
The point of character which, beyond any other, fits
the people of this country for representative government, is that they have almost universally the contrary characteristic. They are very jealous of any
attempt to exercise power over them not sanctioned
by long usage and by their own opinion of right, but
they in general care very little for the exercise of
power over others. Not having the smallest sympathy with the passion for governing, while they are but
too well acquainted with the motives of private inter-

est from which that office is sought, they prefer that it should be performed by those to whom it comes without seeking, as a consequence of social position. If foreigners understood this, it would account to them for some of the apparent contradictions in the political feelings of Englishmen; their unhesitating readiness to let themselves be governed by the higher classes, coupled with so little personal subservience to them, that no people are so fond of resisting authority when it oversteps certain prescribed limits, or so determined to make their rulers always remember that they will only be governed in the way they themselves like best. Place-hunting, accordingly, is a form of ambition to which the English, considered nationally, are almost strangers. If we except the few families or connections of whom official employment lies directly in the way, Englishmen's views of advancement in life take an altogether different direction— that of success in business or in a profession. They have the strongest distaste for any mere struggle for office by political parties or individuals; and there are few things to which they have a greater aversion than to the multiplication of public employments; a thing, on the contrary, always popular with the bureaucracy-ridden nations of the Continent, who would rather pay higher taxes than diminish, by the smallest fraction, their individual chances of a place for themselves or their relatives, and among whom a cry for retrenchment never means abolition of offices, but the reduction of the salaries of those which are too considerable for the ordinary citizen to have any chance of being appointed to them.

CHAPTER V.

OF THE PROPER FUNCTIONS OF REPRESENTATIVE BODIES.

In treating of representative government, it is above all necessary to keep in view the distinction between its idea or essence, and the particular forms in which the idea has been clothed by accidental historical developments, or by the notions current at some particular period.

The meaning of representative government is, that the whole people, or some numerous portion of them, exercise, through deputies periodically elected by themselves, the ultimate controlling power, which, in every constitution, must reside somewhere. This ultimate power they must possess in all its completeness. They must be masters, whenever they please, of all the operations of government. There is no need that the constitutional law should itself give them this mastery. It does not in the British Constitution. But what it does give practically amounts to this: the power of final control is as essentially single, in a mixed and balanced government, as in a pure monarchy or democracy. This is the portion of truth in the opinion of the ancients, revived by great authorities in our own time, that a balanced constitution is impossible. There is almost always a balance, but the scales never hang exactly even. Which of them preponderates is not always apparent on the face of the political institutions. In the British Constitution, each of the three co-ordinate members of the sovereignty is invested with powers which, if fully exercised, would enable it to stop all the machinery of government. Nominally, therefore, each is invested with equal power of thwarting and obstructing the others; and if, by exerting that power, any of the three could hope to better its position, the ordinary course of human affairs forbids us to doubt that the power would be exercised. There can be no question that the full powers of each would be employed defensively, if it found· itself assailed by one or both of the others. What, then, prevents the same powers from being exerted aggressively? The unwritten maxims of the Constitution—in other words, the positive political morality of the country; and this positive political morality is what we must look to if we would know in whom the really supreme power in the Constitution resides.

By constitutional law, the crown can refuse its assent to any act of Parliament, and can appoint to office and maintain in it any minister, in opposition to the remonstrances of Parliament. But the constitutional morality of the country nullifies these powers, preventing them from being ever used; and, by requiring that the head of the administration should always be virtually appointed by the House of Commons, makes that body the real sovereign of the state.

These unwritten rules, which limit the use of lawful powers, are, however, only effectual, and maintain themselves in existence on condition of harmonizing with the actual distribution of real political strength. There is in every constitution a strongest power—one which would gain the victory if the compromises by which the Constitution habitually works were suspended, and there came a trial of strength. Constitutional maxims are adhered to, and are practically operative, so long as they give the predominance in the Constitution to that one of the powers which has the preponderance of active power out of doors. This, in England, is the popular power. If, therefore, the legal provisions of the British Constitution, together with the unwritten maxims by which the conduct of the different political authorities is in fact regulated, did not give to the popular element in the Constitution that substantial supremacy over every department of the government which corresponds to its real power in the country, the Constitution would not possess the stability which characterizes it; either the laws or the unwritten maxims would soon have to be changed. The British government is thus a representative government in the correct sense of the term; and the powers which it leaves in hands not directly accountable to the people can only be considered as precautions which the ruling power is willing should be taken against its own errors. Such precautions have existed in all well-constructed democracies. The Athenian Constitution had many such provisions, and so has that of the United States.

But while it is essential to representative government that the practical supremacy in the state should reside in the representatives of the people, it is an open question what actual functions, what precise part in the machinery of government, shall be directly and personally discharged by the representative body. Great varieties in this respect are compatible with the essence of representative government, provided the functions are such as secure to the representative body the control of every thing in the last resort.

There is a radical distinction between controlling the business of government and actually doing it. The same person or body may be able to control every thing, but can not possibly do every thing; and in many cases its control over every thing will be more perfect the less it personally attempts to do. The commander of an army could not direct its movements so effectually if he himself fought in the ranks or led an assault. It is the same with bodies of men. Some things can not be done except by bodies; other things can not be well done by them. It is one question, therefore, what a popular assembly should control, another what it should itself do. It should, as we have already seen, control all the operations of government. But, in order to determine through what channel this general control may most expediently be exercised, and what portion of the business of government the representative assembly should hold in its own hands, it is necessary to consider what kinds of business a numerous body is competent to perform properly. That alone which it can do well it ought to take personally upon itself. With regard to the rest, its proper province is not to do it, but to take means for having it well done by others.

For example, the duty which is considered as belonging more peculiarly than any other to an assembly representative of the people is that of voting the taxes. Nevertheless, in no country does the representative body undertake, by itself or its delegated officers, to prepare the estimates. Though the supplies can only be voted by the House of Commons, and though the sanction of the House is also required for the appropriation of the revenues to the different items of the public expenditure, it is the maxim and the uniform practice of the Constitution that money can be granted only on the proposition of the crown. It has, no doubt, been felt that moderation as to the amount, and care and judgment in the detail of its application, can only be expected when the executive government, through whose hands it is to pass, is made responsible for the plans and calculations on which the disbursements are grounded. Parliament, accordingly, is not expected, nor even permitted, to originate directly either taxation or expenditure. All it is asked for is its consent, and the sole power it possesses is that of refusal.

The principles which are involved and recognized in this constitutional doctrine, if followed as far as they will go, are a guide to the limitation and definition of the general functions of representative assemblies. In the first place, it is admitted in all countries in which the representative system is practically understood, that numerous representative bodies ought not to administer. The maxim is grounded not only on the most essential principles of good government, but on those of the successful conduct of business of any description. No body of men, unless organized and under command, is fit for action, in the proper sense. Even a select board, composed of few members, and these specially conversant with the business to be done, is always an inferior instrument to some one individual who could be found among them, and would be improved in character if that one person were made the chief, and all the others reduced to subordinates. What can be done better by a body than by any individual is deliberation. When it is necessary or important to secure hearing and consideration to many conflicting opinions, a deliberative body is indispensable. Those bodies, therefore, are frequently useful, even for administrative business, but in general only as advisers; such business being, as a rule, better conducted under the responsibility of one. Even a joint-stock company has always in practice, if not in theory, a managing director; its good or bad management depends essentially on some one person's qualifications, and the remaining directors, when of any use, are so by their suggestions to him, or by the power they possess of watching him, and restraining or removing him in case of misconduct. That they are ostensibly equal sharers with him in the management is no advantage, but a considerable set-off against any good which they are capable of doing: it weakens greatly the sense in his own mind, and in those of other people, of that individual responsibility in which he should stand forth personally and undividedly.

But a popular assembly is still less fitted to administer, or to dictate in detail to those who have the charge of administration. Even when honestly meant, the interference is almost always injurious. Every branch of public administration is a skilled business, which has its own peculiar principles and traditional rules, many of them not even known in any effectual way except to those who have at some time had a hand in carrying on the business, and none of them likely to be duly appreciated by persons not practically acquainted with the department. I do not mean that the transaction of public business has esoteric mysteries, only to be understood by the initiated. Its principles are all intelligible to any person of good sense, who has in his mind a true picture of the circumstances and conditions to be dealt with; but to have this, he must know those circumstances and conditions; and the knowledge does not come by intuition. There are many rules of the greatest importance in every branch of public business (as there are in every private occupation), of which a person fresh to the subject neither knows the reason nor even suspects the existence, because they are intended to meet dangers or provide against inconveniences which never entered into his thoughts. I have known public men, ministers of more than ordinary mental capacity, who, on their first introduction to a department of business new to them, have excited the mirth of their inferiors by the air with which they announced as a truth hitherto set at naught, and brought to light by themselves, something which was probably the first thought of every body who ever looked at the subject, given up as soon as he had got on to a second. It is true that a great statesman is he who knows when to depart from traditions, as well as when to adhere to them; but it is a great mistake to suppose that he will do this better for being ignorant of the traditions. No one who does not thoroughly know the modes of action which common experience has sanctioned is capable of judging of the circumstances which require a departure from those ordinary modes of action. The interests dependent on the acts done by a public department, the consequences liable to follow from any particular mode of conducting it, require for weighing and estimating them a kind of knowledge, and of specially exercised judgment, almost as rarely found in those not bred to it, as the capacity to reform the law in those who have not professionally studied it. All these difficulties are sure to be ignored by a representative assembly which attempts to decide on special acts of administration. At its best, it is inexperience sitting in judgment on experience, ignorance on knowledge; ignorance which, never suspecting the existence of what it does not know, is equally careless and supercilious, making light of, if not resenting, all pretensions to have a judgment better worth attending to than its own. Thus it is when no interested motives intervene; but when they do, the result is jobbery more unblushing and audacious than the worst corruption which can well take place in a public office under a government of publicity. It is not necessary that the interested bias should extend to the majority of the assembly. In any particular case it is often enough that it affects two or three of their number. Those two or three will have a greater interest in misleading the body than any other of its members are likely to have in putting it right. The bulk of the assembly may keep their hands clean, but they can not keep their minds vigilant or their judgments discerning in matters they know nothing about; and an indolent majority, like an indolent individual, belongs to the person who takes most pains with it. The bad measures or bad appointments of a minister may be checked by Parliament; and the interests of ministers in defending, and of rival partisans in attacking, secure a tolerably equal discussion ; but *quis custodiet custodes?* who shall check the Parliament? A minister, a head of an office, feels himself under some responsibility. An assembly in such cases feels under no responsibility at all ; for when did any member of Parliament lose his seat for the vote he gave on any detail of administration? To a minister, or the head of an office, it is of more importance what will be thought of his proceedings some time hence, than what is thought of them at the instant; but an assembly, if the cry of the moment goes with it, however hastily raised or artificially stirred up, thinks itself, and is thought by every body, to be completely exculpated, however disastrous may be the consequences. Besides, an assembly never personally experiences the inconveniences of its bad measures until they have reached the dimensions of national evils. Ministers and administrators see them approaching, and have to bear all the annoy-ance and trouble of attempting to ward them off.

The proper duty of a representative assembly in regard to matters of administration is not to decide them by its own vote, but to take care that the persons who have to decide them shall be the proper persons. Even this they can not advantageously do by nomi-nating the individuals. There is no act which more imperatively requires to be performed under a strong sense of individual responsibility than the nomina-tion to employments. The experience of every per-son conversant with public affairs bears out the asser-tion that there is scarcely any act respecting which the conscience of an average man is less sensitive; scarce-ly any case in which less consideration is paid to quali-fications, partly because men do not know, and partly because they do not care for, the difference in quali-fications between one person and another. When a minister makes what is meant to be an honest appoint-ment, that is, when he does not actually job it for his personal connections or his party, an ignorant person might suppose that he would try to give it to the person best qualified. No such thing. An ordinary minister thinks himself a miracle of virtue if he gives it to a person of merit, or who has a claim on the public on any account, though the claim or the merit may be of the most opposite description to that re-quired. *Il fallait un calculateur, ce fut un danseur qui l'obtint,* is hardly more of a caricature than in the days of Figaro; and the minister doubtless thinks himself not only blameless, but meritorious, if the man dances well. Besides, the qualifications which fit special individuals for special duties can only be recognized by those who know the individuals, or who make it their business to examine and judge of persons from what they have done, or from the evidence of those who are in a position to judge. When these conscientious obligations are so little regarded by great public officers who can be made responsible for their appointments, how must it be with assemblies who can not? Even now, the worst appointments are those which are made for the sake of gaining support or disarming opposition in the representative body; what might we expect if they were made by the body itself? Numerous bodies never regard special qualifications at all. Unless a man is fit for the gallows, he is thought to be about as fit as other people for almost any thing for which he can offer himself as a candidate. When appointments made by a popular body are not decided, as they almost always are, by party connection or private jobbing, a man is appointed either because he has a reputation, often quite undeserved, for *general* ability, or oftener for no better reason than that he is personally popular.

It has never been thought desirable that Parliament should itself nominate even the members of a cabinet. It is enough that it virtually decides who shall be prime minister, or who shall be the two or three individuals from whom the prime minister shall be chosen. In doing this, it merely recognizes the fact that a certain person is the candidate of the party whose general policy commands its support. In reality, the only thing which Parliament decides is, which of two, or at most three, parties or bodies of men shall furnish the executive government: the opinion of the party itself decides which of its members is fittest to be placed at the head. According to the existing practice of the British Constitution, these things seem to be on as good a footing as they can be. Parliament does not nominate any minister, but the crown appoints the head of the administration in conformity to the general wishes and inclinations manifested by Parliament, and the other ministers on the recommend‧ation of the chief, while every minister has the un‧divided moral responsibility of appointing fit persons to the other offices of administration which are not permanent. In a republic, some other management would be necessary; but the nearer it approached in practice to that which has long existed in England, the more likely it would be to work well. Either, as in the American republic, the head of the executive must be elected by some agency entirely independent of the representative body, or the body must content itself with naming the prime minister, and making him responsible for the choice of his associates and subordinates. In all these considerations, at least theoretically, I fully anticipate a general assent; though, practically, the tendency is strong in representative bodies to interfere more and more in the details of administration, by virtue of the general law, that whoever has the strongest power is more and more tempt‧ed to make an excessive use of it; and this is one of the practical dangers to which the futurity of repre‧sentative governments will be exposed.

But it is equally true, though only of late and slowly beginning to be acknowledged, that a numerous assembly is as little fitted for the direct business of legislation as for that of administration. There is hardly any kind of intellectual work which so much needs to be done not only by experienced and exercised minds, but by minds trained to the task through long and laborious study, as the business of making laws. This is a sufficient reason, were there no other, why they can never be well made but by a committee of very few persons. A reason no less conclusive is, that every provision of a law requires to be framed with the most accurate and long-sighted perception of its effect on all the other provisions; and the law, when made, should be capable of fitting into a consistent whole with the previously existing laws. It is impossible that these conditions should be in any degree fulfilled when laws are voted clause by clause in a miscellaneous assembly. The incongruity of such a mode of legislating would strike all minds, were it not that our laws are already, as to form and construction, such a chaos, that the confusion and contradiction seem incapable of being made greater by any addition to the mass. Yet even now, the utter unfitness of our legislative machinery for its purpose is making itself practically felt every year more and more. The mere time necessarily occupied in getting through bills, renders Parliament more and more incapable of passing any, except on detached and narrow points. If a bill is prepared which even attempts to deal with the whole of any subject (and it is impossible to legislate properly on any part without having the whole present to the mind), it hangs over from session to session through sheer impossibility of finding time to dispose of it. It matters not though the bill may have been deliberately drawn up by the authority deemed the best qualified, with all appliances and means to boot, or by a select commission, chosen for their conversancy with the subject, and having employed years in considering and digesting the particular measure: it can not be passed, because the House of Commons will not forego the precious privilege of tinkering it with their clumsy hands. The custom has of late been to some extent introduced, when the principle of a bill has been affirmed on the second reading, of referring it for consideration in detail to a select committee; but it has not been found that this practice causes much less time to be lost afterward in carrying it through the committee of the whole House: the opinions or private crotchets which have been overruled by knowledge always insist on giving themselves a second chance before the tribunal of ignorance. Indeed, the practice itself has been adopted principally by the House of Lords, the members of which are less busy and fond of meddling, and less jealous of the importance of their individual voices, than those of the elective House. And when a bill of many clauses does succeed in getting itself discussed in detail, what can depict the state in which it comes out of committee! Clauses omitted which are essential to the working of the rest; incongruous ones inserted to conciliate some private interest, or

some crotchety member who threatens to delay the
bill; articles foisted in on the motion of some sciolist
with a mere smattering of the subject, leading to consequences which the member who introduced or those
who supported the bill did not at the moment fore-
see, and which need an amending act in the next session to correct their mischiefs. It is an evil inherent
in the present mode of managing these things, that
the explaining and defending of a bill, and of its various provisions, is scarcely ever performed by the
person from whose mind they emanated, who probably has not a seat in the House. Their defense rests
upon some minister or member of Parliament who did
not frame them, who is dependent on cramming for
all his arguments but those which are perfectly obvious, who does not know the full strength of his
case, nor the best reasons by which to support it, and
is wholly incapable of meeting unforeseen objections.
This evil, as far as government bills are concerned,
admits of remedy, and has been remedied in some
representative constitutions by allowing the government to be represented in either House by persons in
its confidence, having a right to speak, though not to
vote.

If that, as yet considerable, majority of the House
of Commons who never desire to move an amendment
or make a speech would no longer leave the whole
regulation of business to those who do; if they would
bethink themselves that better qualifications for legislation exist, and may be found if sought for, than a
fluent tongue, and the faculty of getting elected by a

constituency, it would soon be recognized that, in legislation as well as administration, the only task to
which a representative assembly can possibly be competent is not that of doing the work, but of causing it
to be done; of determining to whom or to what sort
of people it shall be confided, and giving or withholding the national sanction to it when performed.
Any government fit for a high state of civilization
would have as one of its fundamental elements a small
body, not exceeding in number the members of a cabinet, who should act as a Commission of Legislation,
having for its appointed office to make the laws. If
the laws of this country were, as surely they will soon
be, revised and put into a connected form, the Commission of Codification by which this is effected should
remain as a permanent institution, to watch over the
work, protect it from deterioration, and make farther
improvements as often as required. No one would
wish that this body should of itself have any power
of *enacting* laws; the commission would only embody
the element of intelligence in their construction; Parliament would represent that of will. No measure
would become a law until expressly sanctioned by
Parliament; and Parliament, or either house, would
have the power not only of rejecting, but of sending
back a bill to the commission for reconsideration and
improvement. Either house might also exercise its
initiative by referring any subject to the commission,
with directions to prepare a law. The commission, of
course, would have no power of refusing its instru-
mentality to any legislation which the country de-

sired. Instructions, concurred in by both houses, to draw up a bill which should effect a particular purpose, would be imperative on the commissioners, unless they preferred to resign their office. Once framed, however, Parliament should have no power to alter the measure, but solely to pass or reject it, or, if partially disapproved of, remit it to the commission for reconsideration. The commissioners should be appointed by the crown, but should hold their offices for a time certain, say five years, unless removed on an address from the two houses of Parliament, grounded either on personal misconduct (as in the case of judges), or on refusal to draw up a bill in obedience to the demands of Parliament. At the expiration of the five years a member should cease to hold office unless reappointed, in order to provide a convenient mode of getting rid of those who had not been found equal to their duties, and of infusing new and younger blood into the body.

The necessity of some provision corresponding to this was felt even in the Athenian Democracy, where, in the time of its most complete ascendency, the popular Ecclesia could pass psephisms (mostly decrees on single matters of policy), but laws, so called, could only be made or altered by a different and less numerous body, renewed annually, called the Nomothetæ, whose duty it also was to revise the whole of the laws, and keep them consistent with one another. In the English Constitution there is great difficulty in introducing any arrangement which is new both in form and in substance, but comparatively little repugnance

is felt to the attainment of new purposes by an adaptation of existing forms and traditions. It appears to
me that the means might be devised of enriching the
Constitution with this great improvement through
the machinery of the House of Lords. A commission for preparing bills would in itself be no more an
innovation on the Constitution than the Board for
the administration of the Poor Laws, or the Inclosure
Commission. If, in consideration of the great importance and dignity of the trust, it were made a rule
that every person appointed a member of the Legislative Commission, unless removed from office on an
address from Parliament, should be a peer for life, it
is probable that the same good sense and taste which
leave the judicial functions of the peerage practically
to the exclusive care of the law lords would leave
the business of legislation, except on questions involving political principles and interests, to the professional legislators; that bills originating in the Upper House would always be drawn up by them; that
the government would devolve on them the framing
of all its bills; and that private members of the
House of Commons would gradually find it convenient, and likely to facilitate the passing of their
measures through the two houses, if, instead of bringing in a bill and submitting it directly to the House,
they obtained leave to introduce it and have it refer-
red to the Legislative Commission; for it would, of
course, be open to the House to refer for the consideration of that body not a subject merely, but any
specific proposal, or a draft of a bill *in extenso*, when

any member thought himself capable of preparing one
such as ought to pass; and the House would doubtless refer every such draft to the commission, if only
as materials, and for the benefit of the suggestions it
might contain, as they would, in like manner, refer
every amendment or objection which might be proposed in writing by any member of the House after
a measure had left the commissioners' hands. The
alteration of bills by a committee of the whole House
would cease, not by formal abolition, but by desue-
tude; the right not being abandoned, but laid up in
the same armory with the royal veto, the right of
withholding the supplies, and other ancient instruments of political warfare, which no one desires to see
used, but no one likes to part with, lest they should at
any time be found to be still needed in an extraordinary emergency. By such arrangements as these,
legislation would assume its proper place as a work
of skilled labor and special study and experience;
while the most important liberty of the nation, that
of being governed only by laws assented to by its
elected representatives, would be fully preserved, and
made more valuable by being detached from the serious, but by no means unavoidable drawbacks which
now accompany it in the form of ignorant and ill-
considered legislation.

Instead of the function of governing, for which it
is radically unfit, the proper office of a representative
assembly is to watch and control the government; to
throw the light of publicity on its acts; to compel a
full exposition and justification of all of them which

any one considers questionable; to censure them if
found condemnable, and, if the men who compose the
government abuse their trust, or fulfill it in a manner
which conflicts with the deliberate sense of the nation,
to expel them from office, and either expressly or virtually appoint their successors.   This is surely ample
power, and security enough for the liberty of the nation.   In addition to this, the Parliament has an office not inferior even to this in importance; to be
at once the nation's Committee of Grievances and its
Congress of Opinions; an arena in which not only
the general opinion of the nation, but that of every
section of it, and, as far as possible, of every eminent
individual whom it contains, can produce itself in full
light and challenge discussion; where every person in
the country may count upon finding somebody who
speaks his mind as well or better than he could speak
it himself—not to friends and partisans exclusively,
but in the face of opponents, to be tested by adverse
controversy; where those whose opinion is overruled feel satisfied that it is heard, and set aside not
by a mere act of will, but for what are thought superior reasons, and commend themselves as such to the
representatives of the majority of the nation; where
every party or opinion in the country can muster its
strength, and be cured of any illusion concerning the
number or power of its adherents; where the opinion
which prevails in the nation makes itself manifest as
prevailing, and marshals its hosts in the presence of
the government, which is thus enabled and compelled
to give way to it on the mere manifestation, without

the actual employment of its strength; where statesmen can assure themselves, far more certainly than
by any other signs, what elements of opinion and
power are growing and what declining, and are enabled to shape their measures with some regard not
solely to present exigencies, but to tendencies in progress. Representative assemblies are often taunted by
their enemies with being places of mere talk and
bavardage. There has seldom been more misplaced
derision. I know not how a representative assembly
can more usefully employ itself than in talk, when
the subject of talk is the great public interests of the
country, and every sentence of it represents the opinion either of some important body of persons in the
nation, or of an individual in whom some such body
have reposed their confidence. A place where every
interest and shade of opinion in the country can have
its cause even passionately pleaded, in the face of the
government and of all other interests and opinions,
can compel them to listen, and either comply, or state
clearly why they do not, is in itself, if it answered no
other purpose, one of the most important political institutions that can exist any where, and one of the
foremost benefits of free government. Such "talking" would never be looked upon with disparagement
if it were not allowed to stop "doing;" which it
never would, if assemblies knew and acknowledged
that talking and discussion are their proper business,
while *doing,* as the result of discussion, is the task not
of a miscellaneous body, but of individuals specially
trained to it; that the fit office of an assembly is to

see that those individuals are honestly and intelligently chosen, and to interfere no farther with them, except by unlimited latitude of suggestion and criticism, and by applying or withholding the final seal of national assent. It is for want of this judicious reserve that popular assemblies attempt to do what they can not do well — to govern and legislate — and provide no machinery but their own for much of it, when of course every hour spent in talk is an hour withdrawn from actual business. But the very fact which most unfits such bodies for a council of legislation, qualifies them the more for their other office—namely, that they are not a selection of the greatest political minds in the country, from whose opinions little could with certainty be inferred concerning those of the nation, but are, when properly constituted, a fair sample of every grade of intellect among the people which is at all entitled to a voice in public affairs. Their part is to indicate wants, to be an organ for popular demands, and a place of adverse discussion for all opinions relating to public matters, both great and small; and, along with this, to check by criticism, and eventually by withdrawing their support, those high public officers who really conduct the public business, or who appoint those by whom it is conducted. Nothing but the restriction of the function of representative bodies within these rational limits will enable the benefits of popular control to be enjoyed in conjunction with the no less important requisites (growing ever more important as human affairs increase in scale and in complexity) of skilled legisla-

tion and administration. There are no means of combining these benefits except by separating the functions which guarantee the one from those which essentially require the other; by disjoining the office
of control and criticism from the actual conduct of affairs, and devolving the former on the representatives
of the Many, while securing for the latter, under strict
responsibility to the nation, the acquired knowledge
and practiced intelligence of a specially trained and
experienced Few.

The preceding discussion of the functions which
ought to devolve on the sovereign representative assembly of the nation would require to be followed by
an inquiry into those properly vested in the minor
representative bodies, which ought to exist for purposes that regard only localities. And such an inquiry forms an essential part of the present treatise;
but many reasons require its postponement, until we
have considered the most proper composition of the
great representative body, destined to control as sovereign the enactment of laws and the administration
of the general affairs of the nation.

CHAPTER VI.

OF THE INFIRMITIES AND DANGERS TO WHICH REPRESENTATIVE GOVERNMENT IS LIABLE.

THE defects of any form of government may be either negative or positive. It is negatively defective if it does not concentrate in the hands of the authorities power sufficient to fulfill the necessary offices of a government, or if it does not sufficiently develop by exercise the actual capacities and social feelings of the individual citizens. On neither of these points is it necessary that much should be said at this stage of our inquiry.

The want of an amount of power in the government adequate to preserve order and allow of progress in the people is incident rather to a wild and rude state of society generally than to any particular form of political union. When the people are too much attached to savage independence to be tolerant of the amount of power to which it is for their good that they should be subject, the state of society (as already observed) is not yet ripe for representative government. When the time for that government has arrived, sufficient power for all needful purposes is sure to reside in the sovereign assembly; and if enough of it is not intrusted to the executive, this can only arise from a jealous feeling on the part of the assembly toward the administration, never likely to exist but where the constitutional power of the assembly to turn them out of office has not yet sufficiently established itself. Wherever that constitutional right is admitted in principle and fully operative in practice, there is no fear that the assembly will not be willing to trust its own ministers with any amount of power really desirable; the danger is, on the contrary, lest they should grant it too ungrudgingly, and too indefinite in ex· tent, since the power of the minister is the power of the body who make and who keep him so. It is, however, very likely, and is one of the dangers of a controlling assembly, that it may be lavish of powers, but afterward interfere with their exercise; may give power by wholesale, and take it back in detail, by multiplied single acts of interference in the business of administration. The evils arising from this assumption of the actual function of governing, in lieu of that of criticising and checking those who govern, have been sufficiently dwelt upon in the preceding chapter. No safeguard can in the nature of things be provided against this improper meddling, except a strong and general conviction of its injurious character.

The other negative defect which may reside in a government, that of not bringing into sufficient exercise the individual faculties, moral, intellectual, and active, of the people, has been exhibited generally in setting forth the distinctive mischiefs of despotism. As between one form of popular government and another, the advantage in this respect lies with that which most widely diffuses the exercise of public functions;

on the one hand, by excluding fewest from the suf·
frage; on the other, by opening to all classes of pri·
vate citizens, so far as is consistent with other equally
important objects, the widest participation in the details of judicial and administrative business; as by
jury-trial, admission to municipal offices, and, above
all, by the utmost possible publicity and liberty of discussion, whereby not merely a few individuals in succession, but the whole public, are made, to a certain
extent, participants in the government, and sharers in
the instruction and mental exercise derived from it.
The farther illustration of these benefits, as well as of
the limitations under which they must be pursued,
will be better deferred until we come to speak of the
details of administration.

The *positive* evils and dangers of the representative,
as of every other form of government, may be reduced
to two heads: .first, general ignorance and incapacity,
or, to speak more moderately, insufficient mental qualifications in the controlling body ; secondly, the danger of its being under the influence of interests not
identical with the general welfare of the community.

The former of these evils, deficiency in high mental
qualifications, is one to which it is generally supposed
that popular government is liable in a greater degree
than any other.   The energy of a monarch, the stead-
iness and prudence of an aristocracy, are thought to
contrast most favorably with the vacillation and short-
sightedness of even the most qualified democracy.
These propositions, however, are not by any means so
well founded as they at first sight appear.

Compared with simple monarchy, representative government is in these respects at no disadvantage. Except in a rude age, hereditary monarchy, when it is really such, and not aristocracy in disguise, much surpasses democracy in all the forms of incapacity supposed to be characteristic of the last. I say except in a rude age, because in a really rude state of society there is a considerable guaranty for the intellectual and active capacities of the sovereign. His personal will is constantly encountering obstacles from the willfulness of his subjects, and of powerful individuals among their number. The circumstances of society do not afford him much temptation to mere luxurious self-indulgence; mental and bodily activity, especially political and military, are his principal excitements; and among turbulent chiefs and lawless followers he has little authority, and is seldom long secure of his throne, unless he possesses a considerable amount of personal daring, dexterity, and energy. The reason why the average of talent is so high among the Henries and Edwards of our history may be read in the tragical fate of the second Edward and the second Richard, and the civil wars and disturbances of the reigns of John and his incapable successor. The troubled period of the Reformation also produced several eminent hereditary monarchs—Elizabeth, Henri Quatre, Gustavus Adolphus; but they were mostly bred up in adversity, succeeded to the throne by the unexpected failure of nearer heirs, or had to contend with great difficulties in the commencement of their reign. Since European life assumed a settled aspect, any thing above mediocrity in a hereditary king has become extremely rare, while the general average has been even below mediocrity, both in talent and in vigor of character. A monarchy constitutionally absolute now only maintains itself in existence (except temporarily in the minds of some active-minded usurper) through the mental qualifications of a permanent bureaucracy. The Russian and Austrian governments, and even the French government in its normal condition, are oligarchies of officials, of whom the head of the state does little more than select the chiefs. I am speaking of the regular course of their administration; for the will of the master of course determines many of their particular acts.

The governments which have been remarkable in history for sustained mental ability and vigor in the conduct of affairs have generally been aristocracies. But they have been, without any exception, aristocracies of public functionaries. The ruling bodies have been so narrow, that each member, or at least each influential member, of the body was able to make, and did make, public business an active profession, and the principal occupation of his life. The only aristocracies which have manifested high governing capacities, and acted on steady maxims of policy through many generations, are those of Rome and Venice. But at Venice, though the privileged order was numerous, the actual management of affairs was rigidly concentrated in a small oligarchy within the oligarchy, whose whole lives were devoted to the study and conduct of the affairs of state.   The Roman government partook more of the character of an open aristocracy like our own.   But the really governing body, the Senate, was exclusively composed of persons who had exercised public functions, and had either already filled, or were looking forward to fill the highest offices of the state, at the peril of a severe responsibility in case of incapacity and failure.   When once members of the Senate, their lives were pledged to the conduct of public affairs; they were not permitted even to leave Italy except in the discharge of some public trust; and unless turned out of the Senate by the censors for character or conduct deemed disgraceful, they retained their powers and responsibilities to the end of life.   In an aristocracy thus constituted, every member felt his personal importance entirely bound up with the dignity and estimation of the commonwealth which he administered, and with the part he was able to play in its councils.   This dignity and estimation were quite different things from the prosperity and happiness of the general body of the citizens, and were often wholly incompatible with it.   But they were closely linked with the external success and aggrandizement of the state; and it was, consequently, in the pursuit of that object almost exclusively, that either the Roman or the Venetian aristocracies manifested the systematically wise collective policy and the great individual capacities for government for which history has deservedly given them credit.

It thus appears that the only governments, not rep-

resentative, in which high political skill and ability
have been other than exceptional, whether under monarchical or aristocratic forms, have been essentially
bureaucracies.   The work of government has been in
the hands of governors by profession, which is the
essence and meaning of bureaucracy.   Whether the
work is done by them because they have been trained
to it, or they are trained to it because it is to be done
by them, makes a great difference in many respects,
but none at all as to the essential character of the rule.
Aristocracies, on the other hand, like that of England,
in which the class who possessed the power derived
it merely from their social position, without being
specially trained or devoting themselves exclusively
to it (and in which, therefore, the power was not exercised directly, but through representative institutions
oligarchically constituted), have been, in respect to
intellectual endowments, much on a par with democracies; that is, they have manifested such qualities in
any considerable degree only during the temporary
ascendency which great and popular talents, united
with a distinguished position, have given to some one
man.   Themistocles and Pericles, Washington and
Jefferson, were not more completely exceptions in
their several democracies, and were assuredly much
more brilliant exceptions, than the Chathams and
Peels of the representative aristocracy of Great Britain, or even the Sullys and Colberts of the aristocratic
monarchy of France.   A great minister in the aristocratic governments of modern Europe is almost as
rare a phenomenon as a great king.

The comparison, therefore, as to the intellectual attributes of a government has to be made between a representative democracy and a bureaucracy; all other governments may be left out of the account. And here it must be acknowledged that a bureaucratic government has, in some important respects, greatly the advantage. It accumulates experience, acquires well-tried and well-considered traditional maxims, and makes provision for appropriate practical knowledge in those who have the actual conduct of affairs. But it is not equally favorable to individual energy of mind. The disease which afflicts bureaucratic governments, and which they usually die of, is routine. They perish by the immutability of their maxims, and, still more, by the universal law that whatever becomes a routine loses its vital principle, and, having no longer a mind acting within it, goes on revolving mechanically, though the work it is intended to do remains undone. A bureaucracy always tends to become a pedantocracy. When the bureaucracy is the real government, the spirit of the corps (as with the Jesuits) bears down the individuality of its more distinguished members. In the profession of government, as in other professions, the sole idea of the majority is to do what they have been taught; and it requires a popular government to enable the conceptions of the man of original genius among them to prevail over the obstructive spirit of trained mediocrity. Only in a popular government (setting apart the accident of a highly intelligent despot) could Sir Rowland Hill have been victorious over the Post-office.

A popular government installed him *in* the Post-office, and made the body, in spite of itself, obey the impulse given by the man who united special knowledge with individual vigor and originality. That the Roman aristocracy escaped this characteristic disease of a bureaucracy was evidently owing to its popular element. All special offices, both those which gave a seat in the Senate and those which were sought by senators, were conferred by popular election. The Russian government is a characteristic exemplification of both the good and bad side of bureaucracy: its fixed maxims, directed with Roman perseverance to the same unflinchingly-pursued ends from age to age; the remarkable skill with which those ends are generally pursued; the frightful internal corruption, and the permanent organized hostility to improvements from without, which even the autocratic power of a vigorous-minded emperor is seldom or never sufficient to overcome; the patient obstructiveness of the body being in the long run more than a match for the fitful energy of one man. The Chinese government, a bureaucracy of Mandarins, is, as far as known to us, another apparent example of the same qualities and defects.

In all human affairs, conflicting influences are required to keep one another alive and efficient even for their own proper uses; and the exclusive pursuit of one good object, apart from some other which should accompany it, ends not in excess of one and defect of the other, but in the decay and loss even of that which has been exclusively cared for. Government by trained officials can not do for a country the things which can be done by a free government, but it might be supposed capable of doing some things which free government of itself can not do.   We find, however, that an outside element of freedom is necessary to enable it to do effectually or permanently even its own business.   And so, also, freedom can not produce its best effects, and often breaks down altogether, unless means can be found of combining it with trained and skilled administration.   There could not be a moment's hesitation between representative government, among a people in any degree ripe for it, and the most perfect imaginable bureaucracy.   But it is, at the same time, one of the most important ends of political institutions to attain as many of the qualities of the one as are consistent with the other; to secure, as far as they can be made compatible, the great advantage of the conduct of affairs by skilled persons, bred to it as an intellectual profession, along with that of a general control vested in, and seriously exercised by, bodies representative of the entire people.   Much would be done toward this end by recognizing the line of separation, discussed in the preceding chapter, between the work of government properly so called, which can only be well performed after special cultivation, and that of selecting, watching, and, when needful, controlling the governors, which in this case, as in all others, properly devolves, not on those who do the work, but on those for whose benefit it ought to be done.   No progress at all can be made toward obtaining a skilled democracy, unless the democracy are willing that the work which requires skill should be done by those who possess it. A democracy has enough to do in providing itself with an amount of mental competency sufficient for its own proper work, that of superintendence and check.

How to obtain and secure this amount is one of the questions to be taken into consideration in judging of the proper constitution of a representative body. In proportion as its composition fails to secure this amount, the assembly will encroach, by special acts, on the province of the executive; it will expel a good, or elevate and uphold a bad ministry; it will connive at, or overlook in them, abuses of trust, will be deluded by their false pretenses, or will withhold support from those who endeavor to fulfill their trust conscientiously; it will countenance or impose a selfish, a capricious and impulsive, a short-sighted, ignorant, and prejudiced general policy, foreign and domestic; it will abrogate good laws or enact bad ones; let in new evils, or cling with perverse obstinacy to old; it will even, perhaps, under misleading impulses, momentary or permanent, emanating from itself or from its constituents, tolerate or connive at proceedings which set law aside altogether in cases where equal justice would not be agreeable to popular feeling. Such are among the dangers of representative government, arising from a constitution of the representation which does not secure an adequate amount of intelligence and knowledge in the representative assembly.

We next proceed to the evils arising from the prevalence of modes of action in the representative body, dictated by sinister interests (to employ the useful phrase introduced by Bentham), that is, interests conflicting more or less with the general good of the community.

It is universally admitted that, of the evils incident to monarchical and aristocratic governments, a large proportion arise from this cause. The interest of the monarch, or the interest of the aristocracy, either collective or that of its individual members, is promoted, or they themselves think that it will be promoted, by conduct opposed to that which the general interest of the community requires. The interest, for example, of the government is to tax heavily; that of the community is to be as little taxed as the necessary expenses of good government permit. The interest of the king and of the governing aristocracy is to possess and exercise unlimited power over the people; to enforce, on their part, complete conformity to the will and preferences of the rulers. The interest of the people is to have as little control exercised over them in any respect as is consistent with attaining the legitimate ends of government. The interest, or apparent and supposed interest of the king or aristocracy, is to permit no censure of themselves, at least in any form which they may consider either to threaten their power or seriously to interfere with their free agency. The interest of the people is that there should be full liberty of censure on every public officer, and on every public act or measure. The interest of a ruling class, whether in an aristocracy or an aristocratic monarchy, is to assume to themselves an endless variety of unjust privileges, sometimes benefiting their pockets at the expense of the people, sometimes merely tending to exalt them above others, or, what is the same thing in different words, to degrade others below themselves. If the people are disaffected, which under such a government they are very likely to be, it is the interest of the king or aristocracy to keep them at a low level of intelligence and education, foment dissensions among them, and even prevent them from being too well off, lest they should "wax fat and kick," agreeably to the maxim of Cardinal Richelieu in his celebrated "Testament Politique." All these things are for the interest of a king or aristocracy, in a purely selfish point of view, unless a sufficiently strong counter-interest is created by the fear of provoking resistance. All these evils have been, and many of them still are, produced by the sinister interests of kings and aristocracies, where their power is sufficient to raise them above the opinion of the rest of the community; nor is it rational to expect, as the consequence of such a position, any other conduct.

These things are superabundantly evident in the case of a monarchy or an aristocracy, but it is sometimes rather gratuitously assumed that the same kind of injurious influences do not operate in a democracy. Looking at democracy in the way in which it is commonly conceived as the rule of the numerical majority, it is surely possible that the ruling power may be under the dominion of sectional or class interests,

pointing to conduct different from that which would
be dictated by impartial regard for the interest of all.
Suppose the majority to be whites, the minority ne-
groes, or *vice versâ:* is it likely that the majority
would allow equal justice to the minority?   Suppose
the majority Catholics, the minority Protestants, or
the reverse: will there not be the same danger?   Or
let the majority be English, the minority Irish, or the
contrary: is there not a great probability of similar
evil?   In all countries there is a majority of poor,
a minority who, in contradistinction, may be called
rich.   Between these two classes, on many questions,
there is complete opposition of apparent interest.
We will suppose the majority sufficiently intelligent
to be aware that it is not for their advantage to
weaken the security of property, and that it would
be weakened by any act of arbitrary spoliation.   But
is there not a considerable danger lest they should
throw upon the possessors of what is called realized
property, and upon the larger incomes, an unfair
share, or even the whole, of the burden of taxation,
and having done so, add to the amount without scruple, expending the proceeds in modes supposed to
conduce to the profit and advantage of the laboring
class?   Suppose, again, a minority of skilled laborers, a majority of unskilled: the experience of many
Trade Unions, unless they are greatly calumniated,
justifies the apprehension that equality of earnings
might be imposed as an obligation, and that piece-
work, and all practices which enable superior industry or abilities to gain a superior reward, might be

put down. Legislative attempts to raise wages, limitation of competition in the labor market, taxes or restrictions on machinery, and on improvements of all kinds tending to dispense with any of the existing labor—even, perhaps, protection of the home producer against foreign industry — are very natural (I do not venture to say whether probable) results of a feeling of class interest in a governing majority of manual laborers.

It will be said that none of these things are for the *real* interest of the most numerous class: to which I answer, that if the conduct of human beings was determined by no other interested considerations than those which constitute their "real" interest, neither monarchy nor oligarchy would be such bad governments as they are; for assuredly very strong arguments may be, and often have been, adduced to show that either a king or a governing senate are in much the most enviable position when ruling justly and vigilantly over an active, wealthy, enlightened, and high-minded people. But a king only now and then, and an oligarchy in no known instance, have taken this exalted view of their self-interest; and why should we expect a loftier mode of thinking from the laboring classes? It is not what their interest is, but what they suppose it to be, that is the important consideration with respect to their conduct; and it is quite conclusive against any theory of government that it assumes the numerical majority to do habitually what is never done, nor expected to be done, save in very exceptional cases, by any other depositaries of power — namely, to direct their conduct by their real ultimate interest, in opposition to their immediate and apparent interest. No one, surely, can doubt that the pernicious measures above enumerated, and many others as bad, would be for the immediate interest of the general body of unskilled laborers. It is quite possible that they would be for the selfish interest of the whole existing generation of the class. The relaxation of industry and activity, and diminished encouragement to saving, which would be their ultimate consequence, might perhaps be little felt by the class of unskilled laborers in the space of a single lifetime. Some of the most fatal changes in human affairs have been, as to their more manifest immediate effects, beneficial. The establishment of the despotism of the Cæsars was a great benefit to the entire generation in which it took place. It put a stop to civil war, abated a vast amount of malversation and tyranny by prætors and proconsuls; it fostered many of the graces of life, and intellectual cultivation in all departments not political; it produced monuments of literary genius dazzling to the imaginations of shallow readers of history, who do not reflect that the men to whom the despotism of Augustus (as well as of Lorenzo de' Medici and of Louis XIV.) owes its brilliancy were all formed in the generation preceding. The accumulated riches, and the mental energy and activity produced by centuries of freedom, remained for the benefit of the first generation of slaves. Yet this was the commencement of a *régime* by whose gradual operation all the civilization which had been gained insensibly faded away, until the empire which had conquered and embraced the world in its grasp so completely lost even its military efficiency that invaders whom three or four legions had always sufficed to coerce were able to overrun and occupy nearly the whole of its vast territory. The fresh impulse given by Christianity came but just in time to save arts and letters from perishing, and the human race from sinking back into perhaps endless night.

When we talk of the interest of a body of men, or even of an individual man, as a principle determining their actions, the question what would be considered their interest by an unprejudiced observer is one of the least important parts of the whole matter. As Coleridge observes, the man makes the motive, not the motive the man. What it is the man's interest to do or refrain from depends less on any outward circumstances than upon what sort of man he is. If you wish to know what is practically a man's interest, you must know the cast of his habitual feelings and thoughts. Every body has two kinds of interests— interests which he cares for and interests which he does not care for. Every body has selfish and unselfish interests, and a selfish man has cultivated the habit of caring for the former and not caring for the latter. Every one has present and distant interests, and the improvident man is he who cares for the present interests and does not care for the distant. It matters little that on any correct calculation the latter may be the more considerable, if the habits of his mind lead him to fix his thoughts and wishes solely on the former. It would be vain to attempt to persuade a man who beats his wife and ill-treats his children that he would be happier if he lived in love and kindness with them. He would be happier if he were the kind of person who *could* so live; but he is not, and it is probably too late for him to become that kind of person. Being as he is, the gratification of his love of domineering and the indulgence of his ferocious temper are to his perceptions a greater good to himself than he would be capable of deriving from the pleasure and affection of those dependent on him. He has no pleasure in their pleasure, and does not care for their affection. His neighbor, who does, is probably a happier man than he; but could he be persuaded of this, the persuasion would, most likely, only still farther exasperate his malignity or his irritability. On the average, a person who cares for other people, for his country, or for mankind, is a happier man than one who does not; but of what use is it to preach this doctrine to a man who cares for nothing but his own ease or his own pocket? He can not care for other people if he would. It is like preaching to the worm who crawls on the ground how much better it would be for him if he were an eagle.

Now it is a universally observed fact that the two evil dispositions in question, the disposition to prefer a man's selfish interests to those which he shares with other people, and his immediate and direct interests to those which are indirect and remote, are characteristics most especially called forth and fostered by the possession of power. The moment a man, or a class of men, find themselves with power in their hands, the man's individual interest, or the class's separate interest, acquires an entirely new degree of importance in their eyes. Finding themselves worshiped by others, they become worshipers of themselves, and think themselves entitled to be counted at a hundred times the value of other people, while the facility they acquire of doing as they like without regard to consequences insensibly weakens the habits which make men look forward even to such consequences as affect themselves. This is the meaning of the universal tradition, grounded on universal experience, of men's being corrupted by power. Every one knows how absurd it would be to infer from what a man is or does when in a private station, that he will be and do exactly the like when a despot on a throne; where the bad parts of his human nature, instead of being restrained and kept in subordination by every circumstance of his life and by every person surrounding him, are courted by all persons, and ministered to by all circumstances. It would be quite as absurd to entertain a similar expectation in regard to a class of men; the Demos, or any other. Let them be ever so modest and amenable to reason while there is a power over them stronger than they, we ought to expect a total change in this respect when they themselves become the strongest power.

Governments must be made for human beings as they are, or as they are capable of speedily becoming; and in any state of cultivation which mankind, or any class among them, have yet attained, or are likely soon to attain, the interests by which they will be led, when they are thinking only of self-interest, will be almost exclusively those which are obvious at first sight, and which operate on their present condition. It is only a disinterested regard for others, and especially for what comes after them, for the idea of posterity, of their country, or of mankind, whether grounded on sympathy or on a conscientious feeling, which ever directs the minds and purposes of classes or bodies of men toward distant or unobvious interests; and it can not be maintained that any form of government would be rational which required as a condition that these exalted principles of action should be the guiding and master motives in the conduct of average human beings. A certain amount of conscience and of disinterested public spirit may fairly be calculated on in the citizens of any community ripe for representative government, but it would be ridiculous to expect such a degree of it, combined with such intellectual discernment, as would be proof against any plausible fallacy tending to make that which was for their class interest appear the dictate of justice and of the general good. We all know what specious fallacies may be urged in defense of every act of injustice yet proposed for the imaginary benefit of the mass. We know how many, not otherwise fools or bad men, have thought it justifiable to repudiate the national debt. We know how many, not destitute of ability and of considerable popular influence, think it fair to throw the whole burden of taxation upon savings, under the name of realized

property, allowing those whose progenitors and themselves have always spent all they received, to remain,
as a reward for such exemplary conduct, wholly un-
taxed. We know what powerful arguments, the more
dangerous because there is a portion of truth in them,
may be brought against all inheritance, against the
power of bequest, against every advantage which one
person seems to have over another. We know how
easily the uselessness of almost every branch of knowledge may be proved to the complete satisfaction of
those who do not possess it. How many, not altogether stupid men, think the scientific study of languages useless, think ancient literature useless, all eru-
dition useless, logic and metaphysics useless, poetry
and the fine arts idle and frivolous, political economy
purely mischievous? Even history has been pronounced useless and mischievous by able men. Nothing but that acquaintance with external nature, empirically acquired, which serves directly for the production of objects necessary to existence or agreeable
to the senses, would get its utility recognized if people had the least encouragement to disbelieve it. Is
it reasonable to think that even much more cultivated
minds than those of the numerical majority can be expected to be, will have so delicate a conscience, and
so just an appreciation of what is against their own
apparent interest, that they will reject these and the
innumerable other fallacies which will press in upon
them from all quarters as soon as they come into
power, to induce them to follow their own selfish inclinations and short-sighted notions of their own good,

in opposition to justice, at the expense of all other classes and of posterity?

One of the greatest dangers, therefore, of democracy, as of all other forms of government, lies in the sinister interest of the holders of power: it is the danger of class legislation, of government intended for (whether really effecting it or not) the immediate benefit of the dominant class, to the lasting detriment of the whole. And one of the most important questions demanding consideration in determining the best constitution of a representative government is how to provide efficacious securities against this evil.

If we consider as a class, politically speaking, any number of persons who have the same sinister interest—that is, whose direct and apparent interest points toward the same description of bad measures — the desirable object would be that no class, and no combination of classes likely to combine, shall be able to exercise a preponderant influence in the government. A modern community, not divided within itself by strong antipathies of race, language, or nationality, may be considered as in the main divisible into two sections, which, in spite of partial variations, correspond on the whole with two divergent directions of apparent interest. Let us call them (in brief general terms) laborers on the one hand, employers of labor on the other; including, however, along with employers of labor not only retired capitalists and the possessors of inherited wealth, but all that highly-paid description of laborers (such as the professions) whose education and way of life assimilate them with the rich, and whose prospect and ambition it is to raise themselves into that class.   With the laborers, on the other hand, may be ranked those smaller employers of labor who by interests, habits, and educational impressions are assimilated in wishes, tastes, and objects to the laboring classes, comprehending a large proportion of petty tradesmen.   In a state of society thus composed, if the representative system could be made ideally perfect, and if it were possible to maintain it in that state, its organization must be such that these two classes, manual laborers and their affinities on one side, employers of labor and their affinities on the other, should be, in the arrangement of the representative system, equally balanced, each influencing about an equal number of votes in Parliament; since, assuming that the majority of each class, in any difference between them, would be mainly governed by their class interests, there would be a minority of each in whom that consideration would be subordinate to reason, justice, and the good of the whole; and this minority of either, joining with the whole of the other, would turn the scale against any demands of their own majority which were not such as ought to prevail.   The reason why, in any tolerably constituted society, justice and the general interest mostly in the end carry their point, is that the separate and selfish interests of mankind are almost always divided; some are interested in what is wrong, but some, also, have their private interest on the side of what is right; and those who are governed by higher considerations, though too few and weak to prevail alone, usually, after sufficient discussion and agitation, become strong enough to turn the balance in favor of the body of private interests which is on the same side with them. The representative system ought to be so constituted as to maintain this state of things; it ought not to allow any of the various sectional interests to be so powerful as to be capable of prevailing against truth and justice, and the other sectional interests combined. There ought always to be such a balance preserved among personal interests as may render any one of them dependent for its successes on carrying with it at least a large proportion of those who act upon higher motives, and more comprehensive and distant views.

CHAPTER VII.

OF TRUE AND FALSE DEMOCRACY; REPRESENTATION
OF ALL, AND REPRESENTATION OF THE MAJORITY
ONLY.

IT has been seen that the dangers incident to a representative democracy are of two kinds: danger of a low grade of intelligence in the representative body, and in the popular opinion which controls it; and danger of class legislation on the part of the numerical majority, these being all composed of the same class. We have next to consider how far it is possible so to organize the democracy as, without interfering materially with the characteristic benefits of democratic government, to do away with these two great evils, or at least to abate them in the utmost degree attainable by human contrivance.

The common mode of attempting this is by limiting the democratic character of the representation through a more or less restricted suffrage. But there is a previous consideration which, duly kept in view, considerably modifies the circumstances which are supposed to render such a restriction necessary. A completely equal democracy, in a nation in which a single class composes the numerical majority, can not be divested of certain evils; but those evils are greatly aggravated by the fact that the democracies which at present exist are not equal, but systematically unequal in favor of the predominant class. Two very different ideas are usually confounded under the name democracy. The pure idea of democracy, according to its definition, is the government of the whole people by the whole people, equally represented. Democracy, as commonly conceived and hitherto practiced, is the government of the whole people by a mere majority of the people exclusively represented. The former is synonymous with the equality of all citizens; the latter, strangely confounded with it, is a government of privilege in favor of the numerical majority, who alone possess practically any voice in the state. This is the inevitable consequence of the manner in which the votes are now taken, to the complete disfranchisement of minorities.

The confusion of ideas here is great, but it is so easily cleared up that one would suppose the slightest indication would be sufficient to place the matter in its true light before any mind of average intelligence. It would be so but for the power of habit; owing to which, the simplest idea, if unfamiliar, has as great difficulty in making its way to the mind as a far more complicated one. That the minority must yield to the majority, the smaller number to the greater, is a familiar idea; and accordingly, men think there is no necessity for using their minds any farther, and it does not occur to them that there is any medium between allowing the smaller number to be equally powerful with the greater, and blotting out the smaller number altogether. In a representative body actually deliberating, the minority must of course be overruled; and in an equal democracy (since the opinions of the constituents, when they insist on them, determine those of the representative body), the majority of the people, through their representatives, will outvote and prevail over the minority and their representatives. But does it follow that the minority should have no representatives at all? Because the majority ought to prevail over the minority, must the majority have all the votes, the minority none? Is it necessary that the minority should not even be heard? Nothing but habit and old association can reconcile any reasonable being to the needless injustice. In a really equal democracy, every or any section would be represented, not disproportionately, but proportionately. A majority of the electors would always have a majority of the representatives, but a minority of the electors would always have a minority of the representatives. Man for man, they would be as fully represented as the majority. Unless they are, there is not equal government, but a government of inequality and privilege: one part of the people rule over the rest: there is a part whose fair and equal share of influence in the representation is withheld from them, contrary to all just government, but, above all, contrary to the principle of democracy, which professes equality as its very root and foundation.

The injustice and violation of principle are not less flagrant because those who suffer by them are a minority, for there is not equal suffrage where every single individual does not count for as much as any other single individual in the community. But it is not only the minority who suffer. Democracy, thus constituted, does not even attain its ostensible object, that of giving the powers of government in all cases to the numerical majority. It does something very different; it gives them to a majority of the majority, who may be, and often are, but a minority of the whole. All principles are most effectually tested by extreme cases. Suppose, then, that, in a country governed by equal and universal suffrage, there is a contested election in every constituency, and every election is carried by a small majority. The Parliament thus brought together represents little more than a bare majority of the people. This Parliament proceeds to legislate, and adopts important measures by a bare majority of itself. What guarantee is there that these measures accord with the wishes of a majority of the people? Nearly half the electors, having been outvoted at the hustings, have had no influence at all in the decision; and the whole of these may be, a majority of them probably are, hostile to the measures, having voted against those by whom they have been carried. Of the remaining electors, nearly half have chosen representatives who, by supposition, have voted against the measures. It is possible, therefore, and even probable, that the opinion which has prevailed was agreeable only to a minority of the nation, though a majority of that portion of it whom the institutions of the country have erected into a ruling class. If democracy means the certain ascendency of the majority, there are no means of insuring that, but by allowing every individual figure to tell equally in the summing up. Any minority left out, either purposely or by the play of the machinery, gives the power not to a majority, but to a minority in some other part of the scale.

The only answer which can possibly be made to this reasoning is, that as different opinions predominate in different localities, the opinion which is in a minority in some places has a majority in others; and, on the whole, every opinion which exists in the constituencies obtains its fair share of voices in the representation. And this is roughly true in the present state of the constituency; if it were not, the discordance of the House with the general sentiment of the country would soon become evident. But it would be no longer true if the present constituency were much enlarged, still less if made co-extensive with the whole population; for in that case the majority in every locality would consist of manual laborers; and when there was any question pending on which these classes were at issue with the rest of the community, no other class could succeed in getting represented any where. Even now, is it not a great grievance that in every Parliament a very numerous portion of the electors, willing and anxious to be represented, have no member in the House for whom they have voted? Is it just that every elector of Marylebone is obliged to be represented by two nominees of the vestries, every elector of Finsbury or Lambeth by those (as is generally believed) of the publicans? The constituencies to which most of the highly educated and pub-

lic-spirited persons in the country belong, those of the
large towns, are now, in great part, either unrepresented or misrepresented. The electors who are on a different side in party politics from the local majority are
unrepresented. Of those who are on the same side,
a large proportion are misrepresented, having been
obliged to accept the man who had the greatest number of supporters in their political party, though his
opinions may differ from theirs on every other point.
The state of things is, in some respects, even worse
than if the minority were not allowed to vote at all;
for then, at least the majority might have a member
who would represent their own best mind; while now,
the necessity of not dividing the party, for fear of let-
ting in its opponents, induces all to vote either for the
person who first presents himself wearing their colors,
or for the one brought forward by their local leaders;
and these, if we pay them the compliment, which they
very seldom deserve, of supposing their choice to be
unbiased by their personal interests, are compelled,
that they may be sure of mustering their whole
strength, to bring forward a candidate whom none of
the party will strongly object to—that is, a man without any distinctive peculiarity, any known opinions
except the shibboleth of the party. This is strikingly
exemplified in the United States, where, at the election
of President, the strongest party never dares put forward any of its strongest men, because every one of
these, from the mere fact that he has been long in the
public eye, has made himself objectionable to some
portion or other of the party, and is therefore not so

sure a card for rallying all their votes as a person who
has never been heard of by the public at all until he
is produced as the candidate. Thus the man who is
chosen, even by the strongest party, represents perhaps the real wishes only of the narrow margin by
which that party outnumbers the other. Any section
whose support is necessary to success possesses a veto
on the candidate. Any section which holds out more
obstinately than the rest can compel all the others to
adopt its nominee; and this superior pertinacity is unhappily more likely to be found among those who are
holding out for their own interest than for that of the
public. Speaking generally, the choice of the majority is determined by that portion of the body who are
the most timid, the most narrow-minded and prejudiced, or who cling most tenaciously to the exclusive
class interest; and the electoral rights of the minority,
while useless for the purposes for which votes are
given, serve only for compelling the majority to accept
the candidate of the weakest or worst portion of themselves.

That, while recognizing these evils, many should
consider them as the necessary price paid for a free
government, is in no way surprising; it was the opinion of all the friends of freedom up to a recent period.
But the habit of passing them over as irremediable
has become so inveterate, that many persons seem to
have lost the capacity of looking at them as things
which they would be glad to remedy if they could.
From despairing of a cure, there is too often but one
step to denying the disease; and from this follows

dislike to having a remedy proposed, as if the pro-
poser were creating a mischief instead of offering relief from one. People are so inured to the evils that
they feel as if it were unreasonable, if not wrong, to
complain of them. Yet, avoidable or not, he must be
a purblind lover of liberty on whose mind they do
not weigh; who would not rejoice at the discovery
that they could be dispensed with. Now nothing is
more certain than that the virtual blotting out of the
minority is no necessary or natural consequence of
freedom; that, far from having any connection with
democracy, it is diametrically opposed to the first principle of democracy, representation in proportion to
numbers. It is an essential part of democracy that
minorities should be adequately represented. No real
democracy, nothing but a false show of democracy, is
possible without it.

Those who have seen and felt, in some degree, the
force of these considerations, have proposed various
expedients by which the evil may be, in a greater or
less degree, mitigated. Lord John Russell, in one of
his Reform Bills, introduced a provision that certain
constituencies should return three members, and that
in these each elector should be allowed to vote only
for two; and Mr. Disraeli, in the recent debates, revived the memory of the fact by reproaching him for
it, being of opinion, apparently, that it befits a Conservative statesman to regard only means, and to dis-
own scornfully all fellow-feeling with any one who is
betrayed, even once, into thinking of ends.* Others

* This blunder of Mr. Disraeli (from which, greatly to his credit,

have proposed that each elector should be allowed to vote only for one. By either of these plans, a minority equaling or exceeding a third of the local constituency would be able, if it attempted no more, to return one out of three members. The same result might be attained in a still better way if, as proposed in an able pamphlet by Mr. James Garth Marshall, the elector retained his three votes, but was at liberty to bestow them all upon the same candidate. These schemes, though infinitely better than none at all, are yet but makeshifts, and attain the end in a very imperfect manner, since all local minorities of less than a third, and all minorities, however numerous, which are made up from several constituencies, would remain unrepresented. It is much to be lamented, however, that none of these plans have been carried into

Sir John Pakington took an opportunity soon after of separating himself) is a speaking instance, among many, how little the Conservative leaders understand Conservative principles. Without presuming to require from political parties such an amount of virtue and discernment as that they should comprehend, and know when to apply, the principles of their opponents, we may yet say that it would be a great improvement if each party understood and acted upon its own. Well would it be for England if Conservatives voted consistently for every thing conservative, and Liberals for every thing liberal. We should not then have to wait long for things which, like the present and many other great measures, are eminently both the one and the other. The Conservatives, as being by the law of their existence the stupidest party, have much the greatest sins of this description to answer for; and it is a melancholy truth, that if any measure were proposed on any subject truly, largely, and far-sightedly conservative, even if Liberals were willing to vote for it, the great bulk of the Conservative party would rush blindly in and prevent it from being carried.

effect, as any of them would have recognized the right principle, and prepared the way for its more complete application. But real equality of representation is not obtained unless any set of electors amounting to the average number of a constituency, wherever in the country they happen to reside, have the power of combining with one another to return a representative. This degree of perfection in representation appeared impracticable until a man of great capacity, fitted alike for large general views and for the contrivance of practical details—Mr. Thomas Hare—had proved its possibility by drawing up a scheme for its accomplishment, embodied in a Draft of an Act of Parliament; a scheme which has the almost unparalleled merit of carrying out a great principle of government in a manner approaching to ideal perfection as regards the special object in view, while it attains incidentally several other ends of scarcely inferior importance.

According to this plan, the unit of representation, the quota of electors who would be entitled to have a member to themselves, would be ascertained by the ordinary process of taking averages, the number of voters being divided by the number of seats in the House; and every candidate who obtained that quota would be returned, from however great a number of local constituencies it might be gathered. The votes would, as at present, be given locally, but any elector would be at liberty to vote for any candidate, in whatever part of the country he might offer himself. Those electors, therefore, who did not wish to be represented by any of the local candidates, might aid by their vote in the return of the person they liked best among all those throughout the country who had expressed a willingness to be chosen. This would so far give reality to the electoral rights of the otherwise virtually disfranchised minority. But it is important that not those alone who refuse to vote for any of the local candidates, but those also who vote for one of them and are defeated, should be enabled to find elsewhere the representation which they have not succeeded in obtaining in their own district. It is therefore provided that an elector may deliver a voting paper containing other names in addition to the one which stands foremost in his preference. His vote would only be counted for one candidate; but if the object of his first choice failed to be returned, from not having obtained the quota, his second perhaps might be more fortunate. He may extend his list to a greater number in the order of his preference, so that if the names which stand near the top of the list either can not make up the quota, or are able to make it up without his vote, the vote may still be used for some one whom it may assist in returning. To obtain the full number of members required to complete the House, as well as to prevent very popular candidates from engrossing nearly all the suffrages, it is necessary, however many votes a candidate may obtain, that no more of them than the quota should be counted for his return; the remainder of those who voted for him would have their votes counted for the next person on their respective lists who needed them, and could by their aid complete the quota. To determine which of a candidate's votes should be used for his return, and which set free for others, several methods are proposed, into which we shall not here enter. He would, of course, retain the votes of all those who would not otherwise be represented; and for the remainder, drawing lots, in default of better, would be an unobjectionable expedient. The voting papers would be conveyed to a central office, where the votes would be counted, the number of first, second, third, and other votes given for each candidate ascertained, and the quota would be allotted to every one who could make it up, until the number of the House was complete; first votes being preferred to second, second to third, and so forth. The voting papers, and all the elements of the calculation, would be placed in public repositories, accessible to all whom they concerned; and if any one who had obtained the quota was not duly returned, it would be in his power easily to prove it.

These are the main provisions of the scheme. For a more minute knowledge of its very simple machinery, I must refer to Mr. Hare's "Treatise on the Election of Representatives" (a small volume published in 1859), and to a pamphlet by Mr. Henry Fawcett, published in 1860, and entitled "Mr. Hare's Reform Bill simplified and explained." This last is a very clear and concise exposition of the plan, reduced to its simplest elements by the omission of some of Mr. Hare's original provisions, which, though in themselves beneficial, were thought to take more from the simplicity of the scheme than they added to its practical advantages. The more these works are studied, the stronger, I venture to predict, will be the impression of the perfect feasibility of the scheme and its transcendent advantages. Such and so numerous are these, that, in my conviction, they place Mr. Hare's plan among the very greatest improvements yet made in the theory and practice of government.

In the first place, it secures a representation, in proportion to numbers, of every division of the electoral body: not two great parties alone, with perhaps a few large sectional minorities in particular places, but every minority in the whole nation, consisting of a sufficiently large number to be, on principles of equal justice, entitled to a representative. Secondly, no elector would, as at present, be nominally represented by some one whom he had not chosen. Every member of the House would be the representative of a unanimous constituency. He would represent a thousand electors, or two thousand, or five thousand, or ten thousand, as the quota might be, every one of whom would have not only voted for him, but selected him from the whole country, not merely from the assortment of two or three perhaps rotten oranges, which may be the only choice offered to him in his local market. Under this relation the tie between the elector and the representative would be of a strength and a value of which at present we have no experience. Every one of the electors would be personally identified with his representative, and the representative with his constituents. Every elector who voted for him would have done so either because he is the person, in the whole list of candidates for Parliament, who best expresses the voter's own opinions, or because he is one of those whose abilities and character the voter most respects, and whom he most willingly trusts to think for him. The member would represent persons, not the mere bricks and mortar of the town—the voters themselves, not a few vestrymen or parish notabilities merely. All, however, that is worth preserving in the representation of places would be preserved. Though the Parliament of the nation ought to have as little as possible to do with purely local affairs, yet, while it has to do with them, there ought to be members specially commissioned to look after the interests of every important locality; and these there would still be. In every locality which contained many more voters than the quota (and there probably ought to be no local constituency which does not), the majority would generally prefer to be represented by one of themselves; by a person of local knowledge, and residing in the locality, if there is any such person to be found among the candidates, who is otherwise eligible as their representative. It would be the minorities chiefly, who, being unable to return the local member, would look out elsewhere for a candidate likely to obtain other votes in addition to their own.

Of all modes in which a national representation can possibly be constituted, this one affords the best security for the intellectual qualifications desirable in the representatives. At present, by universal admission, it is becoming more and more difficult for any one who has only talents and character to gain admission into the House of Commons. The only persons who can get elected are those who possess local influence, or make their way by lavish expenditure, or who, on the invitation of three or four tradesmen or attorneys, are sent down by one of the two great parties from their London clubs as men whose votes the party can depend on under all circumstances. On Mr. Hare's system, those who did not like the local candidates would fill up their voting papers by a selection from all the persons of national reputation on the list of candidates with whose general political principles they were in sympathy. Almost every person, therefore, who had made himself in any way honorably distinguished, though devoid of local influence, and having sworn allegiance to no political party, would have a fair chance of making up the quota, and with this encouragement such persons might be expected to offer themselves in numbers hitherto undreamed of. Hundreds of able men of independent thought, who would have no chance whatever of being chosen by the majority of any existing constituency, have by their writings, or their exertions in some field of public usefulness, made themselves known and approved by a few persons in almost every district of the kingdom; and if every vote that would be given for them in every place could be counted for their election, they might be able to complete the number of the quota. In no other way which it seems possible to suggest would Parliament be so certain of containing the very *élite* of the country.

And it is not solely through the votes of minorities that this system of election would raise the intellectual standard of the House of Commons. Majorities would be compelled to look out for members of a much higher calibre. When the individuals composing the majority would no longer be reduced to Hobson's choice, of either voting for the person brought forward by their local leaders, or not voting at all; when the nominee of the leaders would have to encounter the competition not solely of the candidate of the minority, but of all the men of established reputation in the country who were willing to serve, it would be impossible any longer to foist upon the electors the first person who presents himself with the catchwords of the party in his mouth, and three or four thousand pounds in his pocket. The majority would insist on having a candidate worthy of their choice, or they would carry their votes somewhere else, and the minority would prevail. The slavery of the majority to the least estimable portion of their numbers would be at an end; the very best and most capable of the local notabilities would be put forward by preference; if possible, such as were known in some advantageous way beyond the locality, that their local strength might have a chance of being fortified by stray votes from elsewhere. Constituencies would become competitors for the best candidates, and would vie with one another in selecting from among the men of local knowledge and connections those who were most distinguished in every other respect.

The natural tendency of representative government,

as of modern civilization, is toward collective mediocrity; and this tendency is increased by all reductions
and extensions of the franchise, their effect being to
place the principal power in the hands of classes more
and more below the highest level of instruction in the
community. But, though the superior intellects and
characters will necessarily be outnumbered, it makes
a great difference whether or not they are heard. In
the false democracy which, instead of giving representation to all, gives it only to the local majorities, the
voice of the instructed minority may have no organs
at all in the representative body. It is an admitted
fact that in the American democracy, which is constructed on this faulty model, the highly-cultivated
members of the community, except such of them as
are willing to sacrifice their own opinions and modes
of judgment, and become the servile mouthpieces of
their inferiors in knowledge, do not even offer themselves for Congress or the State Legislatures, so certain is it that they would have no chance of being returned. Had a plan like Mr. Hare's by good fortune
suggested itself to the enlightened and disinterested
founders of the American Republic, the federal and
state assemblies would have contained many of these
distinguished men, and democracy would have been
spared its greatest reproach and one of its most formidable evils. Against this evil the system of personal
representation proposed by Mr. Hare is almost a specific. The minority of instructed minds scattered
through the local constituencies would unite to return
a number, proportioned to their own numbers, of the

very ablest men the country contains. They would be under the strongest inducement to choose such men, since in no other mode could they make their small numerical strength tell for any thing considerable. The representatives of the majority, besides that they would themselves be improved in quality by the operation of the system, would no longer have the whole field to themselves. They would indeed outnumber the others, as much as the one class of electors outnumbers the other in the country : they could always outvote them, but they would speak and vote in their presence, and subject to their criticism. When any difference arose, they would have to meet the arguments of the instructed few by reasons, at least apparently, as cogent; and since they could not, as those do who are speaking to persons already unanimous, simply assume that they are in the right, it would occasionally happen to them to become convinced that they were in the wrong. As they would in general be well-meaning (for thus much may reasonably be expected from a fairly-chosen national representation), their own minds would be insensibly raised by the influence of the minds with which they were in contact, or even in conflict. The champions of unpopular doctrines would not put forth their arguments merely in books and periodicals, read only by their own side; the opposing ranks would meet face to face and hand to hand, and there would be a fair comparison of their intellectual strength in the presence of the country. It would then be found out whether the opinion which prevailed by counting votes would also prevail if the votes were weighed as well as counted. The multitude have often a true instinct for distinguishing an able man when he has the means of displaying his ability in a fair field before them. If such a man fails to obtain any portion whatever of his just weight, it is through institutions or usages which keep him out of sight. In the old democracies there were no means of keeping out of sight any able man; the bema was open to him; he needed nobody's consent to become a public adviser. It is not so in a representative government; and the best friends of representative democracy can hardly be without misgivings that the Themistocles or Demosthenes whose counsels would have saved the nation, might be unable during his whole life ever to obtain a seat. But if the presence in the representative assembly can be insured of even a few of the first minds in the country, though the remainder consist only of average minds, the influence of these leading spirits is sure to make itself insensibly felt in the general deliberations, even though they be known to be, in many respects, opposed to the tone of popular opinion and feeling. I am unable to conceive any mode by which the presence of such minds can be so positively insured* as by that proposed by Mr. Hare.

This portion of the assembly would also be the appropriate organ of a great social function, for which there is no provision in any existing democracy, but which in no government can remain permanently unfulfilled without condemning that government to infallible degeneracy and decay. This may be called

the function of Antagonism. In every government
there is some power stronger than all the rest, and
the power which is strongest tends perpetually to become the sole power. Partly by intention and partly unconsciously, it is ever striving to make all other
things bend to itself, and is not content while there is
any thing which makes permanent head against it,
any influence not in agreement with its spirit. Yet,
if it succeeds in suppressing all rival influences, and
moulding every thing after its own model, improvement, in that country, is at an end, and decline com-
mences. Human improvement is a product of many
factors, and no power ever yet constituted among
mankind includes them all: even the most beneficent
power only contains in itself some of the requisites
of good, and the remainder, if progress is to continue,
must be derived from some other source. No community has ever long continued progressive but while
a conflict was going on between the strongest power
in the community and some rival power; between
the spiritual and temporal authorities; the military
or territorial and the industrious classes; the king
and the people; the orthodox and religious reformers. When the victory on either side was so complete as to put an end to the strife, and no other conflict took its place, first stagnation followed, and then
decay. The ascendency of the numerical majority is
less unjust, and, on the whole, less mischievous than
many others, but it is attended with the very same
kind of dangers, and even more certainly; for when
the government is in the hands of One or a Few, the

Many are always existent as a rival power, which may not be strong enough ever to control the other, but whose opinion and sentiment are a moral, and even a social support to all who, either from conviction or contrariety of interest, are opposed to any of the tendencies of the ruling authority. But when the democracy is supreme, there is no One or Few strong enough for dissentient opinions and injured or menaced interests to lean upon. The great difficulty of democratic government has hitherto seemed to be, how to provide in a democratic society — what circumstances have provided hitherto in all the societies which have maintained themselves ahead of others— a social support, a *point d'appui*, for individual resistance to the tendencies of the ruling power; a protection, a rallying-point for opinions and interests which the ascendant public opinion views with disfavor. For want of such a *point d'appui*, the older societies, and all but a few modern ones, either fell into dissolution or became stationary (which means slow deterioration) through the exclusive predominance of a part only of the conditions of social and mental well-being.

Now this great want the system of Personal Representation is fitted to supply in the most perfect manner which the circumstances of modern society admit of. The only quarter in which to look for a supplement, or completing corrective to the instincts of a democratic majority, is the instructed minority; but, in the ordinary mode of constituting democracy, this minority has no organ: Mr. Hare's system provides one. The representatives who would be returned to Parliament by the aggregate of minorities would afford that organ in its greatest perfection. A separate organization of the instructed classes, even if practicable, would be invidious, and could only escape from being offensive by being totally without influence. But if the *élite* of these classes formed part of the Parliament, by the same title as any other of its members—by representing the same number of citizens, the same numerical fraction of the national will—their presence could give umbrage to nobody, while they would be in the position of highest vantage, both for making their opinions and counsels heard on all important subjects, and for taking an active part in public business. Their abilities would probably draw to them more than their numerical share of the actual administration of government; as the Athenians did not confide responsible public functions to Cleon or Hyperbolus (the employment of Cleon at Pylus and Amphipolis was purely exceptional), but Nicias, and Theramenes, and Alcibiades were in constant employment both at home and abroad, though known to sympathize more with oligarchy than with democracy. The instructed minority would, in the actual voting, count only for their numbers, but as a moral power they would count for much more, in virtue of their knowledge, and of the influence it would give them over the rest. An arrangement better adapted to keep popular opinion within reason and justice, and to guard it from the various deteriorating influences which assail the weak side of democracy, could scarcely by human ingenuity be devised. A democratic people would in this way be provided with what in any other way it would almost certainly miss —leaders of a higher grade of intellect and character than itself. Modern democracy would have its occasional Pericles, and its habitual group of superior and guiding minds.

With all this array of reasons, of the most fundamental character, on the affirmative side of the question, what is there on the negative? Nothing that will sustain examination when people can once be induced to bestow any real examination upon a new thing. Those indeed, if any such there be, who, under pretense of equal justice, aim only at substituting the class ascendency of the poor for that of the rich, will of course be unfavorable to a scheme which places both on a level. But I do not believe that any such wish exists at present among the working classes of this country, though I would not answer for the effect which opportunity and demagogic artifices may hereafter have in exciting it. In the United States, where the numerical majority have long been in full possession of collective despotism, they would probably be as unwilling to part with it as a single despot or an aristocracy. But I believe that the English democracy would as yet be content with protection against the class legislation of others, without claiming the power to exercise it in their turn.

Among the ostensible objectors to Mr. Hare's scheme, some profess to think the plan unworkable; but these, it will be found, are generally people who have barely heard of it, or have given it a very slight and cursory examination. Others are unable to reconcile themselves to the loss of what they term the local character of the representation. A nation does not seem to them to consist of persons, but of artificial units, the creation of geography and statistics. Parliament must represent towns and counties, not human beings. But no one seeks to annihilate towns and counties. Towns and counties, it may be presumed, are represented when the human beings who inhabit them are represented. Local feelings can not exist without somebody who feels them, nor local interests without somebody interested in them. If the human beings whose feelings and interests these are have their proper share of representation, these feelings and interests are represented in common with all other feelings and interests of those persons. But I can not see why the feelings and interests which arrange mankind according to localities should be the only ones thought worthy of being represented, or why people who have other feelings and interests, which they value more than they do their geographical ones, should be restricted to these as the sole principle of their political classification. The notions that Yorkshire and Middlesex have rights apart from those of their inhabitants, or that Liverpool and Exeter are the proper objects of the legislator's care, in contradistinction to the population of those places, is a curious specimen of delusion produced by words.

In general, however, objectors cut the matter short by affirming that the people of England will never consent to such a system. What the people of England are likely to think of those who pass such a summary sentence on their capacity of understand-

ing and judgment, deeming it superfluous to consider
whether a thing is right or wrong before affirming
that they are certain to reject it, I will not undertake
to say. For my own part, I do not think that the
people of England have deserved to be, without trial,
stigmatized as insurmountably prejudiced against any
thing which can be proved to be good either for themselves or for others. It also appears to me that when
prejudices persist obstinately, it is the fault of nobody
so much as of those who make a point of proclaiming
them insuperable, as an excuse to themselves for never joining in an attempt to remove them. Any prejudice whatever will be insurmountable if those who
do not share it themselves truckle to it, and flatter it,
and accept it as a law of nature. I believe, however,
that of prejudice, properly speaking, there is in this
case none except on the lips of those who talk about
it, and that there is in general, among those who have
yet heard of the proposition, no other hostility to it
than the natural and healthy distrust attaching to all
novelties which have not been sufficiently canvassed
to make generally manifest all the pros and cons of
the question. The only serious obstacle is the unfamiliarity: this, indeed, is a formidable one, for the imagination much more easily reconciles itself to a great
alteration in substance than to a very small one in
names and forms. But unfamiliarity is a disadvantage which, when there is any real value in an idea, it
only requires time to remove; and in these days of
discussion and generally awakened interest in improvement, what formerly was the work of centuries
often requires only years.

CHAPTER VIII.

OF THE EXTENSION OF THE SUFFRAGE.

SUCH a representative democracy as has now been sketched—representative of all, and not solely of the majority—in which the interests, the opinions, the grades of intellect which are outnumbered would nevertheless be heard, and would have a chance of obtaining by weight of character and strength of argument an influence which would not belong to their numerical force—this democracy, which is alone equal, alone impartial, alone the government of all by all, the only true type of democracy, would be free from the greatest evils of the falsely-called democracies which now prevail, and from which the current idea of democracy is exclusively derived. But even in this democracy, absolute power, if they chose to exercise it, would rest with the numerical majority, and these would be composed exclusively of a single class, alike in biases, prepossessions, and general modes of thinking, and a class, to say no more, not the most highly cultivated. The constitution would therefore still be liable to the characteristic evils of class government; in a far less degree, assuredly, than that exclusive government by a class which now usurps the name of democracy, but still under no effective restraint except what might be found in the good sense, moderation, and forbear-

ance of the class itself. If checks of this description
are sufficient, the philosopy of constitutional government is but solemn trifling. All trust in constitutions
is grounded on the assurance they may afford, not that
the depositaries of power will not, but that they can
not misemploy it. Democracy is not the ideally best
form of government unless this weak side of it can
be strengthened; unless it can be so organized that
no class, not even the most numerous, shall be able
to reduce all but itself to political insignificance, and
direct the course of legislation and administration by
its exclusive class interest. The problem is to find
the means of preventing this abuse without sacrificing
the characteristic advantages of popular government.

These twofold requisites are not fulfilled by the expedient of a limitation of the suffrage, involving the
compulsory exclusion of any portion of the citizens
from a voice in the representation. Among the foremost benefits of free government is that education of
the intelligence and of the sentiments which is carried down to the very lowest ranks of the people when
they are called to take a part in acts which directly
affect the great interests of their country. On this
topic I have already dwelt so emphatically that I
only return to it because there are few who seem to
attach to this effect of popular institutions all the
importance to which it is entitled. People think it
fanciful to expect so much from what seems so slight
a cause—to recognize a potent instrument of mental
improvement in the exercise of political franchises by
manual laborers. Yet, unless substantial mental cul-

tivation in the mass of mankind is to be a mere vision, this is the road by which it must come. If any one supposes that this road will not bring it, I call to witness the entire contents of M. de Tocqueville's great work, and especially his estimate of the Americans. Almost all travelers are struck by the fact that every American is in some sense both a patriot and a person of cultivated intelligence; and M. de Tocqueville has shown how close the connection is between these qualities and their democratic institutions. No such wide diffusion of the ideas, tastes, and sentiments of educated minds has ever been seen elsewhere, or even conceived of as attainable. Yet this is nothing to what we might look for in a government equally democratic in its unexclusiveness, but better organized in other important points. For political life is indeed in America a most valuable school, but it is a school from which the ablest teachers are excluded; the first minds in the country being as effectually shut out from the national representation, and from public functions generally, as if they were under a formal disqualification. The Demos, too, being in America the one source of power, all the selfish ambition of the country gravitates toward it, as it does in despotic countries toward the monarch; the People, like the despot, is pursued with adulation and sycophancy, and the corrupting effects of power fully keep pace with its improving and ennobling influences. If, even with this alloy, democratic institutions produce so marked a superiority of mental development in the lowest class of Americans, compared with the corresponding

classes in England and elsewhere, what would it be
if the good portion of the influence could be retained
without the bad? And this, to a certain extent, may
be done, but not by excluding that portion of the
people who have fewest intellectual stimuli of other
kinds from so inestimable an introduction to large,
distant, and complicated interests as is afforded by
the attention they may be induced to bestow on political affairs. It is by political discussion that the
manual laborer, whose employment is a routine, and
whose way of life brings him in contact with no variety of impressions, circumstances, or ideas, is taught
that remote causes, and events which take place far
off, have a most sensible effect even on his personal
interests; and it is from political discussion and collective political action that one whose daily occupations concentrate his interests in a small circle round
himself, learns to feel for and with his fellow-citizens,
and becomes consciously a member of a great community. But political discussions fly over the heads
of those who have no votes, and are not endeavoring
to acquire them. Their position, in comparison with
the electors, is that of the audience in a court of justice compared with the twelve men in the jury-box.
It is not *their* suffrages that are asked, it is not their
opinion that is sought to be influenced; the appeals
are made, the arguments addressed, to others than
them; nothing depends on the decision *they* may arrive at, and there is no necessity and very little inducement to them to come to any. Whoever, in an
otherwise popular government, has no vote, and no

prospect of obtaining it, will either be a permanent
malcontent, or will feel as one whom the general affairs of society do not concern ; for whom they are to
be managed by others; who "has no business with
the laws except to obey them," nor with public interests and concerns except as a looker-on. What he
will know or care about them from this position may
partly be measured by what an average woman of the
middle class knows and cares about politics compared
with her husband or brothers.

Independently of all these considerations, it is a personal injustice to withhold from any one, unless for
the prevention of greater evils, the ordinary privilege
of having his voice reckoned in the disposal of affairs
in which he has the same interest as other people.
If he is compelled to pay, if he may be compelled to
fight, if he is required implicitly to obey, he should
be legally entitled to be told what for; to have his
consent asked, and his opinion counted at its worth,
though not at more than its worth. There ought to
be no pariahs in a full-grown and civilized nation ;
no persons disqualified except through their own default. Every one is degraded, whether aware of it or
not, when other people, without consulting him, take
upon themselves unlimited power to regulate his destiny. And even in a much more improved state than
the human mind has ever yet reached, it is not in nature that they who are thus disposed of should meet
with as fair play as those who have a voice. Rulers
and ruling classes are under a necessity of considering
the interests and wishes of those who have the suf-

frage; but of those who are excluded, it is in their
option whether they will do so or not; and, however
honestly disposed, they are, in general, too fully occupied with things which they *must* attend to to have
much room in their thoughts for any thing which
they can with impunity disregard. No arrangement
of the suffrage, therefore, can be permanently satisfactory in which any person or class is peremptorily
excluded—in which the electoral privilege is not open
to all persons of full age who desire to obtain it.

There are, however, certain exclusions, required by
positive reasons, which do not conflict with this principle, and which, though an evil in themselves, are
only to be got rid of by the cessation of the state of
things which requires them. I regard it as wholly
inadmissible that any person should participate in the
suffrage without being able to read, write, and, I will
add, perform the common operations of arithmetic.
Justice demands, even when the suffrage does not depend on it, that the means of attaining these elementary acquirements should be within the reach of every
person, either gratuitously, or at an expense not exceeding what the poorest, who can earn their own
living, can afford. If this were really the case, people
would no more think of giving the suffrage to a man
who could not read, than of giving it to a child who
could not speak; and it would not be society that
would exclude him, but his own laziness. When society has not performed its duty by rendering this
amount of instruction accessible to all, there is some
hardship in the case, but it is a hardship that ought

to be borne. If society has neglected to discharge two solemn obligations, the more important and more fundamental of the two must be fulfilled first; universal teaching must precede universal enfranchisement. No one but those in whom an *à priori* theory has silenced common sense will maintain that power over others, over the whole community, should be imparted to people who have not acquired the commonest and most essential requisites for taking care of themselves — for pursuing intelligently their own interests, and those of the persons most nearly allied to them. This argument, doubtless, might be pressed farther, and made to prove much more. It would be eminently desirable that other things besides reading, writing, and arithmetic could be made necessary to the suffrage; that some knowledge of the conformation of the earth, its natural and political divisions, the elements of general history, and of the history and institutions of their own country, could be required from all electors. But these kinds of knowledge, however indispensable to an intelligent use of the suffrage, are not, in this country, nor probably any where save in the Northern United States, accessible to the whole people, nor does there exist any trustworthy machinery for ascertaining whether they have been acquired or not. The attempt, at present, would lead to partiality, chicanery, and every kind of fraud. It is better that the suffrage should be conferred indiscriminately, or even withheld indiscriminately, than that it should be given to one and withheld from another at the discretion of a public officer. In regard, however, to read-

ing, writing, and calculating, there need be no difficulty. It would be easy to require from every one
who presented himself for registry that he should, in
the presence of the registrar, copy a sentence from an
English book, and perform a sum in the rule of three;
and to secure, by fixed rules and complete publicity,
the honest application of so very simple a test. This
condition, therefore, should in all cases accompany
universal suffrage; and it would, after a few years,
exclude none but those who cared so little for the
privilege that their vote, if given, would not be an indication of any real political opinion.

It is also important that the assembly which votes
the taxes, either general or local, should be elected
exclusively by those who pay something toward the
taxes imposed. Those who pay no taxes, disposing
by their votes of other people's money, have every
motive to be lavish and none to economize. As far
as money matters are concerned, any power of voting
possessed by them is a violation of the fundamental
principle of free government, a severance of the power
of control from the interest in its beneficial exercise.
It amounts to allowing them to put their hands into
other people's pockets for any purpose which they
think fit to call a public one, which, in the great
towns of the United States, is known to have produced a scale of local taxation onerous beyond example, and wholly borne by the wealthier classes. That
representation should be coextensive with taxation,
not stopping short of it, but also not going beyond it,
is in accordance with the theory of British institutions.

But to reconcile this, as a condition annexed to the representation, with universality, it is essential, as it is on many other accounts desirable, that taxation, in a visible shape, should descend to the poorest class. In this country, and in most others, there is probably no laboring family which does not contribute to the indirect taxes by the purchase of tea, coffee, sugar, not to mention narcotics or stimulants. But this mode of defraying a share of the public expenses is hardly felt: the payer, unless a person of education and reflection, does not identify his interest with a low scale of public expenditure as closely as when money for its support is demanded directly from himself; and even supposing him to do so, he would doubtless take care that, however lavish an expenditure he might, by his vote, assist in imposing upon the government, it should not be defrayed by any additional taxes on the articles which he himself consumes. It would be better that a direct tax, in the simple form of a capitation, should be levied on every grown person in the community, or that every such person should be admitted an elector on allowing himself to be rated *extra ordinem* to the assessed taxes, or that a small annual payment, rising and falling with the gross expenditure of the country, should be required from every registered elector, that so every one might feel that the money which he assisted in voting was partly his own, and that he was interested in keeping down its amount.

However this may be, I regard it as required by first principles that the receipt of parish relief should be a peremptory disqualification for the franchise. He who can not by his labor suffice for his own support, has no claim to the privilege of helping himself to the money of others. By becoming dependent on the re. maining members of the community for actual sub sistence, he abdicates his claim to equal rights with them in other respects. Those to whom he is in. debted for the continuance of his very existence may justly claim the exclusive management of those com- mon concerns to which he now brings nothing, or less than he takes away. As a condition of the fran- chise, a term should be fixed, say five years previous to the registry, during which the applicant's name has not been on the parish books as a recipient of relief. To be an uncertificated bankrupt, or to have taken the benefit of the Insolvent Act, should disqualify for the franchise until the person has paid his debts, or at least proved that he is not now, and has not for some long period been, dependent on eleemosynary support. Non-payment of taxes, when so long per- sisted in that it can not have arisen from inadvertence, should disqualify while it lasts. These exclusions are not in their nature permanent. They exact such con- ditions only as all are able, or ought to be able, to ful- fill if they choose. They leave the suffrage accessible to all who are in the normal condition of a human be- ing; and if any one has to forego it, he either does not care sufficiently for it to do for its sake what he is already bound to do, or he is in a general condition of depression and degradation in which this slight ad- dition, necessary for the security of others, would be unfelt, and on emerging from which this mark of inferiority would disappear with the rest.

In the long run, therefore (supposing no restrictions to exist but those of which we have now treated), we might expect that all, except that (it is to be hoped) progressively diminishing class, the recipients of parish relief, would be in possession of votes, so that the suffrage would be, with that slight abatement, universal. That it should be thus widely expanded is, as we have seen, absolutely necessary to an enlarged and elevated conception of good government. Yet in this state of things, the great majority of voters in most countries, and emphatically in this, would be manual laborers, and the twofold danger, that of too low a standard of political intelligence, and that of class legislation, would still exist in a very perilous degree. It remains to be seen whether any means exist by which these evils can be obviated.

They are capable of being obviated if men sincerely wish it; not by any artificial contrivance, but by carrying out the natural order of human life, which recommends itself to every one in things in which he has no interest or traditional opinion running counter to it. In all human affairs, every person directly interested, and not under positive tutelage, has an admitted. claim to a voice, and when his exercise of it is not inconsistent with the safety of the whole, can not justly be excluded from it. But (though every one ought to have a voice) that every one should have an equal voice is a totally different proposition. When two persons who have a joint interest in any business dif-

fer in opinion, does justice require that both opinions
should be held of exactly equal value? If with equal
virtue, one is superior to the other in knowledge and
intelligence—or if with equal intelligence, one excels
the other in virtue—the opinion, the judgment of the
higher moral or intellectual being is worth more than
that of the inferior; and if the institutions of the
country virtually assert that they are of the same value, they assert the thing which is not. One of the
two, as the wiser or better man, has a claim to superior weight: the difficulty is in ascertaining which of
the two it is; a thing impossible as between individuals, but, taking men in bodies and in numbers, it can
be done with a sufficient approach to accuracy. There
would be no pretense for applying this doctrine to any
case which can with reason be considered as one of
individual and private right. In an affair which concerns only one of two persons, that one is entitled to
follow his own opinion, however much wiser the other
may be than himself. But we are speaking of things
which equally concern them both; where, if the more
ignorant does not yield his share of the matter to the
guidance of the wiser man, the wiser man must resign
his to that of the more ignorant. Which of these
modes of getting over the difficulty is most for the interest of both, and most conformable to the general
fitness of things? If it be deemed unjust that either
should have to give way, which injustice is greatest?
that the better judgment should give way to the worse,
or the worse to the better?

Now national affairs are exactly such a joint concern, with the difference that no one needs ever be called upon for a complete sacrifice of his own opinion. It can always be taken into the calculation, and counted at a certain figure, a higher figure being assigned to the suffrages of those whose opinion is entitled to greater weight. There is not in this arrangement any thing necessarily invidious to those to whom it assigns the lower degrees of influence. Entire exclusion from a voice in the common concerns is one thing; the concession to others of a more potential voice, on the ground of greater capacity for the management of the joint interests, is another. The two things are not merely different, they are incommensurable. Every one has a right to feel insulted by being made a nobody, and stamped as of no account at all. No one but a fool, and only a fool of a peculiar description, feels offended by the acknowledgment that there are others whose opinion, and even whose wish, is entitled to a greater amount of consideration than his. To have no voice in what are partly his own concerns is a thing which nobody willingly submits to; but when what is partly his concern is also partly another's, and he feels the other to understand the subject better than himself, that the other's opinion should be counted for more than his own accords with his expectations, and with the course of things which in all other affairs of life he is accustomed to acquiesce in. It is only necessary that this superior influence should be assigned on grounds which he can comprehend, and of which he is able to perceive the justice.

I hasten to say that I consider it entirely inadmissible, unless as a temporary makeshift, that the superiority of influence should be conferred in consideration of property. I do not deny that property is a kind of test; education, in most countries, though any thing but proportional to riches, is on the average better in the richer half of society than in the poorer. But the criterion is so imperfect; accident has so much more to do than merit with enabling men to rise in the world; and it is so impossible for any one, by acquiring any amount of instruction, to make sure of the corresponding rise in station, that this foundation of electoral privilege is always, and will continue to be, supremely odious. To connect plurality of votes with any pecuniary qualification would be not only objectionable in itself, but a sure mode of compromising the principle, and making its permanent maintenance impracticable. The democracy, at least of this country, are not at present jealous of personal superiority, but they are naturally and most justly so of that which is grounded on mere pecuniary circumstances. The only thing which can justify reckoning one person's opinion as equivalent to more than one is individual mental superiority, and what is wanted is some approximate means of ascertaining that. If there existed such a thing as a really national education or a trustworthy system of general examination, education might be tested directly. In the absence of these, the nature of a person's occupation is some test. An employer of labor is on the average more intelligent than a laborer; for he must labor with his head, and not solely with his hands. A foreman is generally more intelligent than an ordinary laborer, and a laborer in the skilled trades than in the unskilled. A banker, merchant, or manufacturer is likely to be more intelligent than a tradesman, because he has larger and more complicated interests to manage. In all these cases it is not the having merely undertaken the superior function, but the successful performance of it, that tests the qualifications; for which reason, as well to prevent persons from engaging nominally in an occupation for the sake of the vote, it would be proper to require that the occupation should have been persevered in for some length of time (say three years). Subject to some such condition, two or more votes might be allowed to every person who exercises any of these superior functions. The liberal professions, when really and not nominally practiced, imply, of course, a still higher degree of instruction; and whenever a sufficient examination, or any serious conditions of education, are required before entering on a profession, its members could be admitted at once to a plurality of votes. The same rule might be applied to graduates of universities, and even to those who bring satisfactory certificates of having passed through the course of study required by any school at which the higher branches of knowledge are taught, under proper securities that the teaching is real, and not a mere pretense. The "local" or "middle class" examinations for the degree of associate, so laudably and public-spiritedly established by the University of Oxford, and any similar ones which may be instituted by

other competent bodies (provided they are fairly open
to all comers), afford a ground on which plurality of
votes might with great advantage be accorded to those
who have passed the test. All these suggestions are
open to much discussion in the detail, and to objections
which it is of no use to anticipate. The time is not
come for giving to such plans a practical shape, nor
should I wish to be bound by the particular proposals
which I have made. But it is to me evident that in
this direction lies the true ideal of representative government, and that to work toward it by the best practical contrivances which can be found is the path of
real political improvement.

If it be asked to what length the principle admits
of being carried, or how many votes might be accorded to an individual on the ground of superior qualifications, I answer, that this is not in itself very material, provided the distinctions and gradations are not
made arbitrarily, but are such as can be understood
and accepted by the general conscience and understanding. But it is an absolute condition not to over-
pass the limit prescribed by the fundamental principle
laid down in a former chapter as the condition of excellence in the constitution of a representative system.
The plurality of votes must on no account be carried
so far that those who are privileged by it, or the class
(if any) to which they mainly belong, shall outweigh
by means of it all the rest of the community. The
distinction in favor of education, right in itself, is farther and strongly recommended by its preserving the
educated from the class legislation of the uneducated;

but it must stop short of enabling them to practice class legislation on their own account. Let me add that I consider it an absolutely necessary part of the plurality scheme that it be open to the poorest individual in the community to claim its privileges, if he can prove that, in spite of all difficulties and obstacles, he is, in point of intelligence, entitled to them. There ought to be voluntary examinations at which any person whatever might present himself, might prove that he came up to the standard of knowledge and ability laid down as sufficient, and be admitted, in consequence, to the plurality of votes. A privilege which is not refused to any one who can show that he has realized the conditions on which in theory and principle it is dependent, would not be repugnant to any one's sentiment of justice; but it would certainly be so if, while conferred on general presumptions not always infallible, it were denied to direct proof.

Plural voting, though practiced in vestry elections and those of poor-law guardians, is so unfamiliar in elections to Parliament that it is not likely to be soon or willingly adopted; but as the time will certainly arrive when the only choice will be between this and equal universal suffrage, whoever does not desire the last can not too soon begin to reconcile himself to the former. In the mean time, though the suggestion, for the present, may not be a practical one, it will serve to mark what is best in principle, and enable us to judge of the eligibility of any indirect means, either existing or capable of being adopted, which may promote in a less perfect manner the same end. A per-

son may have a double vote by other means than that
of tendering two votes at the same hustings ; he may
have a vote in each of two different constituencies;
and though this exceptional privilege at present belongs rather to superiority of means than of intelligence, I would not abolish it where it exists, since, until a truer test of education is adopted, it would be
unwise to dispense with even so imperfect a one as is
afforded by pecuniary circumstances. Means might
be found of giving a farther extension to the privilege, which would connect it in a more direct manner
with superior education. In any future Reform Bill
which lowers greatly the pecuniary conditions of the
suffrage, it might be a wise provision to allow all graduates of universities, all persons who had passed cred-
itably through the higher schools, all members of the
liberal professions, and perhaps some others, to be registered specifically in those characters, and to give
their votes as such in any constituency in which they
chose to register; retaining, in addition, their votes as
simple citizens in the localities in which they reside.

Until there shall have been devised, and until opinion is willing to accept, some mode of plural voting
which may assign to education as such the degree of
superior influence due to it, and sufficient as a counterpoise to the numerical weight of the least educated
class, for so long the benefits of completely universal
suffrage can not be obtained without bringing with
them, as it appears to me, more than equivalent evils.
It is possible, indeed (and this is perhaps one of the
transitions through which we may have to pass in our

progress to a really good representative system), that
the barriers which restrict the suffrage might be entirely leveled in some particular constituencies, whose
members, consequently, would be returned principally
by manual laborers; the existing electoral qualification being maintained elsewhere, or any alteration in
it being accompanied by such a grouping of the constituencies as to prevent the laboring class from becoming preponderant in Parliament. By such a compromise, the anomalies in the representation would not
only be retained, but augmented; this, however, is not
a conclusive objection; for if the country does not
choose to pursue the right ends by a regular system
directly leading to them, it must be content with an
irregular makeshift, as being greatly preferable to a
system free from irregularities, but regularly adapted
to wrong ends, or in which some ends equally necessary with the others have been left out. It is a far
graver objection that this adjustment is incompatible
with the intercommunity of local constituencies which
Mr. Hare's plan requires; that under it every voter
would remain imprisoned within the one or more constituencies in which his name is registered, and, unless
willing to be represented by one of the candidates for
those localities, would not be represented at all.

So much importance do I attach to the emancipation of those who already have votes, but whose votes
are useless, because always outnumbered—so much
should I hope from the natural influence of truth and
reason, if only secured a hearing and a competent
advocacy, that I should not despair of the operation

even of equal and universal suffrage, if made real by
the proportional representation of all minorities, on
Mr. Hare's principle. But if the best hopes which can
be formed on this subject were certainties, I should
still contend for the principle of plural voting. I do
not propose the plurality as a thing in itself unde-
sirable, which, like the exclusion of part of the community from the suffrage, may be temporarily tolerated while necessary to prevent greater evils. I do
not look upon equal voting as among the things which
are good in themselves, provided they can be guarded
against inconveniences. I look upon it as only rela-
tively good; less objectionable than inequality of
privilege grounded on irrelevant or adventitious circumstances, but in principle wrong, because recognizing a wrong standard, and exercising a bad influence
on the voter's mind. It is not useful, but hurtful, that
the constitution of the country should declare ignorance to be entitled to as much political power as
knowledge. The national institutions should place
all things that they are concerned with before the
mind of the citizen in the light in which it is for his
good that he should regard them; and as it for his
good that he should think that every one is entitled
to some influence, but the better and wiser to more
than others, it is important that this conviction should
be professed by the state, and embodied in the national institutions. Such things constitute the *spirit* of
the institutions of a country; that portion of their influence which is least regarded by common, and especially by English thinkers, though the institutions of

every country, not under great positive oppression, produce more effect by their spirit than by any of their direct provisions, since by it they shape the national character. The American institutions have imprinted strongly on the American mind that any one man (with a white skin) is as good as any other, and it is felt that this false creed is nearly connected with some of the more unfavorable points in American character. It is not a small mischief that the constitution of any country should sanction this creed; for the belief in it, whether express or tacit, is almost as detrimental to moral and intellectual excellence as any effect which most forms of government can produce.

It may, perhaps, be said that a constitution which gives equal influence, man for man, to the most and to the least instructed, is nevertheless conducive to progress, because the appeals constantly made to the less instructed classes, the exercise given to their mental powers, and the exertions which the more instructed are obliged to make for enlightening their judgment and ridding them of errors and prejudices, are powerful stimulants to their advance in intelligence. That this most desirable effect really attends the admission of the less educated classes to some, and even to a large share of power, I admit, and have already strenuously maintained. But theory and experience alike prove that a counter current sets in when they are made the possessors of all power. Those who are supreme over every thing, whether they be One, or Few, or Many, have no longer need of the arms of reason; they can make their mere will prevail; and those who can not be resisted are usually far too well satisfied with their own opinions to be willing to change them, or listen without impatience to any one who tells them that they are in the wrong. The position which gives the strongest stimulus to the growth of intelligence is that of rising into power, not that of having achieved it; and of all resting-points, temporary or permanent, in the way to ascendency, the one which develops the best and highest qualities is the position of those who are strong enough to make reason prevail, but not strong enough to prevail against reason. This is the position in which, according to the principles we have laid down, the rich and the poor, the much and the little educated, and all the other classes and denominations which divide society between them, ought as far as practicable to be placed; and by combining this principle with the otherwise just one of allowing superiority of weight to superiority of mental qualities, a political constitution would realize that kind of relative perfection which is alone compatible with the complicated nature of human affairs.

In the preceding argument for universal but graduated suffrage, I have taken no account of difference of sex. I consider it to be as entirely irrelevant to political rights as difference in height, or in the color of the hair. All human beings have the same interest in good government; the welfare of all is alike affected by it, and they have equal need of a voice in

it to secure their share of its benefits. If there be any
difference, women require it more than men, since, being physically weaker, they are more dependent on
law and society for protection. Mankind have long
since abandoned the only premises which will support
the conclusion that women ought not to have votes.
No one now holds that women should be in personal
servitude; that they should have no thought, wish,
or occupation but to be the domestic drudges of hus-
bands, fathers, or brothers. It is allowed to unmar-
ried, and wants but little of being conceded to married women to hold property, and have pecuniary and
business interests in the same manner as men. It is
considered suitable and proper that women should
think, and write, and be teachers. As soon as these
things are admitted, the political disqualification has
no principle to rest on. The whole mode of thought
of the modern world is, with increasing emphasis, pro-
nouncing against the claim of society to decide for individuals what they are and are not fit for, and what
they shall and shall not be allowed to attempt. If
the principles of modern politics and political economy are good for any thing, it is for proving that these
points can only be rightly judged of by the individuals themselves; and that, under complete freedom of
choice, wherever there are real diversities of aptitude,
the greater number will apply themselves to the things
for which they are on the average fittest, and the exceptional course will only be taken by the exceptions.
Either the whole tendency of modern social improvements has been wrong, or it ought to be carried out

to the total abolition of all exclusions and disabilities which close any honest employment to a human being.

But it is not even necessary to maintain so much in order to prove that women should have the suffrage. Were it as right as it is wrong that they should be a subordinate class, confined to domestic occupations and subject to domestic authority, they would not the less require the protection of the suffrage to secure them from the abuse of that authority. Men, as well as women, do not need political rights in order that they may govern, but in order that they may not be misgoverned. The majority of the male sex are, and will be all their lives, nothing else than laborers in corn-fields or manufactories; but this does not render the suffrage less desirable for them, nor their claim to it less irresistible, when not likely to make a bad use of it. Nobody pretends to think that women would make a bad use of the suffrage. The worst that is said is that they would vote as mere dependents, at the bidding of their male relations. If it be so, so let it be. If they think for themselves, great good will be done; and if they do not, no harm. It is a benefit to human beings to take off their fetters, even if they do not desire to walk. It would already be a great improvement in the moral position of women to be no longer declared by law incapable of an opinion, and not entitled to a preference respecting the most important concerns of humanity. There would be some benefit to them individually in having something to bestow which their male relatives can not exact, and are yet desirous to have. It would

also be no small matter that the husband would necessarily discuss the matter with his wife, and that the
vote would not be his exclusive affair, but a joint concern. People do not sufficiently consider how markedly the fact that she is able to have some action on
the outward world independently of him, raises her
dignity and value in a vulgar man's eyes, and makes
her the object of a respect which no personal qualities would ever obtain for one whose social existence
he can entirely appropriate. The vote itself, too,
would be improved in quality. The man would often
be obliged to find honest reasons for his vote, such as
might induce a more upright and impartial character
to serve with him under the same banner. The wife's
influence would often keep him true to his own sincere opinion. Often, indeed, it would be used, not on
the side of public principle, but of the personal interest or worldly vanity of the family. But, wherever
this would be the tendency of the wife's influence, it
is exerted to the full already in that bad direction,
and with the more certainty, since under the present
law and custom she is generally too utter a stranger
to politics in any sense in which they involve principle to be able to realize to herself that there is a point
of honor in them ; and most people have as little sympathy in the point of honor of others, when their own
is not placed in the same thing, as they have in the
religious feelings of those whose religion differs from
theirs. Give the woman a vote, and she comes under
the operation of the political point of honor. She
learns to look on politics as a thing on which she is

allowed to have an opinion, and in which, if one has an opinion, it ought to be acted upon; she acquires a sense of personal accountability in the matter, and will no longer feel, as she does at present, that whatever amount of bad influence she may exercise, if the man can but be persuaded, all is right, and his responsibility covers all. It is only by being herself encouraged to form an opinion, and obtain an intelligent comprehension of the reasons which ought to prevail with the conscience against the temptations of personal or family interest, that she can ever cease to act as a disturbing force on the political conscience of the man. Her indirect agency can only be prevented from being politically mischievous by being exchanged for direct.

I have supposed the right of suffrage to depend, as in a good state of things it would, on personal conditions. Where it depends, as in this and most other countries, on conditions of property, the contradiction is even more flagrant. There is something more than ordinarily irrational in the fact that when a woman can give all the guarantees required from a male elector, independent circumstances, the position of a householder and head of a family, payment of taxes, or whatever may be the conditions imposed, the very principle and system of a representation based on property is set aside, and an exceptionally personal disqualification is created for the mere purpose of excluding her. When it is added that in the country where this is done a woman now reigns, and that the most glorious ruler whom that country ever had was a woman, the picture of unreason and scarcely disguised injustice is complete. Let us hope that as the work proceeds of pulling down, one after another, the remains of the mouldering fabric of monopoly and tyranny, this one will not be the last to disappear; that the opinion of Bentham, of Mr. Samuel Bailey, of Mr. Hare, and many other of the most powerful political thinkers of this age and country (not to speak of others), will make its way to all minds not rendered obdurate by selfishness or inveterate prejudice; and that, before the lapse of another generation, the accident of sex, no more than the accident of skin, will be deemed a sufficient justification for depriving its possessor of the equal protection and just privileges of a citizen.

CHAPTER IX.

SHOULD THERE BE TWO STAGES OF ELECTION?

IN some representative constitutions, the plan has been adopted of choosing the members of the representative body by a double process, the primary electors only choosing other electors, and these electing the member of Parliament. This contrivance was probably intended as a slight impediment to the full sweep of popular feeling, giving the suffrage, and with it the complete ultimate power, to the Many, but compelling them to exercise it through the agency of a comparatively few, who, it was supposed, would be less moved than the Demos by the gusts of popular passion; and as the electors, being already a select body, might be expected to exceed in intellect and character the common level of their constituents, the choice made by them was thought likely to be more careful and enlightened, and would, in any case, be made under a greater feeling of responsibility than election by the masses themselves. This plan of filtering, as it were, the popular suffrage through an intermediate body, admits of a very plausible defense; since it may be said, with great appearance of reason, that less intellect and instruction are required for judging who among our neighbors can be most safely trusted to choose a member of Parliament than who is himself fittest to be one.

In the first place, however, if the dangers incident to popular power may be thought to be in some degree lessened by this indirect management, so also are its benefits; and the latter effect is much more certain than the former. To enable the system to work as desired, it must be carried into effect in the spirit in which it is planned; the electors must use the suffrage in the manner supposed by the theory, that is, each of them must not ask himself who the member of Parliament should be, but only whom he would best like to choose one for him. It is evident that the advantages which indirect is supposed to have over direct election require this disposition of mind in the voter, and will only be realized by his taking the doctrine *au sérieux*, that his sole business is to choose the choosers, not the member himself. The supposition must be, that he will not occupy his thoughts with political opinions and measures or political men, but will be guided by his personal respect for some private individual, to whom he will give a general power of attorney to act for him. Now if the primary electors adopt this view of their position, one of the principal uses of giving them a vote at all is defeated; the political function to which they are called fails of developing public spirit and political intelligence, of making public affairs an object of interest to their feelings and of exercise to their faculties. The supposition, moreover, involves inconsistent conditions; for if the voter feels no interest in the final result, how or why can he be expected to feel any in the process which leads to it? To wish to have a particular individual for his representative in Parliament is possible to a person of a very moderate degree of virtue and intelligence, and to wish to choose an elector who will elect that individual is a natural consequence; but for a person who does not care who is elected, or feels bound to put that consideration in abeyance, to take any interest whatever in merely naming the worthiest person to elect another according to his own judgment, implies a zeal for what is right in the abstract, an habitual principle of dūty for the sake of duty, which is possible only to persons of a rather high grade of cultivation, who, by the very possession of it, show that they may be, and deserve to be, trusted with political power in a more direct shape. Of all public functions which it is possible to confer on the poorer members of the community, this surely is the least calculated to kindle their feelings, and holds out least natural inducement to care for it other than a virtuous determination to discharge conscientiously whatever duty one has to perform; and if the mass of electors cared enough about political affairs to set any value on so limited a participation in them, they would not be likely to be satisfied without one much more extensive.

In the next place, admitting that a person who, from his narrow range of cultivation, can not judge well of the qualifications of a candidate for Parliament, may be a sufficient judge of the honesty and general capacity of somebody whom he may depute to choose a member of Parliament for him, I may remark, that if the voter acquiesces in this estimate of

his capabilities, and really wishes to have the choice
made for him by a person in whom he places reliance,
there is no need of any constitutional provision for
the purpose; he has only to ask this confidential person privately what candidate he had better vote for.
In that case the two modes of election coincide in
their result, and every advantage of indirect election
is obtained under direct.   The systems only diverge
in their operation if we suppose that the voter would
prefer to use his own judgment in the choice of a
representative, and only lets another choose for him
because the law does not allow him a more direct
mode of action.   But if this be his state of mind; if
his will does not go along with the limitation which
the law imposes, and he desires to make a direct
choice, he can do so notwithstanding the law.   He
has only to choose as elector a known partisan of the
candidate he prefers, or some one who will pledge
himself to vote for that candidate.   And this is so
much the natural working of election by two stages,
that, except in a condition of complete political indifference, it can scarcely be expected to act otherwise.
It is in this way that the election of the President of
the United States practically operates.   Nominally
the election is indirect; the population at large does
not vote for the President; it votes for electors who
choose the President.   But the electors are always
chosen under an express engagement to vote for a
particular candidate; nor does a citizen ever vote for
an elector because of any preference for the man; he
votes for the Breckinridge ticket or the Lincoln tick-

et. It must be remembered that the electors are not chosen in order that they may search the country and find the fittest person in it to be President or to be a member of Parliament. There would be something to be said for the practice if this were so; but it is not so, nor ever will be, until mankind in general are of opinion, with Plato, that the proper person to be intrusted with power is the person most unwilling to accept it. The electors are to make choice of one of those who have offered themselves as candidates, and those who choose the electors already know who these are. If there is any political activity in the country, all electors who care to vote at all have made up their minds which of these candidates they would like to have, and will make that the sole consideration in giving their vote. The partisans of each candidate will have their list of electors ready, all pledged to vote for that individual; and the only question practically asked of the primary elector will be, which of these lists he will support.

The case in which election by two stages answers well in practice is when the electors are not chosen solely as electors, but have other important functions to discharge, which precludes their being selected solely as delegates to give a particular vote. This combination of circumstances exemplifies itself in another American institution, the Senate of the United States. That assembly, the Upper House, as it were, of Congress, is considered to represent, not the people directly, but the states as such, and to be the guardian of that portion of their sovereign rights which they have not alienated. As the internal sovereignty of each state is, by the nature of an equal federation, equally sacred whatever be the size or importance of the state, each returns to the Senate the same number of members (two), whether it be little Delaware or the "Empire State" of New York. These members are not chosen by the population, but by the State Legislatures, themselves elected by the people of each state; but as the whole ordinary business of a legislative assembly, internal legislation and the control of the executive, devolves upon these bodies, they are elected with a view to those objects more than to the other; and in naming two persons to represent the state in the federal Senate, they for the most part exercise their own judgment, with only that general reference to public opinion necessary in all acts of the government of a democracy. The elections thus made have proved eminently successful, and are conspicuously the best of all the elections in the United States, the Senate invariably consisting of the most distinguished men among those who have made themselves sufficiently known in public life. After such an example, it can not be said that indirect popular election is never advantageous. Under certain conditions, it is the very best system that can be adopted. But those conditions are hardly to be obtained in practice except in a federal government like that of the United States, where the election can be intrusted to local bodies whose other functions extend to the most important concerns of the nation. The only bodies in any analogous position which exist, or are likely to

exist, in this country, are the municipalities, or any
other boards which have been or may be created for
similar local purposes. Few persons, however, would
think it any improvement in our Parliamentary constitution if the members for the City of London were
chosen by the aldermen and Common Council, and
those for the borough of Marylebone avowedly, as
they already are virtually, by the vestries of the com-
ponent parishes. Even if those bodies, considered
merely as local boards, were far less objectionable
than they are, the qualities that would fit them for
the limited and peculiar duties of municipal or parochial ædileship are no guaranty of any special fitness to judge of the comparative qualifications of candidates for a seat in Parliament. They probably
would not fulfill this duty any better than it is fulfilled by the inhabitants voting directly ; while, on the
other hand, if fitness for electing members of Parliament had to be taken into consideration in selecting
persons for the office of vestrymen or town council-
ors, many of those who are fittest for that more limited duty would inevitably be excluded from it, if only
by the necessity there would be of choosing persons
whose sentiments in general politics agreed with those
of the voters who elected them. The mere indirect
political influence of town councils has already led to
a considerable perversion of municipal elections from
their intended purpose by making them a matter of
party politics. If it were part of the duty of a man's
book-keeper or steward to choose his physician, he
would not be likely to have a better medical attend-

ant than if he chose one for himself, while he would be restricted in his choice of a steward or book-keeper to such as might, without too great danger to his health, be intrusted with the other office.

It appears, therefore, that every benefit of indirect election which is attainable at all is attainable under direct; that such of the benefits expected from it as would not be obtained under direct election will just as much fail to be obtained under indirect; while the latter has considerable disadvantages peculiar to itself. The mere fact that it is an additional and superfluous wheel in the machinery is no trifling objection. Its decided inferiority as a means of cultivating public spirit and political intelligence has already been dwelt upon; and if it had any effective operation at all— that is, if the primary electors did to any extent leave to their nominees the selection of their Parliamentary representative, the voter would be prevented from identifying himself with his member of Parliament, and the member would feel a much less active sense of responsibility to his constituents. In addition to all this, the comparatively small number of persons in whose hands, at last, the election of a member of Parliament would reside, could not but afford great additional facilities to intrigue, and to every form of corruption compatible with the station in life of the electors. The constituencies would universally be reduced, in point of conveniences for bribery, to the condition of the small boroughs at present. It would be sufficient to gain over a small number of persons to be certain of being returned. If it be said that the electors would be responsible to those who elected them, the answer

is obvious, that, holding no permanent office or position in the public eye, they would risk nothing by a
corrupt vote except what they would care little for,
not to be appointed electors again; and the main reliance must still be on the penalties for bribery, the
insufficiency of which reliance, in small constituencies,
experience has made notorious to all the world. The
evil would be exactly proportional to the amount of
discretion left to the chosen electors. The only case
in which they would probably be afraid to employ
their vote for the promotion of their personal interest
would be when they were elected under an express
pledge, as mere delegates, to carry, as it were, the votes
of their constituents to the hustings. The moment
the double stage of election began to have any effect,
it would begin to have a bad effect. And this we
shall find true of the principle of indirect election however applied, except in circumstances similar to those
of the election of senators in the United States.

It is unnecessary, as far as England is concerned,
to say more in opposition to a scheme which has no
foundation in any of the national traditions. An apology may even be expected for saying so much against
a political expedient which perhaps could not, in this
country, muster a single adherent. But a conception
so plausible at the first glance, and for which there are
so many precedents in history, might perhaps, in the
general chaos of political opinions, rise again to the
surface, and be brought forward on occasions when it
might be seductive to some minds; and it could not,
therefore, even if English readers were alone to be
considered, be passed altogether in silence.

CHAPTER X.

OF THE MODE OF VOTING.

THE question of greatest moment in regard to modes of voting is that of secrecy or publicity, and to this we will at once address ourselves.

It would be a great mistake to make the discussion turn on sentimentalities about skulking or cowardice. Secrecy is justifiable in many cases, imperative in some, and it is not cowardice to seek protection against evils which are honestly avoidable. Nor can it be reasonably maintained that no cases are conceivable in which secret voting is preferable to public; but I must contend that these cases, in affairs of a political character, are the exception, not the rule.

The present is one of the many instances in which, as I have already had occasion to remark, the *spirit* of an institution, the impression it makes on the mind of the citizen, is one of the most important parts of its operation. The spirit of vote by ballot—the interpretation likely to be put on it in the mind of an elector, is that the suffrage is given to him for himself—for his particular use and benefit, and not as a trust for the public. For if it is indeed a trust, if the public are entitled to his vote, are not they entitled to know his vote? This false and pernicious impression may well be made on the generality, since it has been made on most of those who of late years have been conspicuous advocates of the ballot. The doctrine was not so understood by its earlier promoters; but the effect of a doctrine on the mind is best shown, not in those who form it, but in those who are formed by it. Mr. Bright and his school of democrats think themselves greatly concerned in maintaining that the franchise is what they term a right, not a trust. Now this one idea, taking root in the general mind, does a moral mischief outweighing all the good that the ballot could do, at the highest possible estimate of it. In whatever way we define or understand the idea of a right, no person can have a right (except in the legal sense) to power over others: every such power which he is allowed to possess is morally, in the fullest force of the term, a trust. But the exercise of any political function, either as an elector or as a representative, is power over others. Those who say that the suffrage is not a trust, but a right, can scarcely have considered the consequences to which their doctrine leads. If it is a right, if it belongs to the voter for his own sake, on what ground can we blame him for selling it, or using it to recommend himself to any one whom it is his interest to please? A person is not expected to consult exclusively the public benefit in the use he makes of his house, or his three per cent. stock, or any thing to which he really has a right. The suffrage is indeed due to him, among other reasons, as a means to his own protection, but only against treatment from which he is equally bound, so far as depends on his vote, to protect every one of his fellow-citizens. His vote is not a thing in which he has an option; it has no more to do with his personal wishes than the verdict of a juryman. It is strictly a matter of duty; he is bound to give it accordingly to his best and most conscientious opinion of the public good. Whoever has any other idea of it is unfit to have the suffrage; its effect on him is to pervert, not to elevate his mind. Instead of opening his heart to an exalted patriotism and the obligation of public duty, it awakens and nourishes in him the disposition to use a public function for his own interest, pleasure, or caprice; the same feelings and purposes, on a humbler scale, which actuate a despot and an oppressor. Now an ordinary citizen in any public position, or on whom there devolves any social function, is certain to think and feel, respecting the obligations it imposes on him, exactly what society appears to think and feel in conferring it. What seems to be expected from him by society forms a standard which he may fall below, but which he certainly will not rise above. And the interpretation which he is almost sure to put upon secret voting is that he is not bound to give his vote with any reference to those who are not allowed to know how he gives it, but may bestow it simply as he feels inclined.

This is the decisive reason why the argument does not hold, from the use of the ballot in clubs and private societies to its adoption in Parliamentary elections. A member of a club is really, what the elector falsely believes himself to be, under no obligation to consider the wishes or interests of any one else. He declares nothing by his vote but that he is or is not willing to associate, in a manner more or less close, with a particular person. This is a matter on which, by universal admission, his own pleasure or inclination is entitled to decide; and that he should be able so to decide it without risking a quarrel is best for every body, the rejected person included. An additional reason rendering the ballot unobjectionable in these cases is that it does not necessarily or naturally lead to lying. The persons concerned are of the same class or rank, and it would be considered improper in one of them to press the other with questions as to how he had voted. It is far otherwise in Parliamentary elections, and is likely to remain so as long as the social relations exist which produce the demand for the ballot—as long as one person is sufficiently the superior of another to think himself entitled to dictate his vote. And while this is the case, silence or an evasive answer is certain to be construed as proof that the vote given has not been that which was desired.

In any political election, even by universal suffrage (and still more obviously in the case of a restricted suffrage), the voter is under an absolute moral obligation to consider the interest of the public, not his private advantage, and give his vote, to the best of his judgment, exactly as he would be bound to do if he were the sole voter, and the election depended upon him alone. This being admitted, it is at least a *primâ facie* consequence that the duty of voting, like any other public duty, should be performed under the eye and criticism of the public; every one of whom has not only an interest in its performance, but a good title to consider himself wronged if it is performed otherwise than honestly and carefully. Undoubtedly neither this nor any other maxim of political morality is absolutely inviolable; it may be overruled by still more cogent considerations; but its weight is such that the cases which admit of a departure from it must be of a strikingly exceptional character.

It may unquestionably be the fact, that if we attempt, by publicity, to make the voter responsible to the public for his vote, he will practically be made responsible for it to some powerful individual, whose interest is more opposed to the general interest of the community than that of the voter himself would be, if, by the shield of secrecy, he were released from responsibility altogether. When this is the condition, in a high degree, of a large proportion of the voters, the ballot may be the smaller evil. When the voters are slaves, any thing may be tolerated which enables them to throw off the yoke. The strongest case for the ballot is when the mischievous power of the Few over the Many is increasing. In the decline of the Roman republic, the reasons for the ballot were irresistible. The oligarchy was yearly becoming richer and more tyrannical, the people poorer and more dependent, and it was necessary to erect stronger and stronger barriers against such abuse of the franchise as rendered it but an instrument the more in the hands of unprincipled persons of consequence. As little can it be doubted that the ballot, so far as it existed, had a beneficial operation in the Athenian constitution. Even in the least unstable of the Grecian common-wealths, freedom might be for the time destroyed by a single unfairly obtained popular vote; and though the Athenian voter was not sufficiently dependent to be habitually coerced, he might have been bribed or intimidated by the lawless outrages of some knot of individuals, such as were not uncommon even at Athens among the youth of rank and fortune. The ballot was in these cases a valuable instrument of order, and conduced to the Eunomia by which Athens was distinguished among the ancient commonwealths.

But in the more advanced states of modern Europe, and especially in this country, the power of coercing voters has declined and is declining; and bad voting is now less to be apprehended from the influences to which the voter is subject at the hands of others, than from the sinister interests and discreditable feelings which belong to himself, either individually or as a member of a class. To secure him against the first, at the cost of removing all restraint from the last, would be to exchange a smaller and a diminishing evil for a greater and increasing one. On this topic, and on the question generally as applicable to England at the present date, I have, in a pamphlet on Parliamentary Reform, expressed myself in terms which, as I do not feel that I can improve upon, I will venture here to transcribe.

"Thirty years ago, it was still true that in the election of members of Parliament the main evil to be guarded against was that which the ballot would ex-

clude—coercion by landlords, employers, and custom-
ers. At present, I conceive, a much greater source of
evil is the selfishness, or the selfish partialities of the
voter himself. A base and mischievous vote is now,
I am convinced, much oftener given from the voter's
personal interest, or class interest, or some mean feeling in his own mind, than from any fear of consequences at the hands of others; and to these influences
the ballot would enable him to yield himself up, free
from all sense of shame or responsibility.

"In times not long gone by, the higher and richer
classes were in complete possession of the government.
Their power was the master grievance of the country.
The habit of voting at the bidding of an employer or
of a landlord was so firmly established that hardly
any thing was capable of shaking it but a strong popular enthusiasm, seldom known to exist but in a good
cause. A vote given in opposition to these influences
was therefore, in general, an honest, a public-spirited
vote; but in any case, and by whatever motive dictated, it was almost sure to be a good vote, for it was
a vote against the monster evil, the overruling influence of oligarchy. Could the voter at that time have
been enabled, with safety to himself, to exercise his
privilege freely, even though neither honestly nor intelligently, it would have been a great gain to reform,
for it would have broken the yoke of the then ruling
power in the country—the power which had created
and which maintained all that was bad in the institutions and administration of the state—the power of
landlords and boroughmongers.

"The ballot was not adopted; but the progress of circumstances has done and is doing more and more, in this respect, the work of the ballot. Both the political and the social state of the country, as they affect this question, have greatly changed, and are changing every day. The higher classes are not now masters of the country. A person must be blind to all the signs of the times who could think that the middle classes are as subservient to the higher, or the working classes as dependent on the higher and middle, as they were a quarter of a century ago. The events of that quarter of a century have not only taught each class to know its own collective strength, but have put the individuals of a lower class in a condition to show a much bolder front to those of a higher. In a majority of cases, the vote of the electors, whether in opposition to or in accordance with the wishes of their superiors, is not now the effect of coercion, which there are no longer the same means of applying, but the expression of their own personal or political partialities. The very vices of the present electoral system are a proof of this. The growth of bribery, so loudly complained of, and the spread of the contagion to places formerly free from it, are evidence that the local influences are no longer paramount; that the electors now vote to please themselves, and not other people. There is, no doubt, in counties and in the smaller boroughs, a large amount of servile dependence still remaining; but the temper of the times is adverse to it, and the force of events is constantly tending to diminish it. A good tenant can now feel that he is as val-

uable to his landlord as his landlord is to him; a
prosperous tradesman can afford to feel independent of
any particular customer. At every election the votes
are more and more the voter's own. It is their minds,
far more than their personal circumstances, that now
require to be emancipated. They are no longer passive instruments of other men's will—mere organs for
putting power into the hands of a controlling oligarchy.
The electors themselves are becoming the oligarchy.

"Exactly in proportion as the vote of the elector is
determined by his own will, and not by that of somebody who is his master, his position is similar to that
of a member of Parliament, and publicity is indispensable. So long as any portion of the community are
unrepresented, the argument of the Chartists against
ballot in conjunction with a restricted suffrage is un-
assailable. The present electors, and the bulk of those
whom any probable Reform Bill would add to the
number, are the middle class, and have as much a
class interest, distinct from the working classes, as
landlords or great manufacturers. Were the suffrage
extended to all skilled laborers, even these would, or
might, still have a class interest distinct from the unskilled. Suppose it extended to all men — suppose
that what was formerly called by the misapplied name
of universal suffrage, and now by the silly title of manhood suffrage, became the law; the voters would still
have a class interest as distinguished from women.
Suppose that there were a question before the Legislature specially affecting women—as whether women
should be allowed to graduate at universities; wheth-

er the mild penalties inflicted on ruffians who beat their wives daily almost to death's door should be exchanged for something more effectual; or suppose that any one should propose in the British Parliament what one state after another in America is enacting, not by a mere law, but by a provision of their revised Constitutions, that married women should have a right to their own property—are not a man's wife and daughters entitled to know whether he votes for or against a candidate who will support these propositions?

" It will of course be objected that these arguments derive all their weight from the supposition of an unjust state of the suffrage: that if the opinion of the non-electors is likely to make the elector vote more honestly or more beneficially than he would vote if left to himself, they are more fit to be electors than he is, and ought to have the franchise; that whoever is fit to influence electors is fit to be an elector; that those to whom voters ought to be responsible should be themselves voters, and, being such, should have the safeguard of the ballot, to shield them from the undue influence of powerful individuals or classes to whom they ought not to be responsible.

" This argument is specious, and I once thought it conclusive. It now appears to me fallacious. All who are fit to influence electors are not, for that reason, fit to be themselves electors. This last is a much greater power than the former, and those may be ripe for the minor political function who could not as yet be safely trusted with the superior. The opinions and wishes of the poorest and rudest class of laborers may

be very useful as one influence among others on the
minds of the voters, as well as on those of the Legislature, and yet it might be highly mischievous to give
them the preponderant influence, by admitting them,
in their present state of morals and intelligence, to the
full exercise of the suffrage. It is precisely this indirect influence of those who have not the suffrage over
those who have, which, by its progressive growth, soft-
ens the transition to every fresh extension of the franchise, and is the means by which, when the time is
ripe, the extension is peacefully brought about. But
there is another and a still deeper consideration, which
should never be left out of the account in political
speculations. The notion is itself unfounded that publicity, and the sense of being answerable to the public,
are of no use unless the public are qualified to form a
sound judgment. It is a very superficial view of the
utility of public opinion to suppose that it does good
only when it succeeds in enforcing a servile conformity to itself. To be under the eyes of others—to have
to defend one's self to others—is never more important than to those who act in opposition to the opinion
of others, for it obliges them to have sure ground of
their own. Nothing has so steadying an influence as
working against pressure. Unless when under the
temporary sway of passionate excitement, no one will
do that which he expects to be greatly blamed for,
unless from a preconceived and fixed purpose of his
own, which is always evidence of a thoughtful and deliberate character, and, except in radically bad men,
generally proceeds from sincere and strong personal

convictions. Even the bare fact of having to give an account of their conduct is a powerful inducement to adhere to conduct of which at least some decent account can be given. If any one thinks that the mere obligation of preserving decency is not a very considerable check on the abuse of power, he has never had his attention called to the conduct of those who do not feel under the necessity of observing that restraint. Publicity is inappreciable, even when it does no more than prevent that which can by no possibility be plausibly defended — than compel deliberation, and force every one to determine, before he acts, what he shall say if called to account for his actions.

"But, if not now (it may be said), at least hereafter, when all are fit to have votes, and when all men and women are admitted to vote in virtue of their fitness, *then* there can no longer be danger of class legislation; then the electors, being the nation, can have no interest apart from the general interest: even if individuals still vote according to private or class inducements, the majority will have no such inducement; and as there will then be no non-electors to whom they ought to be responsible, the effect of the ballot, excluding none but the sinister influences, will be wholly beneficial.

"Even in this I do not agree. I can not think that even if the people were fit for, and had obtained universal suffrage, the ballot would be desirable. First, because it could not, in such circumstances, be supposed to be needful. Let us only conceive the state of things which the hypothesis implies: a people universally educated, and every grown-up human being possessed of a vote. If, even when only a small proportion are electors, and the majority of the population almost uneducated, public opinion is already, as every one now sees that it is, the ruling power in the last resort, it is a chimera to suppose that over a community who all read, and who all have votes, any power could be exercised by landlords and rich people against their own inclination, which it would be at all difficult for them to throw off. But, though the protection of secrecy would then be needless, the control of publicity would be as needful as ever. The universal observation of mankind has been very fallacious, if the mere fact of being one of the community, and not being in a position of pronounced contrariety of interest to the public at large, is enough to insure the performance of a public duty, without either the stimulus or the restraint derived from the opinion of our fellow-creatures. A man's own particular share of the public interest, even though he may have no private interest drawing him in the opposite direction, is not, as a general rule, found sufficient to make him do his duty to the public without other external inducements. Neither can it be admitted that, even if all had votes, they would give their votes as honestly in secret as in public. The proposition that the electors, when they compose the whole of the community, can not have an interest in voting against the interest of the community, will be found, on examination, to have more sound than meaning in it. Though the community, as a whole, can have (as the terms imply)

no other interest than its collective interest, any or
every individual in it may.   A man's interest consists
of whatever he takes interest *in*.   Every body has as
many different interests as he has feelings; likings or
dislikings, either of a selfish or of a better kind.   It
can not be said that any of these, taken by itself, constitutes 'his interest:' he is a good man or a bad according as he prefers one class of his interests or another.   A man who is a tyrant at home will be apt
to sympathize with tyranny (when not exercised over
himself); he will be almost certain not to sympathize
with resistance to tyranny.   An envious man will
vote against Aristides because he is called the Just.
A selfish man will prefer even a trifling individual
benefit to his share of the advantage which his country would derive from a good law, because interests
peculiar to himself are those which the habits of his
mind both dispose him to dwell on and make him
best able to estimate.   A great number of the electors
will have two sets of preferences—those on private
and those on public grounds.   The last are the only
ones which the elector would like to avow.   The best
side of their character is that which people are anxious to show, even to those who are no better than
themselves.   People will give dishonest or mean votes
from lucre, from malice, from pique, from personal ri-
valry, even from the interests or prejudices of class or
sect, more readily in secret than in public.   And cases
exist—they may come to be more frequent—in which
almost the only restraint upon a majority of knaves
consists in their involuntary respect for the opinion

of an honest minority. In such a case as that of the repudiating states of North America, is there not some check to the unprincipled voter in the shame of looking an honest man in the face? Since all this good would be sacrificed by the ballot, even in the circumstances most favorable to it, a much stronger case is requisite than can now be made out for its necessity (and the case is continually becoming still weaker) to make its adoption desirable."*

On the other debatable points connected with the mode of voting, it is not necessary to expend so many words. The system of personal representation, as organized by Mr. Hare, renders necessary the employment of voting papers. But it appears to me indispensable that the signature of the elector should be affixed to the paper at a public polling-place, or, if there be no such place conveniently accessible, at some office open to all the world, and in the presence of a responsible public officer. The proposal which has been thrown out of allowing the voting papers to be filled up at the voter's own residence, and sent by the post, or called for by a public officer, I should regard as fatal. The act would be done in the absence of the salutary and the presence of all the pernicious influences. The briber might, in the shelter of privacy, behold with his own eyes his bargain fulfilled, and the intimidator could see the extorted obedience rendered irrevocably on the spot; while the beneficent counter-influence of the presence of those who knew the voter's real sentiments, and the inspiring effect of the

* "Thoughts on Parliamentary Reform," 2d ed., p. 32-36.

sympathy of those of his own party or opinion, would be shut out.*

The polling-places should be so numerous as to be

* This expedient has been recommended both on the score of saving expense and on that of obtaining the votes of many electors who otherwise would not vote, and who are regarded by the advocates of the plan as a particularly desirable class of voters. The scheme has been carried into practice in the election of poor-law guardians, and its success in that instance is appealed to in favor of adopting it in the more important case of voting for a member of the Legislature. But the two cases appear to me to differ in the point on which the benefits of the expedient depend. In a local election for a special kind of administrative business, which consists mainly in the dispensation of a public fund, it is an object to prevent the choice from being exclusively in the hands of those who actively concern themselves about it; for the public interest which attaches to the election being of a limited kind, and in most cases not very great in degree, the disposition to make themselves busy in the matter is apt to be in a great measure confined to persons who hope to turn their activity to their own private advantage; and it may be very desirable to render the intervention of other people as little onerous to them as possible, if only for the purpose of swamping these private interests. But when the matter in hand is the great business of national government, in which every one must take an interest who cares for any thing out of himself, or who cares even for himself intelligently, it is much rather an object to prevent those from voting who are indifferent to the subject, than to induce them to vote by any other means than that of awakening their dormant minds. The voter who does not care enough about the election to go to the poll is the very man who, if he can vote without that small trouble, will give his vote to the first person who asks for it, or on the most trifling or frivolous inducement. A man who does not care whether he votes is not likely to care much which way he votes; and he who is in that state of mind has no moral right to vote at all; since, if he does so, a vote which is not the expression of a conviction counts for as much, and goes as far in determining the result as one which represents the thoughts and purposes of a life."—*Thoughts*, etc., p. 39.

within easy reach of every voter, and no expenses of conveyance, at the cost of the candidate, should be tolerated under any pretext. The infirm, and they only on medical certificate, should have the right of claiming suitable carriage conveyance at the cost of the state or of the locality. Hustings, poll-clerks, and all the necessary machinery of elections should be at the public charge. Not only the candidate should not be required, he should not be permitted to incur any but a limited and trifling expense for his election. Mr. Hare thinks it desirable that a sum of £50 should be required from every one who places his name on the list of candidates, to prevent persons who have no chance of success, and no real intention of attempting it, from becoming candidates in wantonness or from mere love of notoriety, and perhaps carrying off a few votes which are needed for the return of more serious aspirants. There is one expense which a candidate or his supporters can not help incurring, and which it can hardly be expected that the public should defray for every one who may choose to demand it—that of making his claims known to the electors by advertisements, placards, and circulars. For all necessary expenses of this kind the £50 proposed by Mr. Hare, if allowed to be drawn upon for these purposes (it might be made £100 if requisite), ought to be sufficient. If the friends of the candidate choose to go to expense on committees and canvassing, there are no means of preventing them; but such expenses out of the candidate's own pocket, or any expenses whatever beyond the deposit of £50 (or £100) should be illegal and punishable. If there appeared any likelihood that opinion would refuse to connive at falsehood, a declaration on oath or honor should be required from every member, on taking his seat, that he had not expended, nor would expend, money or money's worth, beyond the £50, directly or indirectly, for the purposes of his election; and if the assertion were proved to be false or the pledge to have been broken, he should be liable to the penalties of perjury. It is probable that those penalties, by showing that the Legislature was in earnest, would turn the course of opinion in the same direction, and would hinder it from regarding, as it has hitherto done, this most serious crime against society as a venial peccadillo. When once this effect had been produced, there need be no doubt that the declaration on oath or honor would be considered binding.* " Opinion tolerates a false disclaim-

---

* Several of the witnesses before the Committee of the House of Commons in 1860, on the operation of the Corrupt Practices Prevention Act, some of them of great practical experience in election matters, were favorable (either absolutely or as a last resort) to the principle of requiring a declaration from members of Parliament, and were of opinion that, if supported by penalties, it would be, to a great degree, effectual.—(*Evidence*, p. 46, 54–7, 67, 123, 198–202, 208.) The chief commissioner of the Wakefield Inquiry said (in reference certainly to a different proposal), "If they see that the Legislature is earnest upon the subject, the machinery will work. . . . I am quite sure that if some personal stigma were applied upon conviction of bribery, it would change the current of public opinion" (p. 26 and 32). A distinguished member of the committee (and of the present cabinet) seemed to think it very objectionable to attach the penalties of perjury to a merely promissory as distinguished from an assertory oath; but he was reminded that the oath taken by a witness in a court of justice

er only when it already tolerates the thing disclaimed."
This is notoriously the case with regard to electoral
corruption.   There has never yet been, among political men, any real and serious attempt to prevent bribery, because there has been no real desire that elections should not be costly.   Their costliness is an advantage to those who can afford the expense by excluding a multitude of competitors; and any thing,
however noxious, is cherished as having a conservative tendency, if it limits the access to Parliament to
rich men.   This is a rooted feeling among our legis-

is a promissory oath; and the rejoinder (that the witness's promise
relates to an act to be done at once, while the member's would be a
promise for all future time) would only be to the purpose if it could
be supposed that the swearer might forget the obligation he had entered into, or could possibly violate it unawares; contingencies which,
in a case like the present, are out of the question.

A more substantial difficulty is, that one of the forms most frequently assumed by election expenditure is that of subscriptions to local
charities or other local objects; and it would be a strong measure to
enact that money should not be given in charity within a place by the
member for it.   When such subscriptions are *bonâ fide*, the popularity which may be derived from them is an advantage which it seems
hardly possible to deny to superior riches.   But the greatest part of
the mischief consists in the fact that money so contributed is employed in bribery, under the euphonious name of keeping up the member's
interest.   To guard against this, it should be part of the member's
promissory declaration that all sums expended by him in the place,
or for any purpose connected with it or with any of its inhabitants
(with the exception perhaps of his own hotel expenses) should pass
through the hands of the election auditor, and be by him (and not by
the member himself or his friends) applied to its declared purpose.

The principle of making all lawful expenses of elections a charge,
not upon the candidate, but upon the locality, was upheld by two of
the best witnesses (p. 20, 65–70, 277).

lators of both political parties, and is almost the only point on which I believe them to be really ill-intentioned. They care comparatively little who votes, as long as they feel assured that none but persons of their own class can be voted for. They know that they can rely on the fellow-feeling of one of their class with another, while the subservience of *nouveaux enrichis* who are knocking at the door of the class is a still surer reliance; and that nothing very hostile to the class interests or feelings of the rich need be apprehended under the most democratic suffrage, as long as democratic persons can be prevented from being elected to Parliament. But, even from their own point of view, this balancing of evil by evil, instead of combining good with good, is a wretched policy. The object should be to bring together the best members of both classes, under such a tenure as shall induce them to lay aside their class preferences, and pursue jointly the path traced by the common interest, instead of allowing the class feelings of the Many to have full swing in the constituencies, subject to the impediment of having to act through persons imbued with the class feelings of the Few.

There is scarcely any mode in which political institutions are more morally mischievous—work greater evil through their spirit—than by representing political functions as a favor to be conferred, a thing which the depositary is to ask for as desiring it for himself, and even pay for as if it were designed for his pecuniary benefit. Men are not fond of paying large sums for leave to perform a laborious duty.

Plato had a much juster view of the conditions of
good government when he asserted that the persons
who should be sought out to be invested with political power are those who are personally most averse
to it, and that the only motive which can be relied on
for inducing the fittest men to take upon themselves
the toils of government is the fear of being governed
by worse men. What must an elector think when he
sees three or four gentlemen, none of them previously
observed to be lavish of their money on projects of
disinterested beneficence, vying with one another in
the sums they expend to be enabled to write M.P.
after their names? Is it likely he will suppose that
it is for *his* interest they incur all this cost? And if
he forms an uncomplimentary opinion of their part
in the affair, what moral obligation is he likely to feel
as to his own? Politicians are fond of treating it as
the dream of enthusiasts that the electoral body will
ever be uncorrupt: truly enough, until they are willing to become so themselves; for the electors, assuredly, will take their moral tone from the candidates.
So long as the elected member, in any shape or manner, pays for his seat, all endeavors will fail to make
the business of election any thing but a selfish bargain on all sides. "So long as the candidate himself,
and the customs of the world, seem to regard the function of a member of Parliament less as a duty to be
discharged than a personal favor to be solicited, no
effort will avail to implant in an ordinary voter the
feeling that the election of a member of Parliament is
also a matter of duty, and that he is not at liberty to

bestow his vote on any other consideration than that of personal fitness."

The same principle which demands that no payment of money for election purposes should be either required or tolerated on the part of the person elected, dictates another conclusion, apparently of contrary tendency, but really directed to the same object. It negatives what has often been proposed as a means of rendering Parliament accessible to persons of all ranks and circumstances — the payment of members of Parliament. If, as in some of our colonies, there are scarcely any fit persons who can afford to attend to an unpaid occupation, the payment should be an indemnity for loss of time or money, not a salary. The greater latitude of choice which a salary would give is an illusory advantage. No remuneration which any one would think of attaching to the post would attract to it those who were seriously engaged in other lucrative professions, with a prospect of succeeding in them. The occupation of a member of Parliament would therefore become an occupation in itself, carried on, like other professions, with a view chiefly to its pecuniary returns, and under the demoralizing influences of an occupation essentially precarious. It would become an object of desire to adventurers of a low class; and 658 persons in possession, with ten or twenty times as many in expectancy, would be incessantly bidding to attract or retain the suffrages of the electors, by promising all things, honest or dishonest, possible or impossible, and rivaling each other in pandering to the meanest feelings and most ignorant prejudices of the vulgarest part of the crowd. The auction between Cleon and the sausage-seller in Aristophanes is a fair caricature of what would be always going on. Such an institution would be a perpetual blister applied to the most peccant parts of human nature. It amounts to offering 658 prizes for the most successful flatterer, the most adroit misleader of a body of his fellow-countrymen. Under no despotism has there been such an organized system of tillage for raising a rich crop of vicious courtiership.* When, by reason of pre-eminent qualifications (as may at any time happen to be the case), it is desirable that a person entirely without independent means, either derived from property or from a trade or profession, should be brought into Parliament to render services which no other person accessible can render as well, there is the resource of a public subscription; he may be supported while in Parliament, like Andrew Marvel, by the contributions of his constituents. This

* "As Mr. Lorimer remarks, by creating a pecuniary inducement to persons of the lowest class to devote themselves to public affairs, the calling of the demagogue would be formally inaugurated. Nothing is more to be deprecated than making it the private interest of a number of active persons to urge the form of government in the direction of its natural perversion. The indications which either a multitude or an individual can give when merely left to their own weaknesses, afford but a faint idea of what those weaknesses would become when played upon by a thousand flatterers. If there were 658 places of certain, however moderate emolument, to be gained by persuading the multitude that ignorance is as good as knowledge, and better, it is terrible odds that they would believe and act upon the lesson."—(Article in *Fraser's Magazine* for April, 1859, headed " Recent Writers on Reform.")

mode is unobjectionable, for such an honor will never
be paid to mere subserviency : bodies of men do not
care so much for the difference between one syco-
phant and another as to go to the expense of his
maintenance in order to be flattered by that particular individual. Such a support will only be given in
consideration of striking and impressive personal qualities, which, though no absolute proof of fitness to be
a national representative, are some presumption of it,
and, at all events, some guaranty for the possession of
an independent opinion and will.

CHAPTER XI.

OF THE DURATION OF PARLIAMENTS.

AFTER how long a term should members of Parliament be subject to re-election? The principles involved are here very obvious; the difficulty lies in their application. On the one hand, the member ought not to have so long a tenure of his seat as to make him forget his responsibility, take his duties easily, conduct them with a view to his own personal advantage, or neglect those free and public conferences with his constituents which, whether he agrees or differs with them, are one of the benefits of representative government. On the other hand, he should have such a term of office to look forward to as will enable him to be judged, not by a single act, but by his course of action. It is important that he should have the greatest latitude of individual opinion and discretion compatible with the popular control essential to free government; and for this purpose it is necessary that the control should be exercised, as in any case it is best exercised, after sufficient time has been given him to show all the qualities he possesses, and to prove that there is some other way than that of a mere obedient voter and advocate of their opinions, by which he can render himself, in the eyes of his constituents, a desirable and creditable representative. It is impossible to fix, by any universal rule, the boundary between these principles. Where the democratic power in the constitution is weak or over-passive, and requires stimulation; where the representative, on leaving his constituents, enters at once into a courtly or aristocratic atmosphere, whose influences all tend to deflect his course into a different direction from the popular one, to tone down any democratic feelings which he may have brought with him, and make him forget the wishes and grow cool to the interests of those who chose him, the obligation of a frequent return to them for a renewal of his commission is indispensable to keeping his temper and character up to the right mark. Even three years, in such circumstances, are almost too long a period, and any longer term is absolutely inadmissible. Where, on the contrary, democracy is the ascendant power, and still tends to increase, requiring rather to be moderated in its exercise than encouraged to any abnormal activity; where unbounded publicity and an ever-present newspaper press give the representative assurance that his every act will be immediately known, discussed, and judged by his constituents, and that he is always either gaining or losing ground in their estimation, while, by the same means, the influence of their sentiments, and all other democratic influences, are kept constantly alive and active in his own mind, less than five years would hardly be a sufficient period to prevent timid subserviency. The change which has taken place in English politics as to all these features explains why annual Parliaments, which forty years ago stood prominently in front of the creed of the more advanced reformers, are so little cared for and so seldom heard of at present. It deserves consideration that, whether the term is short or long, during the last year of it the members are in the position in which they would always be if Parliaments were annual; so that, if the term were very brief, there would virtually be annual Parliaments during a great proportion of all time. As things now are, the period of seven years, though of unnecessary length, is hardly worth altering for any benefit likely to be produced, especially since the possibility, always impending, of an earlier dissolution keeps the motives for standing well with constituents always before the member's eyes.

Whatever may be the term most eligible for the duration of the mandate, it might seem natural that the individual member should vacate his seat at the expiration of that term from the day of his election, and that there should be no general renewal of the whole House. A great deal might be said for this system if there were any practical object in recommending it. But it is condemned by much stronger reasons than can be alleged in its support. One is, that there would be no means of promptly getting rid of a majority which had pursued a course offensive to the nation. The certainty of a general election after a limited, which would often be a nearly expired period, and the possibility of it at any time when the minister either desires it for his own sake, or thinks that it would make him popular with the country, tend to prevent that wide divergence between the feelings of the assembly and those of the constituency, which might subsist indefinitely if the majority of the House had always several years of their term still to run—if it received new infusions drop by drop, which would be more likely to assume than to modify the qualities of the mass they were joined to. It is as essential that the general sense of the House should accord in the main with that of the nation, as it is that distinguished individuals should be able, without forfeiting their seats, to give free utterance to the most unpopular sentiments. There is another reason, of much weight, against the gradual and partial renewal of a representative assembly. It is useful that there should be a periodical general muster of opposing forces to gauge the state of the national mind, and ascertain, beyond dispute, the relative strength of different parties and opinions. This is not done conclusively by any partial renewal, even where, as in some of the French constitutions, a large fraction—a fifth or a third—go out at once.

The reasons for allowing to the executive the power of dissolution will be considered in a subsequent chapter, relating to the constitution and functions of the executive in a representative government.

CHAPTER XII.

OUGHT PLEDGES TO BE REQUIRED FROM MEMBERS OF PARLIAMENT?

SHOULD a member of the Legislature be bound by the instructions of his constituents? Should he be the organ of their sentiments or of his own? their embassador to a congress or their professional agent, empowered not only to act for them, but to judge for them what ought to be done? These two theories of the duty of a legislator in a representative government have each its supporters, and each is the recognized doctrine of some representative governments. In the Dutch United Provinces, the members of the States-General were mere delegates; and to such a length was the doctrine carried, that when any important question arose which had not been provided for in their instructions, they had to refer back to their constituents, exactly as an embassador does to the government from which he is accredited. In this and most other countries which possess representative constitutions, law and custom warrant a member of Parliament in voting according to his opinion of right, however different from that of his constituents; but there is a floating notion of the opposite kind, which has considerable practical operation on many minds, even of members of Parliament, and often makes them, independently of desire for popularity or concern for their re-election, feel bound in conscience to make their conduct on questions on which their constituents have a decided opinion be the expression of that opinion rather than of their own. Abstractedly from positive law, and from the historical traditions of any particular people, which of these notions of the duty of a representative is the true one?

Unlike the questions which we have hitherto treated, this is not a question of constitutional legislation, but of what may more properly be called constitutional morality—the ethics of representative government. It does not so much concern institutions as the temper of mind which the electors ought to bring to the discharge of their functions, the ideas which should prevail as to the moral duties of an elector; for, let the system of representation be what it may, it will be converted into one of mere delegation if the electors so choose. As long as they are free not to vote, and free to vote as they like, they can not be prevented from making their vote depend on any condition they think fit to annex to it. By refusing to elect any one who will not pledge himself to all their opinions, and even, if they please, to consult with them before voting on any important subject not foreseen, they can reduce their representative to their mere mouthpiece, or compel him in honor, when no longer willing to act in that capacity, to resign his seat. And since they have the power of doing this, the theory of the Constitution ought to suppose that they will wish to do it, since the very principle of

constitutional government requires it to be assumed
that political power will be abused to promote the
particular purposes of the holder; not because it always is so, but because such is the natural tendency
of things, to guard against which is the especial use of
free institutions. However wrong, therefore, or however foolish, we may think it in the electors to convert their representative into a delegate, that stretch
of the electoral privilege being a natural and not improbable one, the same precautions ought to be taken
as if it were certain. We may hope that the electors
will not act on this notion of the use of the suffrage;
but a representative government needs to be so framed
that even if they do, they shall not be able to effect
what ought not to be in the power of any body of
persons—class legislation for their own benefit.

When it is said that the question is only one of
political morality, this does not extenuate its importance. Questions of constitutional morality are of no
less practical moment than those relating to the constitution itself. The very existence of some governments, and all that renders others endurable, rests on
the practical observance of doctrines of constitutional
morality; traditional notions in the minds of the several constituted authorities, which modify the use that
might otherwise be made of their powers. In unbal-
anced governments—pure monarchy, pure aristocracy, pure democracy—such maxims are the only barrier which restrains the government from the utmost
excesses in the direction of its characteristic tendency. In imperfectly balanced governments, where

some attempt is made to set constitutional limits to the impulses of the strongest power, but where that power is strong enough to overstep them with at least temporary impunity, it is only by doctrines of constitutional morality, recognized and sustained by opinion, that any regard at all is preserved for the checks and limitations of the constitution. In well-balanced governments, in which the supreme power is divided, and each sharer is protected against the usurpations of the others in the only manner possible, namely, by being armed for defense with weapons as strong as the others can wield for attack, the government can only be carried on by forbearance on all sides to exercise those extreme powers, unless provoked by conduct equally extreme on the part of some other sharer of power; and in this case we may truly say that only by the regard paid to maxims of constitutional morality is the constitution kept in existence. The question of pledges is not one of those which vitally concern the existence of representative governments, but it is very material to their beneficial operation. The laws can not prescribe to the electors the principles by which they shall direct their choice, but it makes a great practical difference by what principles they think they ought to direct it; and the whole of that great question is involved in the inquiry whether they should make it a condition that the representative shall adhere to certain opinions laid down for him by his constituents.

No reader of this treatise can doubt what conclusion, as to this matter, results from the general princi-

ples which it professes. We have from the first affirmed, and unvaryingly kept in view, the coequal importance of two great requisites of government—responsibility to those for whose benefit political power
ought to be, and always professes to be, employed;
and jointly therewith, to obtain, in the greatest measure possible, for the function of government, the benefits of superior intellect, trained by long meditation
and practical discipline to that special task. If this
second purpose is worth attaining, it is worth the necessary price. Superior powers of mind and profound
study are of no use, if they do not sometimes lead a
person to different conclusions from those which are
formed by ordinary powers of mind without study;
and if it be an object to possess representatives in any
intellectual respect superior to average electors, it must
be counted upon that the representative will sometimes differ in opinion from the majority of his constituents, and that when he does, his opinion will be
the oftenest right of the two. It follows that the
electors will not do wisely if they insist on absolute
conformity to their opinions as the condition of his retaining his seat.

The principle is thus far obvious; but there are real
difficulties in its application, and we will begin by
stating them in their greatest force. If it is important that the electors should choose a representative
more highly instructed than themselves, it is no less
necessary that this wiser man should be responsible to
them; in other words, they are the judges of the manner in which he fulfills his trust; and how are they

to judge except by the standard of their own opinions? How are they even to select him, in the first instance, but by the same standard? It will not do to choose by mere brilliancy—by superiority of showy talent. The tests by which an ordinary man can judge of mere ability are very imperfect; such as they are, they have almost exclusive reference to the arts of expression, and little or none to the worth of what is expressed. The latter can not be inferred from the former; and if the electors are to put their own opinions in abeyance, what criterion remains to them of the ability to govern well? Neither, if they could ascertain, even infallibly, the ablest man, ought they to allow him altogether to judge for them, without any reference to their own opinions. The ablest candidate may be a Tory, and the electors Liberals; or a Liberal, and they may be Tories. The political questions of the day may be Church questions, and he may be a High-Churchman or a Rationalist, while they may be Dissenters or Evangelicals, and *vice versâ.* His abilities, in these cases, might only enable him to go greater lengths, and act with greater effect, in what they may conscientiously believe to be a wrong course; and they may be bound, by their sincere convictions, to think it more important that their representative should be kept, on these points, to what they deem the dictate of duty, than that they should be represented by a person of more than average abilities. They may also have to consider, not solely how they can be most ably represented, but how their particular moral position and mental point of view shall be represented at all. The influence of every mode of thinking which is shared by numbers ought to be felt in the Legislature; and the Constitution being supposed to have made due provision that other and conflicting modes of thinking shall be represented likewise, to secure the proper representation for their own mode may be the most important matter which the electors on the particular occasion have to attend to. In some cases, too, it may be necessary that the representative should have his hands tied to keep him true to their interests, or rather to the public interest as they conceive it. This would not be needful under a political system which assured them an indefinite choice of honest and unprejudiced candidates; but under the existing system, in which the electors are almost always obliged, by the expenses of election and the general circumstances of society, to select their representative from persons of a station in life widely different from theirs, and having a different class interest, who will affirm that they ought to abandon themselves to his discretion? Can we blame an elector of the poorer classes, who has only the choice among two or three rich men, for requiring from the one he votes for a pledge to those measures which he considers as a test of emancipation from the class interests of the rich? It will, moreover, always happen to some members of the electoral body to be obliged to accept the representative selected by a majority of their own side. But, though a candidate of their own choosing would have no chance, their votes may be necessary to the success of the one chosen for them,

and their only means of exerting their share of influence on his subsequent conduct may be to make their
support of him dependent on his pledging himself to
certain conditions.

These considerations and counter-considerations are
so intimately interwoven with one another; it is so
important that the electors should choose as their
representatives wiser men than themselves, and should
consent to be governed according to that superior
wisdom, while it is impossible that conformity to
their own opinions, when they have opinions, should
not enter largely into their judgment as to who possesses the wisdom, and how far its presumed possess-
or has verified the presumption by his conduct, that
it seems quite impracticable to lay down for the elect-
or any positive rule of duty; and the result will depend less on any exact prescription or authoritative
doctrine of political morality than on the general
tone of mind of the electoral body in respect to the
important requisite of deference to mental superiority.
Individuals and peoples who are acutely sensible of
the value of superior wisdom are likely to recognize
it, where it exists, by other signs than thinking exactly as they do, and even in spite of considerable differences of opinion; and when they have recognized it
they will be far too desirous to secure it, at any admissible cost, to be prone to impose their own opinion
as a law upon persons whom they look up to as wiser
than themselves.   On the other hand, there is a character of mind which does not look up to any one;
which thinks no other person's opinion much better

than its own, or nearly so good as that of a hundred or a thousand persons like itself. Where this is the turn of mind of the electors, they will elect no one who is not, or at least who does not profess to be, the image of their own sentiments, and will continue him no longer than while he reflects those sentiments in his conduct; and all aspirants to political honors will endeavor, as Plato says in the Gorgias, to fashion themselves after the model of the Demos, and make themselves as like to it as possible. It can not be denied that a complete democracy has a strong tendency to cast the sentiments of the electors in this mould. Democracy is not favorable to the reverential spirit. That it destroys reverence for mere social position must be counted among the good, not the bad part of its influences, though by doing this it closes the principal *school* of reverence (as to merely human relations) which exists in society. But also democracy, in its very essence, insists so much more forcibly on the things in which all are entitled to be considered equally than on those in which one person is entitled to more consideration than another, that respect for even personal superiority is likely to be below the mark. It is for this, among other reasons, I hold it of so much importance that the institutions of the country should stamp the opinions of persons of a more educated class as entitled to greater weight than those of the less educated; and I should still contend for assigning plurality of votes to authenticated superiority of education were it only to give the tone to public feeling, irrespective of any direct political consequences.

When there does exist in the electoral body an adequate sense of the extraordinary difference in value
between one person and another, they will not lack
signs by which to distinguish the persons whose worth
for their purposes is the greatest. Actual public services will naturally be the foremost indication : to have
filled posts of magnitude, and done important things
in them, of which the wisdom has been justified by
the results; to have been the author of measures
which appear from their effects to have been wisely
planned; to have made predictions which have been
often verified by the event, seldom or never falsified
by it; to have given advice, which, when taken, has
been followed by good consequences—when neglected, by bad. There is doubtless a large portion of un-
certainty in these signs of wisdom; but we are seeking for such as can be applied by persons of ordinary
discernment. They will do well not to rely much on
any one indication unless corroborated by the rest,
and, in their estimation of the success or merit of any
practical effort, to lay great stress on the general opinion of disinterested persons conversant with the subject matter. The tests which I have spoken of are
only applicable to tried men, among whom must be
reckoned those who, though untried practically, have
been tried speculatively; who, in public speech or in
print, have discussed public affairs in a manner which
proves that they have given serious study to them.
Such persons may, in the mere character of political
thinkers, have exhibited a considerable amount of the
same titles to confidence as those who have been

proved in the position of practical statesmen. When it is necessary to choose persons wholly untried, the best criteria are, reputation for ability among those who personally know them, and the confidence placed and recommendations given by persons already looked up to. By tests like these, constituencies who sufficiently value mental ability, and eagerly seek for it, will generally succeed in obtaining men beyond mediocrity, and often men whom they can trust to carry on public affairs according to their unfettered judgment; to whom it would be an affront to require that they should give up that judgment at the behest of their inferiors in knowledge. If such persons, honestly sought, are not to be found, then indeed the electors are justified in taking other precautions, for they can not be expected to postpone their particular opinions unless in order that they may be served by a person of superior knowledge to their own. They would do well, indeed, even then, to remember that, when once chosen, the representative, if he devotes himself to his duty, has greater opportunities of correcting an original false judgment than fall to the lot of most of his constituents; a consideration which generally ought to prevent them (unless compelled by necessity to choose some one whose impartiality they do not fully trust) from exacting a pledge not to change his opinion, or, if he does, to resign his seat. But when an unknown person, not certified in unmistakable terms by some high authority, is elected for the first time, the elector can not be expected not to make conformity to his own sentiments the primary requisite. It is enough if he does not regard a subsequent change of those sentiments, honestly avowed, with its grounds undisguisedly stated, as a peremptory reason for withdrawing his confidence.

Even supposing the most tried ability and acknowledged eminence of character in the representative, the private opinions of the electors are not to be placed entirely in abeyance. Deference to mental superiority is not to go the length of self-annihilation—abnegation of any personal opinion. But when the difference does not relate to the fundamentals of politics, however decided the elector may be in his own sentiments, he ought to consider that when an able man differs from him there is at least a considerable chance of his being in the wrong, and that even if otherwise, it is worth while to give up his opinion in things not absolutely essential, for the sake of the inestimable advantage of having an able man to act for him in the many matters in which he himself is not qualified to form a judgment. In such cases he often endeavors to reconcile both wishes by inducing the able man to sacrifice his own opinion on the points of difference; but for the able man to lend himself to this compromise is treason against his especial office—abdication of the peculiar duties of mental supremacy, of which it is one of the most sacred not to desert the cause which has the clamor against it, nor to deprive of his services those of his opinions which need them the most. A man of conscience and known ability should insist on full freedom to act as he in his own judgment deems best, and should not consent to serve on any

other terms. But the electors are entitled to know
how he means to act; what opinions, on all things
which concern his public duty, he intends should
guide his conduct. If some of these are unacceptable
to them, it is for him to satisfy them that he nevertheless deserves to be their representative; and if they
are wise, they will overlook, in favor of his general
value, many and great differences between his opinions and their own. There are some differences, however, which they can not be expected to overlook.
Whoever feels the amount of interest in the government of his country which befits a freeman, has some
convictions on national affairs which are like his life-
blood; which the strength of his belief in their truth,
together with the importance he attaches to them, for-
bid him to make a subject of compromise, or postpone
to the judgment of any person, however greatly his
superior. Such convictions, when they exist in a people, or in any appreciable portion of one, are entitled
to influence in virtue of their mere existence, and not
solely in that of the probability of their being grounded in truth. A people can not be well governed in
opposition to their primary notions of right, even
though these may be in some points erroneous. A
correct estimate of the relation which should subsist
between governors and governed does not require the
electors to consent to be represented by one who intends to govern them in opposition to their fundamental convictions. If they avail themselves of his
capacities of useful service in other respects at a time
when the points on which he is vitally at issue with

them are not likely to be mooted, they are justified in dismissing him at the first moment when a question arises involving these, and on which there is not so assured a majority for what they deem right as to make the dissenting voice of that particular individual unimportant. Thus (I mention names to illustrate my meaning, not for any personal. application) the opinions supposed to be entertained by Mr. Cobden and Mr. Bright on resistance to foreign aggression might be overlooked during the Crimean war, when there was an overwhelming national feeling on the contrary side, and might yet very properly lead to their rejection by the electors at the time of the Chinese quarrel (though in itself a more doubtful question), because it was then for some time a moot point whether their view of the case might not prevail.

As the general result of what precedes, we may affirm that actual pledges should not be required unless, from unfavorable social circumstances or family institutions, the electors are so narrowed in their choice as to be compelled to fix it on a person presumptively under the influence of partialities hostile to their interest: that they are entitled to a full knowledge of the political opinions and sentiments of the candidate; and not only entitled, but often bound to reject one who differs from themselves on the few articles which are the foundation of their political belief: that, in proportion to the opinion they entertain of the mental superiority of a candidate, they ought to put up with his expressing and acting on opinions different from theirs on any number of things not included in their funda-

mental articles of belief: that they ought to be unre-
mitting in their search for a representative of such
calibre as to be intrusted with full power of obeying
the dictates of his own jugdment: that they should
consider it a duty which they owe to their fellow-
countrymen to do their utmost toward placing men
of this quality in the Legislature, and that it is of
much greater importance to themselves to be represented by such a man than by one who professes
agreement in a greater number of their opinions; for
the benefits of his ability are certain, while the hypothesis of his being wrong and their being right on
the points of difference is a very doubtful one.

I have discussed this question on the assumption
that the electoral system, in all that depends on positive institution, conforms to the principles laid down
in the preceding chapters. Even on this hypothesis,
the delegation theory of representation seems to me
false, and its practical operation hurtful, though the
mischief would in that case be confined within certain
bounds. But if the securities by which I have en-
deavored to guard the representative principle are not
recognized by the Constitution; if provision is not
made for the representation of minorities, nor any difference admitted in the numerical value of votes, according to some criterion of the amount of education
possessed by the voters—in that case, no words can
exaggerate the importance in principle of leaving an
unfettered discretion to the representative; for it would
then be the only chance, under universal suffrage, for
any other opinions than those of the majority to be

heard in Parliament. In that falsely called democracy which is really the exclusive rule of the operative classes, all others being unrepresented and unheard, the only escape from class legislation in its narrowest, and political ignorance in its most dangerous form, would lie in such disposition as the uneducated might have to choose educated representatives, and to defer to their opinions. Some willingness to do this might reasonably be expected, and every thing would depend upon cultivating it to the highest point. But, once invested with political omnipotence, if the operative classes voluntarily concurred in imposing upon themselves in this or any other manner any considerable limitation to their self-opinion and self-will, they would prove themselves wiser than any class possessed of absolute power has shown itself, or, we may venture to say, is ever likely to show itself under that corrupting influence.

CHAPTER XIII.

OF A SECOND CHAMBER.

OF all topics relating to the theory of representative government, none have been the subject of more discussion, especially on the Continent, than what is known as the question of the Two Chambers. It has occupied a greater amount of the attention of thinkers than many questions of ten times its importance, and has been regarded as a sort of touchstone which distinguishes the partisans of limited from those of uncontrolled democracy. For my own part, I set little value on any check which a Second Chamber can apply to a democracy otherwise unchecked; and I am inclined to think that if all other constitutional questions are rightly decided, it is of comparatively little importance whether the Parliament consists of two Chambers or only of one.

If there are two chambers, they may either be of similar or of dissimilar composition. If of similar, both will obey the same influences, and whatever has a majority in one of the houses will be likely to have it in the other. It is true that the necessity of obtaining the consent of both to the passing of any measure may at times be a material obstacle to improvement, since, assuming both the houses to be representative and equal in their numbers, a number slightly

exceeding a fourth of the entire representation may
prevent the passing of a bill; while, if there is but
one House, a bill is secure of passing if it has a bare
majority. But the case supposed is rather abstractedly possible than likely to occur in practice. It will
not often happen that, of two houses similarly composed, one will be almost unanimous, and the other
nearly equally divided; if a majority in one rejects a
measure, there will generally have been a large minority unfavorable to it in the other; any improvement, therefore, which could be thus impeded, would
in almost all cases be one which had not much more
than a simple majority in the entire body, and the
worst consequence that could ensue would be to delay for a short time the passing of the measure, or
give rise to a fresh appeal to the electors to ascertain
if the small majority in Parliament corresponded to
an effective one in the country. The inconvenience
of delay, and the advantage of the appeal to the nation, might be regarded in this case as about equally
balanced.

I attach little weight to the argument oftenest urged
for having two Chambers — to prevent precipitancy,
and compel a second deliberation; for it must be a
very ill-constituted representative assembly in which
the established forms of business do not require many
more than two deliberations. The consideration
which tells most, in my judgment, in favor of two
Chambers (and this I do regard as of some moment),
is the evil effect produced upon the mind of any holder of power, whether an individual or an assembly,

by the consciousness of having only themselves to consult. It is important that no set of persons should be able, even temporarily, to make their *sic volo* prevail without asking any one else for his consent. A majority in a single assembly, when it has assumed a permanent character — when composed of the same persons habitually acting together, and always assured of victory in their own House—easily becomes despotic and overweening if released from the necessity of considering whether its acts will be concurred in by another constituted authority. The same reason which induced the Romans to have two consuls, makes it desirable there should be two Chambers— that neither of them may be exposed to the corrupting influence of undivided power even for the space of a single year. One of the most indispensable requisites in the practical conduct of politics, especially in the management of free institutions, is conciliation; a readiness to compromise; a willingness to concede something to opponents, and to shape good measures so as to be as little offensive as possible to persons of opposite views; and of this salutary habit, the mutual give and take (as it has been called) between two houses is a perpetual school — useful as such even now, and its utility would probably be even more felt in a more democratic constitution of the Legislature.

But the houses need not both be of the same composition; they may be intended as a check on one another. One being supposed democratic, the other will naturally be constituted with a view to its being

some restraint upon the democracy. But its efficacy
in this respect wholly depends on the social support
which it can command outside the House. An assembly which does not rest on the basis of some great
power in the country is ineffectual against one which
does. An aristocratic House is only powerful in an
aristocratic state of society. The House of Lords was
once the strongest power in our Constitution, and the
Commons only a checking body; but this was when
the barons were almost the only power out of doors.
I can not believe that, in a really democratic state of
society, the House of Lords would be of any practical
value as a moderator of democracy. When the force
on one side is feeble in comparison with that on the
other, the way to give it effect is not to draw both
out in line, and muster their strength in open field
over against one another. Such tactics would insure
the utter defeat of the less powerful. It can only act
to advantage by not holding itself apart, and compelling every one to declare himself either with or against
it, but taking a position among the crowd rather than
one opposed to it, and drawing to itself the elements
most capable of allying themselves with it on any
given point; not appearing at all as an antagonist
body, to provoke a general rally against it, but working as one of the elements in a mixed mass, infusing
its leaven, and often making what would be the weaker part the stronger, by the addition of its influence.
The really moderating power in a democratic constitution must act in and through the democratic House.

That there should be, in every polity, a centre of

resistance to the predominant power in the Constitution — and in a democratic constitution, therefore, a nucleus of resistance to the democracy — I have already maintained; and I regard it as a fundamental maxim of government. If any people who possess a democratic representation are, from their historical antecedents, more willing to tolerate such a centre of resistance in the form of a Second Chamber or House of Lords than in any other shape, this constitutes a strong reason for having it in that shape. But it does not appear to me the best shape in itself, nor by any means the most efficacious for its object. If there are two houses, one considered to represent the people, the other to represent only a class, or not to be representative at all, I can not think that, where democracy is the ruling power in society, the second House would have any real ability to resist even the aberrations of the first. It might be suffered to exist in deference to habit and association, but not as an effective check. If it exercised an independent will, it would be required to do so in the same general spirit as the other House; to be equally democratic with it, and to content itself with correcting the accidental oversights of the more popular branch of the Legislature, or competing with it in popular measures.

The practicability of any real check to the ascendency of the majority depends henceforth on the distribution of strength in the most popular branch of the governing body; and I have indicated the mode in which, to the best of my judgment, a balance of forces might most advantageously be established there. I have also pointed out that, even if the numerical majority were allowed to exercise complete predominance by means of a corresponding majority in Parliament, yet, if minorities also are permitted to enjoy the equal right due to them on strictly democratic principles, of being represented proportionally to their numbers, this provision will insure the perpetual presence in the House, by the same popular title as its other members, of so many of the first intellects in the country, that without being in any way banded apart, or invested with any invidious prerogative, this portion of the national representation will have a personal weight much more than in proportion to its numerical strength, and will afford, in a most effective form, the moral centre of resistance which is needed. A second Chamber, therefore, is not required for this purpose, and would not contribute to it, but might even, in some degree, tend to compromise it. If, however, for the other reasons already mentioned, the decision were taken that there should be such a Chamber, it is desirable that it should be composed of elements which, without being open to the imputation of class interests adverse to the majority, would incline it to oppose itself to the class interests of the majority, and qualify it to raise its voice with authority against their errors and weaknesses. These conditions evidently are not found in a body constituted in the manner of our House of Lords. So soon as conventional rank and individual riches no longer overawe the democracy, a House of Lords becomes insignificant.

Of all principles on which a wisely conservative

body, destined to moderate and regulate democratic ascendency, could possibly be constructed, the best seems to be that exemplified in the Roman Senate, itself the most consistently prudent and sagacious body that ever administered public affairs. The deficiencies of a democratic assembly, which represents the general public, are the deficiencies of the public itself, want of special training and knowledge. The appropriate corrective is to associate with it a body of which special training and knowledge should be the characteristics. If one House represents popular feeling, the other should represent personal merit, tested and guaranteed by actual public service, and fortified by practical experience. If one is the People's Chamber, the other should be the Chamber of Statesmen—a council composed of all living public men who have passed through any important political office or employment. Such a chamber would be fitted for much more than to be a merely moderating body. It would not be exclusively a check, but also an impelling force. In its hands, the power of holding the people back would be vested in those most competent, and who would then be most inclined to lead them forward in any right course. The council to whom the task would be intrusted of rectifying the people's mistakes would not represent a class believed to be opposed to their interest, but would consist of their own natural leaders in the path of progress. No mode of composition could approach to this in giving weight and efficacy to their function of moderators. It would be impossible to cry down a body always foremost in promoting improvements as a mere obstructive body, whatever amount of mischief it might obstruct.

Were the place vacant in England for such a Senate (I need scarcely say that this is a mere hypothesis), it might be composed of some such elements as the following: All who were or had been members of the Legislative Commission described in a former chapter, and which I regard as an indispensable ingredient in a well constituted popular government. All who were or had been chief justices, or heads of any of the superior courts of law or equity. All who had for five years filled the office of puisne judge. All who had held for two years any cabinet office; but these should also be eligible to the House of Commons, and, if elected members of it, their peerage or senatorial office should be held in suspense. The condition of time is introduced to prevent persons from being named cabinet ministers merely to give them a seat in the Senate; and the period of two years is suggested, that the same term which qualifies them for a pension might entitle them to a senatorship. All who had filled the office of commander-in-chief; and all who, having commanded an army or a fleet, had been thanked by Parliament for military or naval successes. All governors general of India or British America, and all who had held for ten years any colonial governorships. The permanent civil service should also be represented; all should be senators who had filled, during ten years, the important offices of under-secretary to the Treasury, permanent under-secretary of State, or any others equally high and responsible. The functions conferring the senatorial dignity should be limited to those of a legal, political, or military or naval character. Scientific and literary eminence are too indefinite and disputable: they imply a power of selection, whereas the other qualifications speak for themselves; if the writings by which reputation has been gained are unconnected with politics, they are no evidence of the special qualities required, while, if political, they would allow successive ministries to deluge the House with party tools.

The historical antecedents of England render it all but certain that, unless in the improbable case of a violent subversion of the existing Constitution, any second Chamber which could possibly exist would have to be built on the foundation of the House of Lords. It is out of the question to think practically of abolishing that assembly, to replace it by such a Senate as I have sketched or by any other; but there might not be the same insuperable difficulty in aggregating the classes or categories just spoken of to the existing body in the character of peers for life. An ulterior, and perhaps, on this supposition, a necessary step, might be, that the hereditary peerage should be present in the House by their representatives instead of personally; a practice already established in the case of the Scotch and Irish peers, and which the mere multiplication of the order will probably at some time or other render inevitable. An easy adaptation of Mr. Hare's plan would prevent the representative peers from representing exclusively the party which has the majority in the peerage. If, for

example, one representative were allowed for every
ten peers, any ten might be admitted to choose a representative, and the peers might be free to group themselves for that purpose as they pleased. The election
might be thus conducted: All peers who were candidates for the representation of their order should be
required to declare themselves such, and enter their
names in a list. A day and place should be appointed at which peers desirous of voting should be present, either in person, or, in the usual Parliamentary
manner, by their proxies. The votes should be taken,
each peer voting for only one. Every candidate who
had as many as ten votes should be declared elected.
If any one had more, all but ten should be allowed to
withdraw their votes, or ten of the number should be
selected by lot. These ten would form his constituency, and the remainder of his voters would be set
free to give their votes over again for some one else.
This process should be repeated until (so far as possible) every peer present either personally or by proxy
was represented. When a number less than ten remained over, if amounting to five, they might still be
allowed to agree on a representative; if fewer than
five, their votes must be lost, or they might be permitted to record them in favor of somebody already
elected. With this inconsiderable exception, every
representative peer would represent ten members of
the peerage, all of whom had not only voted for him,
but selected him as the one, among all open to their
choice, by whom they were most desirous to be represented. As a compensation to the peers who were

not chosen representatives of their order, they should be eligible to the House of Commons; a justice now refused to Scotch peers, and to Irish peers in their own part of the kingdom, while the representation in the House of Lords of any but the most numerous party in the peerage is denied equally to both.

The mode of composing a Senate which has been here advocated not only seems the best in itself, but is that for which historical precedent and actual brilliant success can to the greatest extent be pleaded. It is not, however, the only feasible plan that might be proposed. Another possible mode of forming a Second Chamber would be to have it elected by the First, subject to the restriction that they should not nominate any of their own members. Such an assembly, emanating, like the American Senate, from popular choice only once removed, would not be considered to clash with democratic institutions, and would probably acquire considerable popular influence. From the mode of its nomination, it would be peculiarly unlikely to excite the jealousy of, or to come into any hostile collision with the popular House. It would, moreover (due provision being made for the representation of the minority), be almost sure to be well composed, and to comprise many of that class of highly capable men who, either from accident or for want of showy qualities, had been unwilling to seek, or unable to obtain, the suffrages of a popular constituency.

The best constitution of a Second Chamber is that which embodies the greatest number of elements exempt from the class interests and prejudices of the majority, but having in themselves nothing offensive to democratic feeling. I repeat, however, that the main reliance for tempering the ascendency of the majority can not be placed in a Second Chamber of any kind. The character of a representative government is fixed by the constitution of the popular House. Compared with this, all other questions relating to the form of government are insignificant.

CHAPTER XIV.

OF THE EXECUTIVE IN A REPRESENTATIVE GOVERN-MENT.

IT would be out of place in this treatise to discuss the question into what departments or branches the executive business of government may most conveniently be divided. In this respect the exigencies of different governments are different; and there is little probability that any great mistake will be made in the classification of the duties when men are willing to begin at the beginning, and do not hold themselves bound by the series of accidents which, in an old government like ours, has produced the existing division of the public business. It may be sufficient to say that the classification of functionaries should correspond to that of subjects, and that there should not be several departments independent of one another, to superintend different parts of the same natural whole, as in our own military administration down to a recent period, and in a less degree even at present. Where the object to be attained is single (such as that of having an efficient army), the authority commissioned to attend to it should be single likewise. The entire aggregate of means provided for one end should be under one and the same control and responsibility. If they are divided among independent authorities, the means with each of those authorities become ends, and it is the business of nobody except the head of the government, who has probably no departmental experience, to take care of the real end. The different classes of means are not combined and adapted to one another under the guidance of any leading idea; and while every department pushes forward its own requirements, regardless of those of the rest, the purpose of the work is perpetually sacrificed to the work itself.

As a general rule, every executive function, whether superior or subordinate, should be the appointed duty of some given individual. It should be apparent to all the world who did every thing, and through whose default any thing was left undone. Responsibility is null when nobody knows who is responsible; nor, even when real, can it be divided without being weakened. To maintain it at its highest, there must be one person who receives the whole praise of what is well done, the whole blame of what is ill. There are, however, two modes of sharing responsibility; by one it is only enfeebled, by the other absolutely destroyed. It is enfeebled when the concurrence of more than one functionary is required to the same act. Each one among them has still a real responsibility; if a wrong has been done, none of them can say he did not do it; he is as much a participant as an accomplice is in an offense : if there has been legal criminality, they may all be punished legally, and their punishment needs not be less severe than if there had been only one person concerned. But it is not so with the penalties any more than with the rewards of opinion; these are always diminished by being shared. Where there has been no definite legal offense, no corruption or malversation, only an error or an imprudence, or what may pass for such, every participator has an excuse to himself and to the world in the fact that other persons are jointly involved with him. There is hardly any thing, even to pecuniary dishonesty, for which men will not feel themselves almost absolved if those whose duty it was to resist and remonstrate have failed to do it, still more if they have given a formal assent.

In this case, however, though responsibility is weakened, there still is responsibility: every one of those implicated has in his individual capacity assented to, and joined in the act. Things are much worse when the act itself is only that of a majority—a board deliberating with closed doors, nobody knowing, or, except in some extreme case, being ever likely to know, whether an individual member voted for the act or against it. Responsibility, in this case, is a mere name. "Boards," it is happily said by Bentham, "are screens." What "the Board" does is the act of nobody, and nobody can be made to answer for it. The Board suffers, even in reputation, only in its collective character; and no individual member feels this farther than his disposition leads him to identify his own estimation with that of the body—a feeling often very strong when the body is a permanent one, and he is wedded to it for better for worse; but the fluctuations of a modern official career give no time for the formation of such an *esprit de corps*, which, if it exists at all, exists only in the obscure ranks of the permanent subordinates. Boards, therefore, are not a fit instrument for executive business, and are only admissible in it when, for other reasons, to give full discretionary power to a single minister would be worse.

On the other hand, it is also a maxim of experience that in the multitude of counselors there is wisdom, and that a man seldom judges right, even in his own concerns, still less in those of the public, when he makes habitual use of no knowledge but his own, or that of some single adviser. There is no necessary incompatibility between this principle and the other. It is easy to give the effective power and the full responsibility to one, providing him when necessary with advisers, each of whom is responsible only for the opinion he gives.

In general, the head of a department of the executive government is a mere politician. He may be a good politician and a man of merit; and, unless this is usually the case, the government is bad. But his general capacity, and the knowledge he ought to possess of the general interests of the country, will not, unless by occasional accident, be accompanied by adequate, and what may be called professional knowledge of the department over which he is called to preside. Professional advisers must therefore be provided for him. Wherever mere experience and attainments are sufficient—wherever the qualities required in a professional adviser may possibly be united in a single well-selected individual (as in the case, for example, of a law officer), one such person for general purposes, and a staff of clerks to supply knowledge of details, meet the demands of the case. But, more frequently, it is not sufficient that the minister should consult some one competent person, and, when himself not conversant with the subject, act implicitly on that person's advice. It is often necessary that he should, not only occasionally, but habitually, listen to a variety of opinions, and inform his judgment by the discussions among a body of advisers. This, for example, is emphatically necessary in military and naval affairs. The military and naval ministers, therefore, and probably several others, should be provided with a council, composed, at least in those two departments, of able and experienced professional men. As a means of obtaining the best men for the purpose under every change of administration, they ought to be permanent; by which I mean that they ought not, like the Lords of the Admiralty, to be expected to resign with the ministry by whom they were appointed; but it is a good rule that all who hold high appointments to which they have risen by selection, and not by the ordinary course of promotion, should retain their office only for a fixed term, unless reappointed, as is now the rule with staff appointments in the British army. This rule renders appointments somewhat less likely to be jobbed, not being a provision for life, and at the same time affords a means, without affront to any one, of getting rid of those who are least worth keeping, and bringing in highly qualified persons of younger standing, for whom there might never be room if death vacancies or voluntary resignations were waited for.

The councils should be consultative merely, in this sense, that the ultimate decision should rest undividedly with the minister himself; but neither ought they to be looked upon, or to look upon themselves as ciphers, or as capable of being reduced to such at his pleasure. The advisers attached to a powerful and perhaps self-willed man ought to be placed under conditions which make it impossible for them, without discredit, not to express an opinion, and impossible for him not to listen to and consider their recommendations, whether he adopts them or not. The relation which ought to exist between a chief and this description of advisers is very accurately hit by the constitution of the Council of the Governor General and those of the different Presidencies in India. These councils are composed of persons who have professional knowledge of Indian affairs, which the governor general and governors usually lack, and which it would not be desirable to require of them. As a rule, every member of council is expected to give an opinion, which is of course very often a simple acquiescence; but if there is a difference of sentiment, it is at the option of every member, and is the invariable practice, to record the reasons of his opinion, the governor general, or governor, doing the same. In ordinary cases the decision is according to the sense of the majority; the council, therefore, has a substantial part in the government; but if the governor general, or governor, thinks fit, he may set aside even their unanimous opinion, recording his reasons. The result is, that the chief is individually and effectively responsible for every act of the government. The members of council have only the responsibility of advisers; but it is always known, from documents capable of being produced, and which, if called for by Parliament or public opinion, always are produced, what each has advised, and what reasons he gave for his advice; while, from their dignified position and ostensible participation in all acts of government, they have nearly as strong motives to apply themselves to the public business, and to form and express a well-considered opinion on every part of it, as if the whole responsibility rested with themselves.

This mode of conducting the highest class of administrative business is one of the most successful instances of the adaptation of means to ends which political history, not hitherto very prolific in works of skill and contrivance, has yet to show. It is one of the acquisitions with which the art of politics has been enriched by the experience of the East India Company's rule; and, like most of the other wise contrivances by which India has been preserved to this country, and an amount of good government produced which is truly wonderful considering the circumstances and the materials, it is probably destined to perish in the general holocaust which the traditions of Indian government seem fated to undergo since they have been placed at the mercy of public ignorance and the presumptuous vanity of political men. Al-

ready an outcry is raised for abolishing the councils
as a superfluous and expensive clog on the wheels of
government; while the clamor has long been urgent,
and is daily obtaining more countenance in the highest quarters, for the abrogation of the professional civil
service, which breeds the men that compose the councils, and the existence of which is the sole guaranty
for their being of any value.

A most important principle of good government in
a popular constitution is that no executive functionaries should be appointed by popular election, neither
by the votes of the people themselves nor by those of
their representatives.   The entire business of government is skilled employment; the qualifications for the
discharge of it are of that special and professional kind
which can not be properly judged of except by persons who have themselves some share of those qualifications, or some practical experience of them.   The
business of finding the fittest persons to fill public employments—not merely selecting the best who offer,
but looking out for the absolutely best, and taking
note of all fit persons who are met with, that they may
be found when wanted — is very laborious, and requires a delicate as well as highly conscientious discernment; and as there is no public duty which is in
general so badly performed, so there is none for which
it is of greater importance to enforce the utmost practicable amount of personal responsibility, by imposing
it as a special obligation on high functionaries in the
several departments.   All subordinate public officers

who are not appointed by some mode of public competition should be selected on the direct responsibility of the minister under whom they serve. The ministers, all but the chief, will naturally be selected by the chief; and the chief himself, though really designated by Parliament, should be, in a regal government, officially appointed by the crown. The functionary who appoints should be the sole person empowered to remove any subordinate officer who is liable to removal, which the far greater number ought not to be, except for personal misconduct, since it would be in vain to expect that the body of persons by whom the whole detail of the public business is transacted, and whose qualifications are generally of much more importance to the public than those of the minister himself, will devote themselves to their profession, and acquire the knowledge and skill on which the minister must often place entire dependence, if they are liable at any moment to be turned adrift for no fault, that the minister may gratify himself, or promote his political interest by appointing somebody else.

To the principle which condemns the appointment of executive officers by popular suffrage, ought the chief of the executive, in a republican government, to be an exception? Is it a good rule which, in the American Constitution, provides for the election of the President once in every four years by the entire people? The question is not free from difficulty. There is unquestionably some advantage, in a country like America, where no apprehension needs be entertained of a *coup d'état*, in making the chief minister constitutionally independent of the legislative body, and rendering the two great branches of the government, while equally popular both in their origin and in their responsibility, an effective check on one another. The plan is in accordance with that sedulous avoidance of the concentration of great masses of power in the same hands, which is a marked characteristic of the American federal Constitution. But the advantage, in this instance, is purchased at a price above all reasonable estimate of its value. It seems far better that the chief magistrate in a republic should be appointed avowedly, as the chief minister in a constitutional monarchy is virtually, by the representative body. In the first place, he is certain, when thus appointed, to be a more eminent man. The party which has the majority in Parliament would then, as a rule, appoint its own leader, who is always one of the foremost, and often the very foremost person in political life; while the President of the United States, since the last survivor of the founders of the republic disappeared from the scene, is almost always either an obscure man, or one who has gained any reputation he may possess in some other field than politics. And this, as I have before observed, is no accident, but the natural effect of the situation. The eminent men of a party, in an election extending to the whole country, are never its most available candidates. All eminent men have made personal enemies, or have done something, or, at the lowest, professed some opinion obnoxious to some local or other considerable division of the community, and likely to tell with fatal effect upon the number of votes; whereas a man without antecedents, of whom nothing is known but that he professes the creed of the party, is readily voted for by its entire strength. Another important consideration is the great mischief of unintermitted electioneering. When the highest dignity in the state is to be conferred by popular election once in every few years, the whole intervening time is spent in what is virtually a canvass. President, ministers, chiefs of parties, and their followers, are all electioneerers: the whole community is kept intent on the mere personalities of politics, and every public question is discussed and decided with less reference to its merits than to its expected bearing on the presidential election. If a system had been devised to make party spirit the ruling principle of action in all public affairs, and create an inducement not only to make every question a party question, but to raise questions for the purpose of founding parties upon them, it would have been difficult to contrive any means better adapted to the purpose.

I will not affirm that it would at all times and places be desirable that the head of the executive should be so completely dependent upon the votes of a representative assembly as the prime minister is in England, and is without inconvenience. If it were thought best to avoid this, he might, though appointed by Parliament, hold his office for a fixed period, independent of a Parliamentary vote, which would be the American system minus the popular election and its evils. There is another mode of giving the head of the administration as much independence of the Legislature as is at all compatible with the essentials of free government. He never could be unduly dependent on a vote of Parliament if he had, as the British prime minister practically has, the power to dissolve the House and appeal to the people; if, instead of being turned out of office by a hostile vote, he could only be reduced by it to the alternative of resignation or dissolution. The power of dissolving Parliament is one which I think it desirable he should possess, even under the system by which his own tenure of office is secured to him for a fixed period. There ought not to be any possibility of that deadlock in politics which would ensue on a quarrel breaking out between a president and an assembly, neither of whom, during an interval which might amount to years, would have any legal means of ridding itself of the other. To get through such a period without a *coup d'état* being attempted, on either side or on both, requires such a combination of the love of liberty and the habit of self-restraint as very few nations have yet shown themselves capable of; and though this extremity were avoided, to expect that the two authorities would not paralyze each other's operations is to suppose that the political life of the country will always be pervaded by a spirit of mutual forbearance and compromise, imperturbable by the passions and excitements of the keenest party struggles. Such a spirit may exist, but even where it does there is imprudence in trying it too far.

Other reasons make it desirable that some power in the state (which can only be the executive) should have the liberty of at any time, and at discretion, calling a new Parliament. When there is a real doubt which of two contending parties has the strongest following, it is important that there should exist a constitutional means of immediately testing the point and setting it at rest. No other political topic has a chance of being properly attended to while this is undecided; and such an interval is mostly an interregnum for purposes of legislative or administrative improvement, neither party having sufficient confidence in its strength to attempt things likely to provoke opposition in any quarter that has either direct or indirect influence in the pending struggle.

I have not taken account of the case in which the vast power centralized in the chief magistrate, and the insufficient attachment of the mass of the people to free institutions, give him a chance of success in an attempt to subvert the Constitution and usurp sovereign power. Where such peril exists, no first magistrate is admissible whom the Parliament can not, by a single vote, reduce to a private station. In a state of things holding out any encouragement to that most audacious and profligate of all breaches of trust, even this entireness of constitutional dependence is but a weak protection.

Of all officers of government, those in whose appointment any participation of popular suffrage is the most objectionable are judicial officers. While there are no functionaries whose special and professional qualifications the popular judgment is less fitted to estimate, there are none in whose case absolute impartiality, and freedom from connection with politicians or sections of politicians, are of any thing like equal importance. Some thinkers, among others Mr. Bentham, have been of opinion that, although it is better that judges should not be appointed by popular election, the people of their district ought to have the power, after sufficient experience, of removing them from their trust. It can not be denied that the irremovability of any public officer to whom great interests are intrusted is in itself an evil. It is far from desirable that there should be no means of getting rid of a bad or incompetent judge, unless for such misconduct as he can be made to answer for in a criminal court, and that a functionary on whom so much depends should have the feeling of being free from responsibility except to opinion and his own conscience. The question however is, whether, in the peculiar position of a judge, and supposing that all practicable securities had been taken for an honest appointment, irresponsibility, except to his own and the public conscience, has not, on the whole, less tendency to pervert his conduct than responsibility to the government or to a popular vote. Experience has long decided this point in the affirmative as regards responsibility to the executive, and the case is quite equally strong when the responsibility sought to be enforced is to the suffrages of electors. Among the good qualities of a popular constituency, those peculiarly incumbent upon a judge, calmness and impartiality, are not numbered. Happily, in that intervention of popular suffrage which is essential to freedom they are not the qualities required. Even the quality of justice, though necessary to all human beings, and therefore to all electors, is not the inducement which decides any popular election. Justice and impartiality are as little wanted for electing a member of Parliament as they can be in any transaction of men. The electors have not to award something which either candidate has a right to, nor to pass judgment on the general merits of the competitors, but to declare which of them has most of their personal confidence, or best represents their political convictions. A judge is bound to treat his political friend, or the person best known to him, exactly as he treats other people; but it would be a breach of duty, as well as an absurdity, if an elector did so. No argument can be grounded on the beneficial effect produced on judges, as on all other functionaries, by the moral jurisdiction of opinion; for even in this respect, that which really exercises a useful control over the proceedings of a judge, when fit for the judicial office, is not (except sometimes in political cases) the opinion of the community generally, but that of the only public by whom his conduct or qualifications can be duly estimated, the bar of his own court. I must not be understood to say that the participation of the general public in the administration of justice is of no importance; it is of the greatest; but in what manner? By the actual discharge of a part of the judicial office in the capacity of jurymen. This is one of the few cases in politics in which it is better that the people should act directly and personally than through their representatives, being almost the only case in which the errors that a person exercising authority may commit can be better borne than the consequences of making him responsible for them.   If a judge could be removed from office by a popular vote, whoever was desirous of supplanting him would make capital for that purpose out of all his judicial decisions; would carry all of them, as far as he found practicable, by irregular appeal before a public opinion wholly incompetent, for want of having heard the case, or from having heard it without either the precautions or the impartiality belonging to a judicial hearing; would play upon popular passion and prejudice where they existed, and take pains to arouse them where they did not. And in this, if the case were interesting, and he took sufficient trouble, he would infallibly be successful, unless the judge or his friends descended into the arena, and made equally powerful appeals on the other side.   Judges would end by feeling that they risked their office upon every decision they gave in a case susceptible of general interest, and that it was less essential for them to consider what decision was just, than what would be most applauded by the public, or would least admit of insidious misrepresentation.   The practice introduced by some of the new or revised State Constitutions in America, of submitting judicial officers to periodical popular re-election, will be found, I apprehend, to be one of the most dangerous errors ever yet committed by democracy; and, were it not that the practical good sense which never totally deserts the people of the United States is said to be producing a reaction, likely in no long time to lead to the

retraction of the error, it might with reason be regarded as the first great downward step in the degenera-
tion of modern democratic government.

With regard to that large and important body
which constitutes the permanent strength of the public service, those who do not change with changes of
politics, but remain, to aid every minister by their experience and traditions, inform him by their knowledge of business, and conduct official details under his
general control — those, in short, who form the class
of professional public servants, entering their profession as others do while young, in the hope of rising
progressively to its higher grades as they advance in
life—it is evidently inadmissible that these should be
liable to be turned out, and deprived of the whole
benefit of their previous service, except for positive,
proved, and serious misconduct.   Not, of course, such
delinquency only as makes them amenable to the
law, but voluntary neglect of duty, or conduct imply-
ing untrustworthiness for the purposes for which their
trust is given them.   Since, therefore, unless in case
of personal culpability, there is no way of getting rid
of them except by quartering them on the public as
pensioners, it is of the greatest importance that the appointments should be well made in the first instance ;
and it remains to be considered by what mode of appointment this purpose can best be attained.

In making first appointments, little danger is to be
apprehended from want of special skill and knowledge
in the choosers, but much from partiality, and private

or political interest. Being all appointed at the commencement of manhood, not as having learned, but in
order that they may learn, their profession, the only
thing by which the best candidates can be discrimi-
nated is proficiency in the ordinary branches of liberal education; and this can be ascertained without difficulty, provided there be the requisite pains and the
requisite impartiality in those who are appointed to
inquire into it. Neither the one nor the other can
reasonably be expected from a minister, who must
rely wholly on recommendations, and, however disinterested as to his personal wishes, never will be proof
against the solicitations of persons who have the power of influencing his election, or whose political adherence is important to the ministry to which he belongs.
These considerations have introduced the practice of
submitting all candidates for first appointments to a
public examination, conducted by persons not engaged
in politics, and of the same class and quality with the
examiners for honors at the Universities. This would
probably be the best plan under any system; and under our Parliamentary government it is the only one
which affords a chance, I do not say of honest appointments, but even of abstinence from such as are
manifestly and flagrantly profligate.

It is also absolutely necessary that the examinations should be competitive, and the appointments
given to those who are most successful. A mere
pass examination never, in the long run, does more
than exclude absolute dunces. When the question,
in the mind of the examiner, lies between blighting

the prospects of an individual and performing a duty
to the public which, in the particular instance, seldom
appears of first-rate importance, and when he is sure
to be bitterly reproached for doing the first, while in
general no one will either know or care whether he
has done the latter, the balance, unless he is a man of
very unusual stamp, inclines to the side of good-na-
ture. A relaxation in one instance establishes a claim
to it in others, which every repetition of indulgence
makes it more difficult to resist; each of these, in succession, becomes a precedent for more, until the standard of proficiency sinks gradually to something almost
contemptible. Examinations for degrees at the two
great Universities have generally been as slender in
their requirements as those for honors are trying and
serious. Where there is no inducement to exceed a
certain minimum, the minimum comes to be the maximum: it becomes the general practice not to aim at
more; and as in every thing there are some who do
not attain all they aim at, however low the standard
may be pitched, there are always several who fall
short of it. When, on the contrary, the appointments
are given to those, among a great number of candidates, who most distinguish themselves, and where
the successful competitors are classed in order of merit, not only each is stimulated to do his very utmost,
but the influence is felt in every place of liberal education throughout the country. It becomes with every schoolmaster an object of ambition and an avenue
to success to have furnished pupils who have gained
a high place in these competitions, and there is hardly

any other mode in which the state can do so much to raise the quality of educational institutions throughout the country. Though the principle of competitive examinations for public employment is of such recent introduction in this country, and is still so imperfectly carried out, the Indian service being as yet nearly the only case in which it exists in its completeness, a sensible effect has already begun to be produced on the places of middle-class education, notwithstanding the difficulties which the principle has encountered from the disgracefully low existing state of education in the country, which these very examinations have brought into strong light. So contemptible has the standard of acquirement been found to be, among the youths who obtain the nomination from a minister, which entitles them to offer themselves as candidates, that the competition of such candidates produces almost a poorer result than would be obtained from a mere pass examination; for no one would think of fixing the conditions of a pass examination so low as is actually found sufficient to enable a young man to surpass his fellow-candidates. Accordingly, it is said that successive years show on the whole a decline of attainments, less effort being made, because the results of former examinations have proved that the exertions then used were greater than would have been sufficient to attain the object. Partly from this decrease of effort, and partly because, even at the examinations which do not require a previous nomination, conscious ignorance reduces the number of competitors to a mere handful, it has so happened that though there have always been a few instances of great proficiency, the lower part of the list of successful candidates represents but a very moderate amount of acquirement; and we have it on the word of the commissioners that nearly all who have been unsuccessful have owed their failure to ignorance, not of the higher branches of instruction, but of its very humblest elements—spelling and arithmetic.

The outcries which continue to be made against these examinations by some of the organs of opinion are often, I regret to say, as little creditable to the good faith as to the good sense of the assailants. They proceed partly by misrepresentation of the kind of ignorance which, as a matter of fact, actually leads to failure in the examinations. They quote with emphasis the most recondite questions* which can be shown to have been ever asked, and make it appear as if unexceptionable answers to all these were made the *sine quâ non* of success. Yet it has been repeated to satiety that such questions are not put because it is expected of every one that he should answer them, but in order that whoever is able to do so may have the means of proving and availing himself of that portion of his knowledge. It is not as a ground of rejection, but as an additional means of success, that this opportunity is given. We are then asked wheth-

* Not always, however, the most recondite; for one of the latest denouncers of competitive examination in the House of Commons had the *naïveté* to produce a set of almost elementary questions in algebra, history, and geography, as a proof of the exorbitant amount of high scientific attainment which the Commissioners were so wild as to exact.

er the kind of knowledge supposed in this, that, or the other question, is calculated to be of any use to the candidate after he has attained his object. People differ greatly in opinion as to what knowledge is useful. There are persons in existence, and a late Foreign Secretary of State is one of them, who think English spelling a useless accomplishment in a diplomatic attaché or a clerk in a government office. About one thing the objectors seem to be unanimous, that general mental cultivation is not useful in these employments, whatever else may be so. If, however (as I presume to think), it is useful, or if any education at all is useful, it must be tested by the tests most likely to show whether the candidate possesses it or not. To ascertain whether he has been well educated, he must be interrogated in the things which he is likely to know if he has been well educated, even though not directly pertinent to the work to which he is to be appointed. Will those who object to his being questioned in classics and mathematics, in a country where the only things regularly taught are classics and mathematics, tell us what they would have him questioned in? There seems, however, to be equal objection to examining him in these, and to examining him in any thing *but* these. If the Commissioners —anxious to open a door of admission to those who have not gone through the routine of a grammar-school, or who make up for the smallness of their knowledge of what is there taught by greater knowledge of something else—allow marks to be gained by proficiency in any other subject of real utility, they are reproached for that too.   Nothing will satisfy the objectors but free admission of total ignorance.

We are triumphantly told that neither Clive nor Wellington could have passed the test which is prescribed for an aspirant to an engineer cadetship; as if, because Clive and Wellington did not do what was not required of them, they could not have done it if it had been required.   If it be only meant to inform us that it is possible to be a great general without these things, so it is without many other things which are very useful to great generals.   Alexander the Great had never heard of Vauban's rules, nor could Julius Cæsar speak French.   We are next informed that book-worms, a term which seems to be held applicable to whoever has the smallest tincture of book-knowledge, may not be good at bodily exercises, or have the habits of gentlemen.   This is a very common line of remark with dunces of condition; but, whatever the dunces may think, they have no monopoly of either gentlemanly habits or bodily activity. Wherever these are needed, let them be inquired into and separately provided for, not to the exclusion of mental qualifications, but in addition.   Meanwhile, I am credibly informed that in the Military Academy at Woolwich the competition cadets are as superior to those admitted on the old system of nomination in these respects as in all others; that they learn even their drill more quickly, as indeed might be expected, for an intelligent person learns all things sooner than a stupid one; and that in general demeanor they contrast so favorably with their predecessors, that the au-

thorities of the institution are impatient for the day
to arrive when the last remains of the old leaven shall
have disappeared from the place. If this be so, and it
is easy to ascertain whether it is so, it is to be hoped
we shall soon have heard for the last time that ignorance is a better qualification than knowledge for the
military, and, *à fortiori*, for every other profession, or
that any one good quality, however little apparently
connected with liberal education, is at all likely to be
promoted by going without it.

Though the first admission to government employment be decided by competitive examination, it would
in most cases be impossible that subsequent promotion
should be so decided; and it seems proper that this
should take place, as it usually does at present, on a
mixed system of seniority and selection. Those whose
duties are of a routine character should rise by seniority to the highest point to which duties merely of that
description can carry them, while those to whom functions of particular trust, and requiring special capacity,
are confided, should be selected from the body on the
discretion of the chief of the office. And this selection will generally be made honestly by him if the
original appointments take place by open competition,
for under that system his establishment will generally
consist of individuals to whom, but for the official connection, he would have been a stranger. If among
them there be any in whom he, or his political friends
and supporters, take an interest, it will be but occasionally, and only when to this advantage of connection is added, as far as the initiatory examination could

test it, at least equality of real merit; and, except when there is a very strong motive to job these appointments, there is always a strong one to appoint the fittest person, being the one who gives to his chief the most useful assistance, saves him most trouble, and helps most to build up that reputation for good management of public business which necessarily and properly redound to the credit of the minister, however much the qualities to which it is immediately owing may be those of his subordinates.

CHAPTER XV.

OF LOCAL REPRESENTATIVE BODIES.

It is but a small portion of the public business of
a country which can be well done or safely attempted
by the central authorities; and even in our own government, the least centralized in Europe, the legislative portion at least of the governing body busies
itself far too much with local affairs, employing the
supreme power of the state in cutting small knots
which there ought to be other and better means of
untying. The enormous amount of private business which takes up the time of Parliament and the
thoughts of its individual members, distracting them
from the proper occupations of the great council of
the nation, is felt by all thinkers and observers as a
serious evil, and, what is worse, an increasing one.

It would not be appropriate to the limited design
of this treatise to discuss at large the great question,
in no way peculiar to representative government, of
the proper limits of governmental action. I have
said elsewhere* what seemed to me most essential respecting the principles by which the extent of that
action ought to be determined. But after subtracting
from the functions performed by most European gov-

* "On Liberty," concluding chapter; and, at greater length, in
the final chapter of "Principles of Political Economy."

ernments those which ought not to be undertaken by
public authorities at all, there still remains so great
and various an aggregate of duties, that, if only on
the principle of division of labor, it is indispensable
to share them between central and local authorities.
Not solely are separate executive officers required for
purely local duties (an amount of separation which
exists under all governments), but the popular control
over those officers can only be advantageously exerted through a separate organ.   Their original appointment, the function of watching and checking them,
the duty of providing or the discretion of withholding the supplies necessary for their operations, should
rest, not with the national Parliament or the national
executive, but with the people of the locality.   That
the people should exercise these functions directly and
personally is evidently inadmissible.   Administration
by the assembled people is a relic of barbarism opposed to the whole spirit of modern life ; yet so much
has the course of English institutions depended on accident, that this primitive mode of local government
remained the general rule in parochial matters up to
the present generation ; and, having never been legally abolished, probably subsists unaltered in many
rural parishes even now.   There remains the plan of
representative sub-Parliaments for local affairs, and
these must henceforth be considered as one of the fundamental institutions of a free government.   They
exist in England but very incompletely, and with
great irregularity and want of system ; in some other
countries much less popularly governed, their consti-

tution is far more rational.   In England there has always been more liberty but worse organization, while
in other countries there is better organization but less
liberty.   It is necessary, then, that, in addition to the
national representation, there should be municipal and
provisional representations; and the two questions
which remain to be resolved are, how the local representative bodies should be constituted, and what
should be the extent of their functions.

In considering these questions, two points require
an equal degree of our attention: how the local business itself can be best done, and how its transaction
can be made most instrumental to the nourishment of
public spirit and the development of intelligence.   In
an earlier part of this inquiry I have dwelt in strong
language—hardly any language is strong enough to
express the strength of my conviction—on the importance of that portion of the operation of free institutions which may be called the public education of
the citizens.   Now of this operation the local administrative institutions are the chief instrument.   Except
by the part they may take as jurymen in the administration of justice, the mass of the population have
very little opportunity of sharing personally in the
conduct of the general affairs of the community.
Reading newspapers, and perhaps writing to them,
public meetings, and solicitations of different sorts addressed to the political authorities, are the extent of
the participation of private citizens in general politics
during the interval between one Parliamentary election and another.   Though it is impossible to exag-

gerate the importance of these various liberties, both as securities for freedom and as means of general cultivation, the practice which they give is more in thinking than in action, and in thinking without the responsibilities of action, which with most people amounts to little more than passively receiving the thoughts of some one else. But in the case of local bodies, besides the function of electing, many citizens in turn have the chance of being elected, and many, either by selection or by rotation, fill one or other of the numerous local executive offices. In these positions they have to act for public interests as well as to think and to speak, and the thinking can not all be done by proxy. It may be added that these local functions, not being in general sought by the higher ranks, carry down the important political education which they are the means of conferring to a much lower grade in society. The mental discipline being thus a more important feature in local concerns than in the general affairs of the state, while there are not such vital interests dependent on the quality of the administration, a greater weight may be given to the former consideration, and the latter admits much more frequently of being postponed to it than in matters of general legislation and the conduct of imperial affairs.

The proper constitution of local representative bodies does not present much difficulty. The principles which apply to it do not differ in any respect from those applicable to the national representation. The same obligation exists, as in the case of the more important function, for making the bodies elective; and the same reasons operate as in that case, but with still greater force, for giving them a widely democratic basis; the dangers being less, and the advantages, in point of popular education and cultivation, in some respects even greater. As the principal duty of the local bodies consists of the imposition and expenditure of local taxation, the electoral franchise should vest in all who contribute to the local rates, to the exclusion of all who do not. I assume that there is no indirect taxation, no *octroi* duties, or that, if there are, they are supplementary only, those on whom their burden falls being also rated to a direct assessment. The representation of minorities should be provided for in the same manner as in the national Parliament, and there are the same strong reasons for plurality of votes; only there is not so decisive an objection, in the inferior as in the higher body, to making the plural voting depend (as in some of the local elections of our own country) on a mere money qualification; for the honest and frugal dispensation of money forms so much larger a part of the business of the local than of the national body, that there is more justice as well as policy in allowing a greater proportional influence to those who have a larger money interest at stake.

In the most recently established of our local representative institutions, the Boards of Guardians, the justices of peace of the district sit *ex officio* along with the elected members, in number limited by law to a third of the whole. In the peculiar constitution of English society, I have no doubt of the beneficial ef-

LOCAL REPRESENTATIVE BODIES.

fect of this provision. It secures the presence in these bodies of a more educated class than it would perhaps be practicable to attract thither on any other terms; and while the limitation in number of the *ex officio* members precludes them from acquiring predominance by mere numerical strength, they, as a virtual representation of another class, having sometimes a different interest from the rest, are a check upon the class interests of the farmers or petty shopkeepers who form the bulk of the elected guardians. A similar commendation can not be given to the constitution of the only provincial boards we possess, the Quarter Sessions, consisting of the justices of peace alone, on whom, over and above their judicial duties, some of the most important parts of the administrative business of the country depend for their performance. The mode of formation of these bodies is most anomalous, they being neither elected, nor, in any proper sense of the term, nominated, but holding their important functions, like the feudal lords to whom they succeeded, virtually by right of their acres; the appointment vested in the crown (or, speaking practically, in one of themselves, the lord lieutenant) being made use of only as a means of excluding any one who it is thought would do discredit to the body, or, now and then, one who is on the wrong side in politics. The institution is the most aristocratic in principle which now remains in England; far more so than the House of Lords, for it grants public money and disposes of important public interests, not in conjunction with a popular assembly, but alone.

It is clung to with proportionate tenacity by our aristocratic classes, but is obviously at variance with all the principles which are the foundation of representative government. In a County Board there is not the same justification as in Boards of Guardians for even an admixture of *ex officio* with elected members, since the business of a county being on a sufficiently large scale to be an object of interest and attraction to country gentlemen, they would have no more difficulty in getting themselves elected to the Board than they have in being returned to Parliament as county members.

In regard to the proper circumscription of the constituencies which elect the local representative bodies, the principle which, when applied as an exclusive and unbending rule to Parliamentary representation, is inappropriate, namely, community of local interests, is here the only just and applicable one. The very object of having a local representation is in order that those who have any interest in common which they do not share with the general body of their countrymen may manage that joint interest by themselves, and the purpose is contradicted if the distribution of the local representation follows any other rule than the grouping of those joint interests. There are local interests peculiar to every town, whether great or small, and common to all its inhabitants; every town, therefore, without distinction of size, ought to have its municipal council. It is equally obvious that every town ought to have but one. The different quarters of the same town have seldom or never any

material diversities of local interest: they all require
to have the same things done, the same expenses incurred; and, except as to their churches, which it is
probably desirable to leave under simply parochial
management, the same arrangements may be made to
serve for all.   Paving, lighting, water supply, drain-
age, port and market regulations, can not, without
great waste and inconvenience, be different for different quarters of the same town.   The subdivision of
London into six or seven independent districts, each
with its separate arrangements for local business (several of them without unity of administration even
within themselves), prevents the possibility of con-
secutive or well-regulated co-operation for common
objects, precludes any uniform principle for the discharge of local duties, compels the general government to take things upon itself which would be best
left to local authorities if there were any whose authority extended to the entire metropolis, and answers
no purpose but to keep up the fantastical trappings
of that union of modern jobbing and antiquated fop-
pery, the Corporation of the City of London.

Another equally important principle is, that in each
local circumscription there should be but one elective
body for all local business, not different bodies for different parts of it.   Division of labor does not mean
cutting up every business into minute fractions; it
means the union of such operations as are fit to be
performed by the same persons, and the separation of
such as can be better performed by different persons.
The executive duties of the locality do indeed require

to be divided into departments for the same reason as
those of the state—because they are of divers kinds,
each requiring knowledge peculiar to itself, and need-
ing, for its due performance, the undivided attention
of a specially qualified functionary. But the reasons
for subdivision which apply to the execution do not
apply to the control. The business of the elective
body is not to do the work, but to see that it is properly done, and that nothing necessary is left undone.
This function can be fulfilled for all departments by
the same superintending body, and by a collective and
comprehensive far better than by a minute and micro-
scopic view. It is as absurd in public affairs as it
would be in private, that every workman should be
looked after by a superintendent to himself. The
government of the crown consists of many departments, and there are many ministers to conduct them,
but those ministers have not a Parliament apiece to
keep them to their duty. The local, like the national
Parliament, has for its proper business to consider the
interest of the locality as a whole, composed of parts
all of which must be adapted to one another, and attended to in the order and ratio of their importance.
There is another very weighty reason for uniting the
control of all the business of a locality under one body.
The greatest imperfection of popular local institutions,
and the chief cause of the failure which so often attends them, is the low calibre of the men by whom
they are almost always carried on. That these should
be of a very miscellaneous character is, indeed, part of
the usefulness of the institution; it is that circumstance

chiefly which renders it a school of political capacity
and general intelligence. But a school supposes teachers as well as scholars: the utility of the instruction
greatly depends on its bringing inferior minds into
contact with superior, a contact which in the ordinary
course of life is altogether exceptional, and the want
of which contributes more than any thing else to keep
the generality of mankind on one level of contented
ignorance. The school, moreover, is worthless, and a
school of evil instead of good, if, through the want of
due surveillance, and of the presence within itself of a
higher order of characters, the action of the body is
allowed, as it so often is, to degenerate into an equally
unscrupulous and stupid pursuit of the self-interest
of its members. Now it is quite hopeless to induce
persons of a high class, either socially or intellectual-
ly, to take a share of local administration in a corner
by piecemeal, as members of a Paving Board or a
Draining Commission. The entire local business of
their town is not more than a sufficient object to induce men whose tastes incline them, and whose knowledge qualifies them for national affairs, to become
members of a mere local body, and devote to it the
time and study which are necessary to render their
presence any thing more than a screen for the jobbing
of inferior persons, under the shelter of their responsibility. A mere Board of Works, though it comprehend the entire metropolis, is sure to be composed of
the same class of persons as the vestries of the London
parishes; nor is it practicable, or even desirable, that
such should not form the majority; but it is import-

ant for every purpose which local bodies are designed to serve, whether it be the enlightened and honest
performance of their special duties, or the cultivation
of the political intelligence of the nation, that every
such body should contain a portion of the very best
minds of the locality, who are thus brought into perpetual contact, of the most useful kind, with minds of
a lower grade, receiving from them what local or professional knowledge they have to give, and, in return,
inspiring them with a portion of their own more enlarged ideas, and higher and more enlightened purposes.

A mere village has no claim to a municipal representation. By a village I mean a place whose inhabitants are not markedly distinguished by occupation
or social relations from those of the rural districts ad-
joining, and for whose local wants the arrangements
made for the surrounding territory will suffice. Such
small places have rarely a sufficient public to furnish
a tolerable municipal council: if they contain any talent or knowledge applicable to public business, it is
apt to be all concentrated in some one man, who there-
by becomes the dominator of the place. It is better
that such places should be merged in a larger circumscription. The local representation of rural districts
will naturally be determined by geographical considerations, with due regard to those sympathies of feeling by which human beings are so much aided to act
in concert, and which partly follow historical boundaries, such as those of counties or provinces, and partly
community of interest and occupation, as in agricul-

tural, maritime, manufacturing, or mining districts. Different kinds of local business may require different areas of representation. The Unions of parishes have been fixed on as the most appropriate basis for the representative bodies which superintend the relief of indigence; while, for the proper regulation of highways, or prisons, or police, a larger extent, like that of an average county, is not more than sufficient. In these large districts, therefore, the maxim that an elective body constituted in any locality should have authority over all the local concerns common to the locality, requires modification from another principle, as well as from the competing consideration of the importance of obtaining for the discharge of the local duties the highest qualifications possible. For example, if it be necessary (as I believe it to be) for the proper administration of the poor-laws that the area of rating should not be more extensive than most of the present Unions, a principle which requires a Board of Guardians for each Union, yet, as a much more highly qualified class of persons is likely to be obtainable for a County Board than those who compose an average Board of Guardians, it may, on that ground, be expedient to reserve for the County Boards some higher descriptions of local business, which might otherwise have been conveniently managed within itself by each separate Union.

Besides the controlling council or local sub-Parliament, local business has its executive department. With respect to this, the same questions arise as with respect to the executive authorities in the state, and they may, for the most part, be answered in the same manner. The principles applicable to all public trusts are in substance the same. In the first place, each executive officer should be single, and singly responsible for the whole of the duty committed to his charge. In the next place, he should be nominated, not elected. It is ridiculous that a surveyor, or a health officer, or even a collector of rates should be appointed by popular suffrage. The popular choice usually depends on interest with a few local leaders, who, as they are not supposed to make the appointment, are not responsible for it; or on an appeal to sympathy, founded on having twelve children, and having been a rate-payer in the parish for thirty years. If, in cases of this description, election by the population is a farce, appointment by the local representative body is little less objectionable. Such bodies have a perpetual tendency to become joint-stock associations for carrying into effect the private jobs of their various members. Appointments should be made on the individual responsibility of the chairman of the body, let him be called mayor, chairman of the Quarter Sessions, or by whatever other title. He occupies in the locality a position analogous to that of the prime minister in the state, and under a well-organized system the appointment and watching of the local officers would be the most important part of his duty; he himself being appointed by the council from its own number, subject either to annual re-election, or to removal by a vote of the body.

From the constitution of the local bodies, I now pass

to the equally important and more difficult subject of their proper attributions. This question divides itself into two parts: what should be their duties, and whether they should have full authority within the sphere of those duties, or should be liable to any, and what, interference on the part of the central government.

It is obvious, to begin with, that all business purely local—all which concerns only a single locality—should devolve upon the local authorities. The paving, lighting, and cleansing of the streets of a town, and, in ordinary circumstances, the draining of its houses, are of little consequence to any but its inhabitants. The nation at large is interested in them in no other way than that in which it is interested in the private well-being of any of its individual citizens. But among the duties classed as local, or performed by local functionaries, there are many which might with equal propriety be termed national, being the share belonging to the locality of some branch of the public administration in the efficiency of which the whole nation is alike interested: the jails, for instance, most of which in this country are under county management; the local police; the local administration of justice, much of which, especially in corporate towns, is performed by officers elected by the locality, and paid from local funds. None of these can be said to be matters of local, as distinguished from national importance. It would not be a matter personally indifferent to the rest of the country if any part of it became a nest of robbers or a focus of demoralization, owing to the maladministration of its police; or if, through the bad regulations of its jail, the punishment which the courts of justice intended to inflict on the criminals confined therein (who might have come from, or committed their offenses in, any other district) might be doubled in intensity or lowered to practical impunity. The points, moreover, which constitute good management of these things are the same every where; there is no good reason why police, or jails, or the administration of justice should be differently managed in one part of the kingdom and in another, while there is great peril that in things so important, and to which the most instructed minds available to the state are not more than adequate, the lower average of capacities which alone can be counted on for the service of the localities might commit errors of such magnitude as to be a serious blot upon the general administration of the country. Security of person and property, and equal justice between individuals, are the first needs of society and the primary ends of government; if these things can be left to any responsibility below the highest, there is nothing except war and treaties which requires a general government at all. Whatever are the best arrangements for securing these primary objects should be made universally obligatory, and, to secure their enforcement, should be placed under central superintendence. It is often useful, and with the institutions of our own country even necessary, from the scarcity, in the localities, of officers representing the general government, that the execution of duties imposed by the central

authority should be intrusted to functionaries appointed for local purposes by the locality. But experience
is daily forcing upon the public a conviction of the
necessity of having at least inspectors appointed by
the general government to see that the local officers
do their duty. If prisons are under local management, the central government appoints inspectors of
prisons, to take care that the rules laid down by Parliament are observed, and to suggest others if the state
of the jails shows them to be requisite, as there are inspectors of factories and inspectors of schools, to watch
over the observance of the Acts of Parliament relating to the first, and the fulfillment of the conditions
on which state assistance is granted to the latter.

But if the administration of justice, police and jails
included, is both so universal a concern, and so much
a matter of general science, independent of local peculiarities, that it may be, and ought to be, uniformly regulated throughout the country, and its regulation enforced by more trained and skillful hands than those
of purely local authorities, there is also business, such
as the administration of the poor-laws, sanitary regulation, and others, which, while really interesting to the
whole country, can not, consistently with the very purposes of local administration, be managed otherwise
than by the localities. In regard to such duties, the
question arises how far the local authorities ought to
be trusted with discretionary power, free from any superintendence or control of the state.

To decide this question, it is essential to consider
what is the comparative position of the central and

the local authorities as to capacity for the work, and security against negligence or abuse. In the first place, the local representative bodies and their officers are almost certain to be of a much lower grade of intelligence and knowledge than Parliament and the national executive. Secondly, besides being themselves of inferior qualifications, they are watched by, and accountable to an inferior public opinion. The public under whose eyes they act, and by whom they are criticised, is both more limited in extent and generally far less enlightened than that which surrounds and admonishes the highest authorities at the capital, while the comparative smallness of the interests involved causes even that inferior public to direct its thoughts to the subject less intently and with less solicitude. Far less interference is exercised by the press and by public discussion, and that which is exercised may with much more impunity be disregarded in the proceedings of local than in those of national authorities. Thus far, the advantage seems wholly on the side of management by the central government; but, when we look more closely, these motives of preference are found to be balanced by others fully as substantial. If the local authorities and public are inferior to the central ones in knowledge of the principles of administration, they have the compensatory advantage of a far more direct interest in the result. A man's neighbors or his landlord may be much cleverer than himself, and not without an indirect interest in his prosperity, but, for all that, his interests will be better attended to in his own keeping than in theirs.

It is farther to be remembered that, even supposing the central government to administer through its own officers, its officers do not act at the centre, but in the locality; and however inferior the local public may be to the central, it is the local public alone which has any opportunity of watching them, and it is the local opinion alone which either acts directly upon their own conduct, or calls the attention of the government to the points in which they may require correction. It is but in extreme cases that the general opinion of the country is brought to bear at all upon details of local administration, and still more rarely has it the means of deciding upon them with any just appreciation of the case. Now the local opinion necessarily acts far more forcibly upon purely local administrators. They, in the natural course of things, are permanent residents, not expecting to be withdrawn from the place when they cease to exercise authority in it; and their authority itself depends, by supposition, on the will of the local public. I need not dwell on the deficiencies of the central authority in detailed knowledge of local persons and things, and the too great engrossment of its time and thoughts by other concerns to admit of its acquiring the quantity and quality of local knowledge necessary even for deciding on complaints, and enforcing responsibility from so great a number of local agents. In the details of management, therefore, the local bodies will generally have the advantage, but in comprehension of the principles even of purely local management, the superiority of the central government, when rightly constituted, ought to be prodigious, not only by reason of the probably great personal superiority of the individuals composing it, and the multitude of thinkers and writers who are at all times engaged in pressing useful ideas upon their notice, but also because the knowledge and experience of any local authority is but local knowledge and experience, confined to their own part of the country and its mode of management, whereas the central government has the means of knowing all that is to be learned from the united experience of the whole kingdom, with the addition of easy access to that of foreign countries.

The practical conclusion from these premises is not difficult to draw. The authority which is most conversant with principles should be supreme over principles, while that which is most competent in details should have the details left to it. The principal business of the central authority should be to give instruction, of the local authority to apply it. Power may be localized, but knowledge, to be most useful, must be centralized; there must be somewhere a focus at which all its scattered rays are collected, that the broken and colored lights which exist elsewhere may find there what is necessary to complete and purify them. To every branch of local administration which affects the general interest there should be a corresponding central organ, either a minister, or some specially appointed functionary under him, even if that functionary does no more than collect information from all quarters, and bring the experience acquired in one locality to the knowledge of another where it is wanted.

But there is also something more than this for the central authority to do. It ought to keep open a perpetual communication with the localities—informing itself by their experience, and them by its own; giving advice freely when asked, volunteering it when seen to be required; compelling publicity and recordation of proceedings, and enforcing obedience to every general law which the Legislature has laid down on the subject of local management. That some such laws ought to be laid down few are likely to deny. The localities may be allowed to mismanage their own interests, but not to prejudice those of others, nor violate those principles of justice between one person and another of which it is the duty of the state to maintain the rigid observance. If the local majority attempts to oppress the minority, or one class another, the state is bound to interpose. For example, all local rates ought to be voted exclusively by the local representative body; but that body, though elected solely by rate-payers, may raise its revenues by imposts of such a kind, or assess them in such a manner, as to throw an unjust share of the burden on the poor, the rich, or some particular class of the population: it is the duty, therefore, of the Legislature, while leaving the mere amount of the local taxes to the discretion of the local body, to lay down authoritatively the mode of taxation and rules of assessment which alone the localities shall be permitted to use. Again, in the administration of public charity, the industry and morality of the whole laboring population depends, to a most serious extent, upon adherence to

certain fixed principles in awarding relief. Though
it belongs essentially to the local functionaries to determine who, according to those principles, is entitled
to be relieved, the national Parliament is the proper
authority to prescribe the principles themselves; and
it would neglect a most important part of its duty if
it did not, in a matter of such grave national concern,
lay down imperative rules, and make effectual provision that those rules should not be departed from.
What power of actual interference with the local administrators it may be necessary to retain, for the due
enforcement of the laws, is a question of detail into
which it would be useless to enter. The laws themselves will naturally define the penalties, and fix the
mode of their enforcement. It may be requisite, to
meet extreme cases, that the power of the central authority should extend to dissolving the local representative council or dismissing the local executive,
but not to making new appointments or suspending
the local institutions. Where Parliament has not in-
terfered, neither ought any branch of the executive to
interfere with authority; but as an adviser and critic,
an enforcer of the laws, and a denouncer to Parliament or the local constituencies of conduct which it
deems condemnable, the functions of the executive
are of the greatest possible value.

Some may think that, however much the central
authority surpasses the local in knowledge of the principles of administration, the great object which has
been so much insisted on, the social and political education of the citizens, requires that they should be left

to manage these matters by their own, however imperfect lights.   To this it might be answered that the education of the citizens is not the only thing to be considered; government and administration do not exist for that alone, great as its importance is. But the objection shows a very imperfect understanding of the function of popular institutions as a means of political instruction.   It is but a poor education that associates ignorance with ignorance, and leaves them, if they care for knowledge, to grope their way to it without help, and to do without it if they do not. What is wanted is the means of making ignorance aware of itself, and able to profit by knowledge; accustoming minds which know only routine to act upon and feel the value of principles; teaching them to compare different modes of action, and learn, by the use of their reason, to distinguish the best.   When we desire to have a good school, we do not eliminate the teacher.   The old remark, " As the schoolmaster is, so will be the school," is as true of the indirect schooling of grown people by public business as of the schooling of youth in academies and colleges.   A government which attempts to do every thing is aptly compared by M. Charles de Rémusat to a schoolmaster who does all the pupils' tasks for them ; he may be very popular with the pupils, but he will teach them little.   A government, on the other hand, which neither does any thing itself that can possibly be done by any one else, nor shows any one else how to do any thing, is like a school in which there is no schoolmaster, but only pupil-teachers who have never themselves been taught.

CHAPTER XVI.

OF NATIONALITY AS CONNECTED WITH REPRESENT- ATIVE GOVERNMENT.

A PORTION of mankind may be said to constitute a nationality if they are united among themselves by common sympathies which do not exist between them and any others—which make them co-operate with each other more willingly than with other people, desire to be under the same government, and desire that it should be government by themselves, or a portion of themselves, exclusively. This feeling of nationality may have been generated by various causes. Sometimes it is the effect of identity of race and descent. Community of language and community of religion greatly contribute to it. Geographical limits are one of its causes. But the strongest of all is identity of political antecedents; the possession of a national history, and consequent community of recollections; collective pride and humiliation, pleasure and regret, connected with the same incidents in the past. None of these circumstances, however, are either indispensable or necessarily sufficient by themselves. Switzerland has a strong sentiment of nationality, though the cantons are of different races, different languages, and different religions. Sicily has hitherto felt itself quite distinct in nationality from Naples, notwithstanding identity of religion, almost identity

of language, and a considerable amount of common
historical antecedents. The Flemish and the Wal-
loon provinces of Belgium, notwithstanding diversity
of race and language, have a much greater feeling of
common nationality than the former have with Holland, or the latter with France. Yet in general the
national feeling is proportionally weakened by the
failure of any of the causes which contribute to it.
Identity of language, literature, and, to some extent,
of race and recollections, have maintained the feeling
of nationality in considerable strength among the different portions of the German name, though they have
at no time been really united under the same government; but the feeling has never reached to making
the separate states desire to get rid of their autonomy.
Among Italians, an identity far from complete of language and literature, combined with a geographical
position which separates them by a distinct line from
other countries, and, perhaps more than every thing
else, the possession of a common name, which makes
them all glory in the past achievements in arts, arms,
politics, religious primacy, science, and literature, of
any who share the same designation, give rise to an
amount of national feeling in the population which,
though still imperfect, has been sufficient to produce
the great events now passing before us, notwithstanding a great mixture of races, and although they have
never, in either ancient or modern history, been under
the same government, except while that government
extended or was extending itself over the greater part
of the known world.

Where the sentiment of nationality exists in any force, there is a *primâ facie* case for uniting all the members of the nationality under the same government, and a government to themselves apart. This is merely saying that the question of government ought to be decided by the governed. One hardly knows what any division of the human race should be free to do if not to determine with which of the various collective bodies of human beings they choose to associate themselves. But, when a people are ripe for free institutions, there is still a more vital consideration. Free institutions are next to impossible in a country made up of different nationalities. Among a people without fellow-feeling, especially if they read and speak different languages, the united public opinion necessary to the working of representative government can not exist. The influences which form opinions and decide political acts are different in the different sections of the country. An altogether different set of leaders have the confidence of one part of the country and of another. The same books, newspapers, pamphlets, speeches, do not reach them. One section does not know what opinions or what instigations are circulating in another. The same incidents, the same acts, the same system of government, affect them in different ways, and each fears more injury to itself from the other nationalities than from the common arbiter, the state. Their mutual antipathies are generally much stronger than dislike of the government. That any one of them feels aggrieved by the policy of the common ruler is sufficient to determine another to support that policy. Even if all are aggrieved, none feel that they can rely on the others for fidelity in a joint resistance; the strength of none is sufficient to resist alone, and each may reasonably think that it consults its own advantage most by bidding for the favor of the government against the rest. Above all, the grand and only reliable security in the last resort against the despotism of the government is in that case wanting—the sympathy of the army with the people. The military are the part of every community in whom, from the nature of the case, the distinction between their fellow-countrymen and foreigners is the deepest and strongest. To the rest of the people foreigners are merely strangers; to the soldier, they are men against whom he may be called, at a week's notice, to fight for life or death. The difference to him is that between friends and enemies—we may almost say between fellow-men and another kind of animals; for, as respects the enemy, the only law is that of force, and the only mitigation the same as in the case of other animals—that of simple humanity. Soldiers to whose feelings half or three fourths of the subjects of the same government are foreigners, will have no more scruple in mowing them down, and no more desire to ask the reason why, than they would have in doing the same thing against declared enemies. An army composed of various nationalities has no other patriotism than devotion to the flag. Such armies have been the executioners of liberty through the whole duration of modern history. The sole bond which holds them together is their officers and the government which they serve, and their only idea, if they have any, of public duty, is obedience to orders. A government thus supported, by keeping its Hungarian regiments in Italy and its Italian in Hungary, can long continue to rule in both places with the iron rod of foreign conquerors.

If it be said that so broadly-marked a distinction between what is due to a fellow-countryman and what is due merely to a human creature is more worthy of savages than of civilized beings, and ought, with the utmost energy, to be contended against, no one holds that opinion more strongly than myself. But this object, one of the worthiest to which human endeavor can be directed, can never, in the present state of civilization, be promoted by keeping different nationalities of any thing like equivalent strength under the same government. In a barbarous state of society the case is sometimes different. The government may then be interested in softening the antipathies of the races, that peace may be preserved and the country more easily governed. But when there are either free institutions, or a desire for them, in any of the peoples artificially tied together, the interest of the government lies in an exactly opposite direction. It is then interested in keeping up and envenoming their antipathies, that they may be prevented from coalescing, and it may be enabled to use some of them as tools for the enslavement of others. The Austrian court has now for a whole generation made these tactics its principal means of government, with what fatal success at the time of the Vienna insurrection and the

Hungarian contest the world knows too well. Happily there are now signs that improvement is too far advanced to permit this policy to be any longer successful.

For the preceding reasons, it is in general a necessary condition of free institutions that the boundaries of governments should coincide in the main with those of nationalities. But several considerations are liable to conflict in practice with this general principle. In the first place, its application is often precluded by geographical hinderances. There are parts even of Europe in which different nationalities are so locally intermingled that it is not practicable for them to be under separate governments. The population of Hungary is composed of Magyars, Slovacks, Croats, Serbs, Roumans, and in some districts Germans, so mixed up as to be incapable of local separation; and there is no course open to them but to make a virtue of necessity, and reconcile themselves to living together under equal rights and laws. Their community of servitude, which dates only from the destruction of Hungarian independence in 1849, seems to be ripening and disposing them for such an equal union. The German colony of East Prussia is cut off from Germany by part of the ancient Poland, and being too weak to maintain separate independence, must, if geographical continuity is to be maintained, be either under a non-German government, or the intervening Polish territory must be under a German one. Another considerable region in which the dominant element of the population is German, the provinces of

Courland, Esthonia, and Livonia, is condemned by its local situation to form part of a Slavonian state. In Eastern Germany itself there is a large Slavonic population; Bohemia is principally Slavonic, Silesia and other districts partially so. The most united country in Europe, France, is far from being homogeneous: independently of the fragments of foreign nationalities at its remote extremities, it consists, as language and history prove, of two portions, one occupied almost exclusively by a Gallo-Roman population, while in the other the Frankish, Burgundian, and other Teutonic races form a considerable ingredient.

When proper allowance has been made for geographical exigencies, another more purely moral and social consideration offers itself. Experience proves that it is possible for one nationality to merge and be absorbed in another; and when it was originally an inferior and more backward portion of the human race, the absorption is greatly to its advantage. Nobody can suppose that it is not more beneficial to a Breton, or a Basque of French Navarre, to be brought into the current of the ideas and feelings of a highly civilized and cultivated people—to be a member of the French nationality, admitted on equal terms to all the privileges of French citizenship, sharing the advantages of French protection, and the dignity and *prestige* of French power—than to sulk on his own rocks, the half-savage relic of past times, revolving in his own little mental orbit, without participation or interest in the general movement of the world. The same remark applies to the Welshman or the Scottish Highlander as members of the British nation.

Whatever really tends to the admixture of nationalities, and the blending of their attributes and peculiarities in a common union, is a benefit to the human race. Not by extinguishing types, of which, in these cases, sufficient examples are sure to remain, but by softening their extreme forms, and filling up the intervals between them. The united people, like a crossed breed of animals (but in a still greater degree, because the influences in operation are moral as well as physical), inherits the special aptitudes and excellencies of all its progenitors, protected by the admixture from being exaggerated into the neighboring vices. But, to render this admixture possible, there must be peculiar conditions. The combinations of circumstances which occur, and which affect the result, are various.

The nationalities brought together under the same government may be about equal in numbers and strength, or they may be very unequal. If unequal, the least numerous of the two may either be the superior in civilization, or the inferior. Supposing it to be superior, it may either, through that superiority, be able to acquire ascendency over the other, or it may be overcome by brute strength and reduced to subjection. This last is a sheer mischief to the human race, and one which civilized humanity with one accord should rise in arms to prevent. The absorption of Greece by Macedonia was one of the greatest misfortunes which ever happened to the world; that of any of the principal countries of Europe by Russia would be a similar one.

If the smaller nationality, supposed to be the more advanced in improvement, is able to overcome the greater, as the Macedonians, re-enforced by the Greeks, did Asia, and the English India, there is often a gain to civilization, but the conquerors and the conquered can not in this case live together under the same free institutions. The absorption of the conquerors in the less advanced people would be an evil: these must be governed as subjects, and the state of things is either a benefit or a misfortune, according as the sub-jugated people have or have not reached the state in which it is an injury not to be under a free govern-ment, and according as the conquerors do or do not use their superiority in a manner calculated to fit the conquered for a higher stage of improvement. This topic will be particularly treated of in a subsequent chapter.

When the nationality which succeeds in overpow-ering the other is both the most numerous and the most improved, and especially if the subdued nation-ality is small, and has no hope of reasserting its inde-pendence, then, if it is governed with any tolerable justice, and if the members of the more powerful na-tionality are not made odious by being invested with exclusive privileges, the smaller nationality is grad-ually reconciled to its position, and becomes amalga-mated with the larger. No Bas-Breton, nor even any Alsatian, has the smallest wish at the present day to be separated from France. If all Irishmen have not yet arrived at the same disposition toward England, it is partly because they are sufficiently numerous to be capable of constituting a respectable nationality by themselves, but principally because, until of late years, they had been so atrociously governed that all their best feelings combined with their bad ones in rousing bitter resentment against the Saxon rule. This disgrace to England and calamity to the whole empire has, it may be truly said, completely ceased for nearly a generation. No Irishman is now less free than an Anglo-Saxon, nor has a less share of every benefit either to his country or to his individual fortunes than if he were sprung from any other portion of the British dominions. The only remaining real grievance of Ireland, that of the State Church, is one which half, or nearly half the people of the larger island have in common with them. There is now next to nothing, except the memory of the past, and the difference in the predominant religion, to keep apart two races perhaps the most fitted of any two in the world to be the completing counterpart of one another. The consciousness of being at last treated not only with equal justice, but with equal consideration, is making such rapid way in the Irish nation as to be wearing off all feelings that could make them insensible to the benefits which the less numerous and less wealthy people must necessarily derive from being fellow-citizens instead of foreigners to those who are not only their nearest neighbors, but the wealthiest, and one of the freest, as well as most civilized and powerful nations of the earth.

The cases in which the greatest practical obstacles exist to the blending of nationalities are when the

nationalities which have been bound together are
nearly equal in numbers and in the other elements of
power. In such cases, each, confiding in its strength,
and feeling itself capable of maintaining an equal
struggle with any of the others, is unwilling to be
merged in it; each cultivates with party obstinacy its
distinctive peculiarities; obsolete customs, and even
declining languages, are revived, to deepen the separation; each deems itself tyrannized over if any authority is exercised within itself by functionaries of a
rival race; and whatever is given to one of the conflicting nationalities is considered to be taken from all
the rest. When nations thus divided are under a despotic government which is a stranger to all of them,
or which, though sprung from one, yet feeling greater
interest in its own power than in any sympathies of
nationality, assigns no privilege to either nation, and
chooses its instruments indifferently from all, in the
course of a few generations identity of situation often
produces harmony of feeling, and the different races
come to feel toward each other as fellow-countrymen,
particularly if they are dispersed over the same tract
of country. But if the era of aspiration to free government arrives before this fusion has been effected,
the opportunity has gone by for effecting it. From
that time, if the unreconciled nationalities are geo-
graphically separate, and especially if their local position is such that there is no natural fitness or convenience in their being under the same government
(as in the case of an Italian province under a French
or German yoke), there is not only an obvious pro-

priety, but, if either freedom or concord is cared for, a necessity for breaking the connection altogether. There may be cases in which the provinces, after separation, might usefully remain united by a federal tie; but it generally happens that if they are willing to forego complete independence, and become members of a federation, each of them has other neighbors with whom it would prefer to connect itself, having more sympathies in common, if not also greater community of interest.

CHAPTER XVII.

OF FEDERAL REPRESENTATIVE GOVERNMENTS.

PORTIONS of mankind who are not fitted or not disposed to live under the same internal government may often, with advantage, be federally united as to their relations with foreigners, both to prevent wars among themselves, and for the sake of more effectual protection against the aggression of powerful states.

To render a federation advisable several conditions are necessary. The first is that there should be a sufficient amount of mutual sympathy among the populations. The federation binds them always to fight on the same side; and if they have such feelings toward one another, or such diversity of feeling toward their neighbors that they would generally prefer to fight on opposite sides, the federal tie is neither likely to be of long duration, nor to be well observed while it subsists. The sympathies available for the purpose are those of race, language, religion, and, above all, of political institutions, as conducing most to a feeling of identity of political interest. When a few free states, separately insufficient for their own defense, are hemmed in on all sides by military or feudal monarchs, who hate and despise freedom even in a neighbor, those states have no chance for preserving liberty and its blessings but by a federal union. The com-

mon interest arising from this cause has in Switzerland, for several centuries, been found adequate to
maintain efficiently the federal bond, in spite not only
of difference of religion when religion was the grand
source of irreconcilable political enmity throughout
Europe, but also in spite of great weakness in the constitution of the federation itself. In America, where
all the conditions for the maintenance of union exist
at the highest point, with the sole drawback of difference of institutions in the single but most important
article of slavery, this one difference goes so far in al-
ienating from each other's sympathies the two divisions of the Union as to be now actually effecting the
disruption of a tie of so much value to them both.

The second condition for the stability of a federal
government is that the separate states be not so powerful as to be able to rely for protection against foreign encroachment on their individual strength. If
they are, they will be apt to think that they do not
gain, by union with others, the equivalent of what
they sacrifice in their own liberty of action; and consequently, whenever the policy of the confederation,
in things reserved to its cognizance, is different from
that which any one of its members would separately
pursue, the internal and sectional breach will, through
absence of sufficient anxiety to preserve the Union,
be in danger of going so far as to dissolve it.

A third condition, not less important than the two
others, is that there be not a very marked inequality of strength among the several contracting states.
They can not, indeed, be exactly equal in resources;

in all federations there will be a gradation of power among the members; some will be more populous, rich, and civilized than others. There is a wide difference in wealth and population between New York and Rhode Island; between Berne, and Zug or Glaris. The essential is, that there should not be any one state so much more powerful than the rest as to be capable of vying in strength with many of them combined. If there be such a one, and only one, it will insist on being master of the joint deliberations; if there be two, they will be irresistible when they agree; and whenever they differ, every thing will be decided by a struggle for ascendency between the rivals. This cause is alone enough to reduce the German Bund to almost a nullity, independently of its wretched internal constitution. It effects none of the real purposes of a confederation. It has never bestowed on Germany a uniform system of customs, nor so much as a uniform coinage, and has served only to give Austria and Prussia a legal right of pouring in their troops to assist the local sovereigns in keeping their subjects obedient to despotism, while, in regard to external concerns, the Bund would make all Germany a dependency of Prussia if there were no Austria, and of Austria if there were no Prussia; and, in the mean time, each petty prince has little choice but to be a partisan of one or the other, or to intrigue with foreign governments against both.

There are two different modes of organizing a federal union. The federal authorities may represent the governments solely, and their acts may be obligatory only on the governments as such, or they may have the power of enacting laws and issuing orders which are binding directly on individual citizens. The former is the plan of the German so-called Confederation, and of the Swiss Constitution previous to 1847. It was tried in America for a few years immediately following the War of Independence. The other principle is that of the existing Constitution of the United States, and has been adopted within the last dozen years by the Swiss Confederacy. The federal Congress of the American Union is a substantive part of the government of every individual state. Within the limits of its attributions, it makes laws which are obeyed by every citizen individually, executes them through its own officers, and enforces them by its own tribunals. This is the only principle which has been found, or which is ever likely to produce an effective federal government. A union between the governments only is a mere alliance, and subject to all the contingencies which render alliances precarious. If the acts of the President and of Congress were binding solely on the governments of New York, Virginia, or Pennsylvania, and could only be carried into effect through orders issued by those governments to officers appointed by them, under responsibility to their own courts of justice, no mandates of the federal government which were disagreeable to a local majority would ever be executed. Requisitions issued to a government have no other sanction or means of enforcement than war, and a federal army would have to be always in readiness to enforce the decrees of the fed.

eration against any recalcitrant state, subject to the probability that other states, sympathizing with the recusant, and perhaps sharing its sentiments on the particular point in dispute, would withhold their contingents, if not send them to fight in the ranks of the disobedient state. Such a federation is more likely to be a cause than a preventive of internal wars; and if such was not its effect in Switzerland until the events of the years immediately preceding 1847, it was only because the federal government felt its weakness so strongly that it hardly ever attempted to exercise any real authority. In America, the experiment of a federation on this principle broke down in the first few years of its existence, happily while the men of enlarged knowledge and acquired ascendency who founded the independence of the republic were still alive to guide it through the difficult transition. The "Federalist," a collection of papers by three of these eminent men, written in explanation and defense of the new federal Constitution while still awaiting the national acceptance, is even now the most instructive treatise we possess on federal government. In Germany, the more imperfect kind of federation, as all know, has not even answered the purpose of maintaining an alliance. It has never, in any European war, prevented single members of the confederation from allying themselves with foreign powers against the rest. Yet this is the only federation which seems possible among monarchical states. A king, who holds his power by inheritance, not by delegation, and who can not be deprived of it, nor made responsible to any one for its use, is not likely to renounce having a separate army, or to brook the exercise of sovereign authority over his own subjects, not through him, but directly by another power. To enable two or more countries under kingly government to be joined together in an effectual confederation, it seems necessary that they should all be under the same king. England and Scotland were a federation of this description during the interval of about a century between the union of the crowns and that of the Parliaments. Even this was effective, not through federal institutions, for none existed, but because the regal power in both Constitutions was so nearly absolute as to enable the foreign policy of both to be shaped according to a single will.

Under the more perfect mode of federation, where every citizen of each particular state owes obedience to two governments, that of his own state and that of the federation, it is evidently necessary not only that the constitutional limits of the authority of each should be precisely and clearly defined, but that the power to decide between them in any case of dispute should not reside in either of the governments, or in any functionary subject to it, but in an umpire independent of both. There must be a Supreme Court of Justice, and a system of subordinate courts in every state of the Union, before whom such questions shall be carried, and whose judgment on them, in the last stage of appeal, shall be final. Every state of the Union, and the federal government itself, as well as every functionary of each, must be liable to be sued in those courts for exceeding their powers, or for non-performance of their federal duties, and must in general be obliged to employ those courts as the instrument for enforcing their federal rights. This involves the remarkable consequence, actually realized in the United States, that a court of justice, the highest federal tribunal, is supreme over the various governments, both state and federal, having the right to declare that any law made, or act done by them, exceeds the powers assigned to them by the federal Constitution, and, in consequence, has no legal validity. It was natural to feel strong doubts, before trial had been made, how such a provision would work; whether the tribunal would have the courage to exercise its constitutional power; if it did, whether it would exercise it wisely, and whether the governments would consent to submit peaceably to its decision. The discussions on the American Constitution, before its final adoption, give evidence that these natural apprehensions were strongly felt; but they are now entirely quieted, since, during the two generations and more which have subsequently elapsed, nothing has occurred to verify them, though there have at times been disputes of considerable acrimony, and which became the badges of parties, respecting the limits of the authority of the federal and state governments. The eminently beneficial working of so singular a provision is probably, as M. de Tocqueville remarks, in a great measure attributable to the peculiarity inherent in a court of justice acting as such—namely, that it does not declare the law *eo nomine* and in the abstract, but waits until a case between man and man is brought before it judicially, involving the point in dispute; from which arises the happy effect that its declarations are not made in a very early stage of the controversy; that much popular discussion usually precedes them; that the court decides after hearing the point fully argued on both sides by lawyers of reputation; decides only as much of the question at a time as is required by the case before it, and its decision, instead of being volunteered for political purposes, is drawn from it by the duty which it can not refuse to fulfill, of dispensing justice impartially between adverse litigants. Even these grounds of confidence would not have sufficed to produce the respectful submission with which all authorities have yielded to the decisions of the Supreme Court on the interpretation of the Constitution, were it not that complete reliance has been felt, not only on the intellectual pre-eminence of the judges composing that exalted tribunal, but on their entire superiority over either private or sectional partialities. This reliance has been in the main justified; but there is nothing which more vitally imports the American people than to guard with the most watchful solicitude against every thing which has the remotest tendency to produce deterioration in the quality of this great national institution. The confidence on which depends the stability of federal institutions has been for the first time impaired by the judgment declaring slavery to be of common right, and consequently lawful in the Territories while not yet constituted as states, even against the will of a majority of their inhabitants. The main pillar of the

American Constitution is scarcely strong enough to bear many more such shocks.

The tribunals which act as umpires between the federal and the state governments naturally also decide all disputes between two states, or between a citizen of one state and the government of another. The usual remedies between nations, war and diplomacy, being precluded by the federal union, it is necessary that a judicial remedy should supply their place. The Supreme Court of the federation dispenses international law, and is the first great example of what is now one of the most prominent wants of civilized society, a real international tribunal.

The powers of a federal government naturally extend not only to peace and war, and all questions which arise between the country and foreign governments, but to making any other arrangements which are, in the opinion of the states, necessary to their enjoyment of the full benefits of union. For example, it is a great advantage to them that their mutual commerce should be free, without the impediment of frontier duties and custom-houses. But this internal freedom can not exist if each state has the power of fixing the duties on interchange of commodities between itself and foreign countries, since every foreign product let in by one state would be let into all the rest; and hence all custom duties and trade regulations in the United States are made or repealed by the federal government exclusively. Again, it is a great convenience to the states to have but one coinage, and but one system of weights and measures, which can only be insured if the regulation of these matters is intrusted to the federal government. The certainty and celerity of post-office communication is impeded, and its expense increased, if a letter has to pass through half a dozen sets of public officers, subject to different supreme authorities: it is convenient, therefore, that all post-offices should be under the federal government; but on such questions the feelings of different communities are liable to be different. One of the American states, under the guidance of a man who has displayed powers as a speculative political thinker superior to any who has appeared in American politics since the authors of the "Federalist,"* claimed a veto for each state on the custom laws of the federal Congress; and that statesman, in a posthumous work of great ability, which has been printed and widely circulated by the Legislature of South Carolina, vindicated this pretension on the general principle of limiting the tyranny of the majority, and protecting minorities by admitting them to a substantial participation in political power. One of the most disputed topics in American politics during the early part of this century was whether the power of the federal government ought to extend, and whether by the Constitution it did extend, to making roads and canals at the cost of the Union. It is only in transactions with foreign powers that the authority of the federal government is of necessity complete. On every other subject the question depends on how closely the people in general wish to draw the federal tie;

* Mr. Calhoun.

what portion of their local freedom of action they are willing to surrender, in order to enjoy more fully the benefit of being one nation.

Respecting the fitting constitution of a federal government within itself, much needs not be said. It of course consists of a legislative branch and an executive, and the constitution of each is amenable to the same principles as that of representative governments generally. As regards the mode of adapting these general principles to a federal government, the provision of the American Constitution seems exceedingly judicious, that Congress should consist of two houses, and that while•one of them is constituted according to population, each state being entitled to representatives in the ratio of the number of its inhabitants, the other should represent not the citizens, but the state governments, and every state, whether large or small, should be represented in it by the same number of members. This provision precludes any undue power from being exercised by the more powerful states over the rest, and guarantees the reserved rights of the state governments by making it impossible, as far as the mode of representation can prevent, that any measure should pass Congress unless approved not only by a majority of the citizens, but by a majority of the states. I have before adverted to the farther incidental advantage obtained of raising the standard of qualifications in one of the houses. Being nominated by select bodies, the Legislatures of the various states, whose choice, for reasons already indicated, is more likely to fall on eminent men than any popu-

lar election — who have not only the power of electing such, but a strong motive to do so, because the
influence of their state in the general deliberations
must be materially affected by the personal weight
and abilities of its representatives — the Senate of
the United States, thus chosen, has always contained
nearly all the political men of established and high
reputation in the Union; while the Lower House of
Congress has, in the opinion of competent observers,
been generally as remarkable for the absence of conspicuous personal merit, as the Upper House for its
presence.

When the conditions exist for the formation of efficient and durable federal unions, the multiplication
of such is always a benefit to the world. It has the
same salutary effect as any other extension of the
practice of co-operation, through which the weak, by
uniting, can meet on equal terms with the strong.
By diminishing the number of those petty states which
are not equal to their own defense, it weakens the
temptations to an aggressive policy, whether working
directly by arms, or through the *prestige* of superior
power. It of course puts an end to war and diplomatic quarrels, and usually also to restrictions on
commerce, between the states composing the Union;
while, in reference to neighboring nations, the increased military strength conferred by it is of a kind
to be almost exclusively available for defensive,
scarcely at all for aggressive purposes. A federal
government has not a sufficiently concentrated authority to conduct with much efficiency any war but

one of self-defense, in which it can rely on the voluntary co-operation of every citizen; nor is there any thing very flattering to national vanity or ambition in acquiring, by a successful war, not subjects, nor even fellow-citizens, but only new, and perhaps troublesome independent members of the confederation. The warlike proceedings of the Americans in Mexico was purely exceptional, having been carried on principally by volunteers, under the influence of the migratory propensity which prompts individual Americans to possess themselves of unoccupied land, and stimulated, if by any public motive, not by that of national aggrandizement, but by the purely sectional purpose of extending slavery. There are few signs in the proceedings of Americans, nationally or individually, that the desire of territorial acquisition for their country as such has any considerable power over them. Their hankering after Cuba is, in the same manner, merely sectional, and the Northern States, those opposed to slavery, have never in any way favored it.

The question may present itself (as in Italy at its present uprising) whether a country which is determined to be united should form a complete or a merely federal union. The point is sometimes necessarily decided by the mere territorial magnitude of the united whole. There is a limit to the extent of country which can advantageously be governed, or even whose government can be conveniently superintended from a single centre. There are vast countries so governed; but they, or at least their distant provinces, are in general deplorably ill administered, and it is only when the inhabitants are almost savages that they could not manage their affairs better separately. This obstacle does not exist in the case of Italy, the size of which does not come up to that of several very efficiently governed single states in past and present times. The question then is, whether the different parts of the nation require to be governed in a way so essentially different that it is not probable the same Legislature, and the same ministry or administrative body, will give satisfaction to them all. Unless this be the case, which is a question of fact, it is better for them to be completely united. That a totally different system of laws and very different administrative institutions may exist in two portions of a country without being any obstacle to legislative unity, is proved by the case of England and Scotland. Perhaps, however, this undisturbed coexistence of two legal systems under one united Legislature, making different laws for the two sections of the country in adaptation to the previous differences, might not be so well preserved, or the same confidence might not be felt in its preservation, in a country whose legislators are more possessed (as is apt to be the case on the Continent) with the mania for uniformity. A people having that unbounded toleration which is characteristic of this country for every description of anomaly, so long as those whose interests it concerns do not feel aggrieved by it, afforded an exceptionally advantageous field for trying this difficult experiment. In most countries, if it was an object to retain different systems of law, it might probably be necessary to retain distinct Legislatures as guardians of them, which is perfectly compatible with a national Parliament and king, or a national Parliament without a king, supreme over the external relations of all the members of the body.

Whenever it is not deemed necessary to maintain permanently, in the different provinces, different systems of jurisprudence, and fundamental institutions grounded on different principles, it is always practicable to reconcile minor diversities with the maintenance of unity of government. All that is needful is to give a sufficiently large sphere of action to the local authorities. Under one and the same central government there may be local governors, and provincial assemblies for local purposes. It may happen, for instance, that the people of different provinces may have preferences in favor of different modes of taxation. If the general Legislature could not be depended on for being guided by the members for each province in modifying the general system of taxation to suit that province, the Constitution might provide that as many of the expenses of government as could by any possibility be made local should be defrayed by local rates imposed by the provincial assemblies, and that those which must of necessity be general, such as the support of an army and navy, should, in the estimates for the year, be apportioned among the different provinces according to some general estimate of their resources, the amount assigned to each being levied by the local assembly on the principles most acceptable to the locality, and paid *en bloc* into the national treasury. A practice approaching to this existed even in the old French monarchy, so far as regarded the *pays d'états*, each of which, having consented or being required to furnish a fixed sum, was left to assess it upon the inhabitants by its own officers, thus escaping the grinding despotism of the royal *intendants* and *subdélégués;* and this privilege is always mentioned as one of the advantages which mainly contributed to render them, as they were, the most flourishing provinces of France.

Identity of central government is compatible with many different degrees of centralization, not only administrative, but even legislative. A people may have the desire and the capacity for a closer union than one merely federal, while yet their local peculiarities and antecedents render considerable diversities desirable in the details of their government. But if there is a real desire on all hands to make the experiment successful, there needs seldom be any difficulty in not only preserving those diversities, but giving them the guaranty of a constitutional provision against any attempt at assimilation except by the voluntary act of those who would be affected by the change.

CHAPTER XVIII.

OF THE GOVERNMENT OF DEPENDENCIES BY A FREE STATE.

FREE states, like all others, may possess dependencies, acquired either by conquest or by colonization, and our own is the greatest instance of the kind in modern history. It is a most important question how such dependencies ought to be governed.

It is unnecessary to discuss the case of small posts, like Gibraltar, Aden, or Heligoland, which are held only as naval or military positions. The military or naval object is in this case paramount, and the inhabitants can not, consistently with it, be admitted to the government of the place, though they ought to be allowed all liberties and privileges compatible with that restriction, including the free management of municipal affairs, and, as a compensation for being locally sacrificed to the convenience of the governing state, should be admitted to equal rights with its native subjects in all other parts of the empire.

Outlying territories of some size and population, which are held as dependencies, that is, which are subject, more or less, to acts of sovereign power on the part of the paramount country, without being equally represented (if represented at all) in its Legislature, may be divided into two classes. Some are composed of people of similar civilization to the ruling country, capable of, and ripe for representative government, such as the British possessions in America and Australia. Others, like India, are still at a great distance from that state.

In the case of dependencies of the former class, this country has at length realized, in rare completeness, the true principle of government. England has always felt under a certain degree of obligation to bestow on such of her outlying populations as were of her own blood and language, and on some who were not, representative institutions formed in imitation of her own; but, until the present generation, she has been on the same bad level with other countries as to the amount of self-government which she allowed them to exercise through the representative institutions that she conceded to them. She claimed to be the supreme arbiter even of their purely internal concerns, according to her own, not their ideas of how those concerns could be best regulated. This practice was a natural corollary from the vicious theory of colonial policy—once common to all Europe, and not yet completely relinquished by any other people—which regarded colonies as valuable by affording markets for our commodities that could be kept entirely to ourselves; a privilege we valued so highly that we thought it worth purchasing by allowing to the colonies the same monopoly of our market for their own productions which we claimed for our commodities in theirs. This notable plan of enriching them and ourselves by making each pay enormous sums to the other, dropping the greatest part by the way, has been for some time abandoned. But the bad habit of meddling in the internal government of the colonies did not at once die out when we relinquished the idea of making any profit by it. We continued to torment them, not for any benefit to ourselves, but for that of a section or faction among the colonists; and this persistence in domineering cost us a Canadian rebellion before we had the happy thought of giving it up. England was like an ill brought-up elder brother, who persists in tyrannizing over the younger ones from mere habit, till one of them, by a spirited resistance, though with unequal strength, gives him notice to desist. We were wise enough not to require a second warning. A new era in the colonial policy of nations began with Lord Durham's Report; the imperishable memorial of that nobleman's courage, patriotism, and enlightened liberality, and of the intellect and practical sagacity of its joint authors, Mr. Wakefield and the lamented Charles Buller.*

It is now a fixed principle of the policy of Great Britain, professed in theory and faithfully adhered to in practice, that her colonies of European race, equally with the parent country, possess the fullest measure of internal self-government. They have been allowed to make their own free representative constitutions by altering in any manner they thought fit the already very popular constitutions which we had given them.

* I am speaking here of the *adoption* of this improved policy, not, of course, of its original suggestion. The honor of having been its earliest champion belongs unquestionably to Mr. Roebuck.

Each is governed by its own Legislature and executive, constituted on highly democratic principles. The veto of the crown and of Parliament, though nominally reserved, is only exercised (and that very rarely) on questions which concern the empire, and not solely the particular colony. How liberal a construction has been given to the distinction between imperial and colonial questions is shown by the fact that the whole of the unappropriated lands in the regions behind our American and Australian colonies have been given up to the uncontrolled disposal of the colonial communities, though they might, without injustice, have been kept in the hands of the imperial government, to be administered for the greatest advantage of future emigrants from all parts of the empire. Every colony has thus as full power over its own affairs as it could have if it were a member of even the loosest federation, and much fuller than would belong to it under the Constitution of the United States, being free even to tax at its pleasure the commodities imported from the mother country. Their union with Great Britain is the slightest kind of federal union; but not a strictly equal federation, the mother country retaining to itself the powers of a federal government, though reduced in practice to their very narrowest limits. This inequality is, of course, as far as it goes, a disadvantage to the dependencies, which have no voice in foreign policy, but are bound by the decisions of the superior country. They are compelled to join England in war without being in any way consulted previous to engaging in it.

Those (now happily not a few) who think that justice is as binding on communities as it is on individuals, and that men are not warranted in doing to other
countries, for the supposed benefit of their own country, what they would not be justified in doing to other men for their own benefit, feel even this limited
amount of constitutional subordination on the part of
the colonies to be a violation of principle, and have
often occupied themselves in looking out for means
by which it may be avoided. With this view it has
been proposed by some that the colonies should return representatives to the British Legislature, and by
others that the powers of our own, as well as of their
Parliaments, should be confined to internal policy, and
that there should be another representative body for
foreign and imperial concerns, in which last the dependencies of Great Britain should be represented in
the same manner, and with the same completeness as
Great Britain itself. On this system there would be
a perfectly equal federation between the mother country and her colonies, then no longer dependencies.

The feelings of equity and conceptions of public
morality from which these suggestions emanate are
worthy of all praise, but the suggestions themselves
are so inconsistent with rational principles of government that it is doubtful if they have been seriously
accepted as a possibility by any reasonable thinker.
Countries separated by half the globe do not present
the natural conditions for being under one government, or even members of one federation. If they
had sufficiently the same interests, they have not, and

never can have, a sufficient habit of taking council together. They are not part of the same public; they do not discuss and deliberate in the same arena, but apart, and have only a most imperfect knowledge of what passes in the minds of one another. They neither know each other's objects, nor have confidence in each other's principles of conduct. Let any Englishman ask himself how he should like his destinies to depend on an assembly of which one third was British American, and another third South African and Australian. Yet to this it must come if there were any thing like fair or equal representation; and would not every one feel that the representatives of Canada and Australia, even in matters of an imperial character, could not know or feel any sufficient concern for the interests, opinions, or wishes of English, Irish, and Scotch? Even for strictly federative purposes the conditions do not exist which we have seen to be essential to a federation. England is sufficient for her own protection without the colonies, and would be in a much stronger, as well as more dignified position, if separated from them, than when reduced to be a single member of an American, African, and Australian confederation. Over and above the commerce which she might equally enjoy after separation, England derives little advantage, except in *prestige*, from her dependencies, and the little she does derive is quite outweighed by the expense they cost her, and the dissemination they necessitate of her naval and military force, which, in case of war, or any real apprehension of it, requires to be double or treble what would be needed for the defense of this country alone.

But, though Great Britain could do perfectly well
without her colonies, and though, on every principle
of morality and justice, she ought to consent to their
separation, should the time come when, after full trial
of the best form of union, they deliberately desire to
be dissevered, there are strong reasons for maintaining the present slight bond of connection so long as
not disagreeable to the feelings of either party. It is
a step, as far as it goes, toward universal peace and
general friendly co-operation among nations. It renders war impossible among a large number of otherwise independent communities, and, moreover, hinders any of them from being absorbed into a foreign
state, and becoming a source of additional aggressive
strength to some rival power, either more despotic or
closer at hand, which may not always be so unambi-
tious or so pacific as Great Britain. It at least keeps
the markets of the different countries open to one another, and prevents that mutual exclusion by hostile
tariffs which none of the great communities of mankind except England have yet outgrown. And in the
case of the British possessions it has the advantage,
specially valuable at the present time, of adding to
the moral influence and weight in the councils of the
world of the power which, of all in existence, best un-
derstands liberty—and, whatever may have been its
errors in the past, has attained to more of conscience
and moral principle in its dealings with foreigners
than any other great nation seems either to conceive
as possible or recognize as desirable. Since, then, the
union can only continue, while it does continue, on

the footing of an unequal federation, it is important to consider by what means this small amount of inequality can be prevented from being either onerous or humiliating to the communities occupying the less exalted position.

The only inferiority necessarily inherent in the case is that the mother country decides, both for the colonies and for herself, on questions of peace and war. They gain, in return, the obligation on the mother country to repel aggressions directed against them; but, except when the minor community is so weak that the protection of a stronger power is indispensable to it, reciprocity of obligation is not a full equivalent for non-admission to a voice in the deliberations. It is essential, therefore, that in all wars, save those which, like the Caffre or New Zealand wars, are incurred for the sake of the particular colony, the colonists should not (unless at their own voluntary request) be made to contribute any thing to the expense except what may be required for the specific local defense of their own ports, shores, and frontiers against invasion. Moreover, as the mother country claims the privilege, at her sole discretion, of taking measures or pursuing a policy which may expose them to attack, it is just that she should undertake a considerable portion of the cost of their military defense even in time of peace; the whole of it, so far as it depends upon a standing army.

But there is a means, still more effectual than these, by which, and in general by which alone, a full equivalent can be given to a smaller community for sink-

ing its individuality, as a substantive power among
nations, in the greater individuality of a wide and
powerful empire. This one indispensable, and, at the
same time, sufficient expedient, which meets at once
the demands of justice and the growing exigencies of
policy, is to open the service of government in all its
departments, and in every part of the empire, on perfectly equal terms, to the inhabitants of the colonies.
Why does no one ever hear a breath of disloyalty
from the islands in the British Channel? By race,
religion, and geographical position they belong less to
England than to France; but, while they enjoy, like
Canada and New South Wales, complete control over
their internal affairs and their taxation, every office or
dignity in the gift of the crown is freely open to the
native of Guernsey or Jersey. Generals, admirals,
peers of the United Kingdom are made, and there is
nothing which hinders prime ministers to be made
from those insignificant islands. The same system
was commenced in reference to the colonies generally
by an enlightened colonial secretary, too early lost,
Sir William Molesworth, when he appointed Mr.
Hinckes, a leading Canadian politician, to a West Indian government. It is a very shallow view of the
springs of political action in a community which
thinks such things unimportant because the number
of those in a position actually to profit by the concession might not be very considerable. That limited
number would be composed precisely of those who
have most moral power over the rest; and men are
not so destitute of the sense of collective degradation

as not to feel the withholding of an advantage from
even one person, because of a circumstance which they
all have in common with him, an affront to all. If we
prevent the leading men of a community from standing forth to the world as its chiefs and representatives
in the general councils of mankind, we owe it both to
their legitimate ambition and to the just pride of the
community to give them in return an equal chance of
occupying the same prominent position in a nation of
greater power and importance. Were the whole service of the British crown opened to the natives of the
Ionian Islands, we should hear no more of the desire
for union with Greece. Such a union is not desirable
for the people, to whom it would be a step backward
in civilization; but it is no wonder if·Corfu, which
has given a minister of European reputation to the
Russian Empire, and a president to Greece itself before the arrival of the Bavarians, should feel it a
grievance that its people are not admissible to the
highest posts in some government or other.

Thus far of the dependencies whose population is
in a sufficiently advanced state to be fitted for representative government; but there are others which
have not attained that state, and which, if held at all,
must be governed by the dominant country, or by
persons delegated for that purpose by it. This mode
of government is as legitimate as any other, if it is
the one which in the existing state of civilization of
the subject people most facilitates their transition to a
higher stage of improvement. There are, as we have
already seen, conditions of society in which a vigorous

despotism is in itself the best mode of government for training the people in what is specifically wanting to render them capable of a higher civilization. There are others in which the mere fact of despotism has indeed no beneficial effect, the lessons which it teaches having already been only too completely learned, but in which, there being no spring of spontaneous improvement in the people themselves, their almost only hope of making any steps in advance depends on the chances of a good despot. Under a native despotism, a good despot is a rare and transitory accident; but when the dominion they are under is that of a more civilized people, that people ought to be able to supply it constantly. The ruling country ought to be able to do for its subjects all that could be done by a succession of absolute monarchs, guaranteed by irresistible force against the precariousness of tenure attendant on barbarous despotisms, and qualified by their genius to anticipate all that experience has taught to the more advanced nation. Such is the ideal rule of a free people over a barbarous or semi-barbarous one. We need not expect to see that ideal realized; but, unless some approach to it is, the rulers are guilty of a dereliction of the highest moral trust which can devolve upon a nation; and if they do not even aim at it, they are selfish usurpers, on a par in criminality with any of those whose ambition and rapacity have sported from age to age with the destiny of masses of mankind.

As it is already a common, and is rapidly tending to become the universal condition of the more back-

ward populations to be either held in direct subjection
by the more advanced, or to be under their complete
political ascendency, there are in this age of the world
few more important problems than how to organize
this rule, so as to make it a good instead of an evil
to the subject people, providing them with the best
attainable present government, and with the conditions most favorable to future permanent improvement. But the mode of fitting the government for
this purpose is by no means so well understood as the
conditions of good government in a people capable of
governing themselves. We may even say that it is
not understood at all.

The thing appears perfectly easy to superficial observers. If India (for example) is not fit to govern
itself, all that seems to them required is that there
should be a minister to govern it, and that this minister, like all other British ministers, should be responsible to the British Parliament. Unfortunately
this, though the simplest mode of attempting to govern a dependency, is about the worst, and betrays in
its advocates a total want of comprehension of the
conditions of good government. To govern a country under responsibility to the people of that country,
and to govern one country under responsibility to the
people of another, are two very different things. What
makes the excellence of the first is, that freedom is
preferable to despotism; but the last *is* despotism.
The only choice the case admits is a choice of despotisms, and it is not certain that the despotism of twenty millions is necessarily better than that of a few or

of one; but it is quite certain that the despotism of those who neither hear, nor see, nor know any thing about their subjects has many chances of being worse than that of those who do. It is not usually thought that the immediate agents of authority govern better because they govern in the name of an absent master, and of one who has a thousand more pressing interests to attend to. The master may hold them to a strict responsibility, enforced by heavy penalties, but it is very questionable if those penalties will often fall in the right place.

It is always under great difficulties, and very imperfectly, that a country can be governed by foreigners, even when there is no extreme disparity in habits and ideas between the rulers and the ruled. Foreigners do not feel with the people. They can not judge, by the light in which a thing appears to their own minds, or the manner in which it affects their feelings, how it will affect the feelings or appear to the minds of the subject population. What a native of the country, of average practical ability, knows as it were by instinct, they have to learn slowly, and, after all, imperfectly, by study and experience. The laws, the customs, the social relations for which they have to legislate, instead of being familiar to them from childhood, are all strange to them. For most of their detailed knowledge they must depend on the information of natives, and it is difficult for them to know whom to trust. They are feared, suspected, probably disliked by the population; seldom sought by them except for interested purposes; and they are prone to think that the servilely submissive are the trustworthy. Their danger is of despising the natives; that of the natives is, of disbelieving that any thing the strangers do can be intended for their good. These are but a part of the difficulties that any rulers have to struggle with, who honestly attempt to govern well a country in which they are foreigners. To overcome these difficulties in any degree will always be a work of much labor, requiring a very superior degree of capacity in the chief administrators, and a high average among the subordinates; and the best organization of such a government is that which will best insure the labor, develop the capacity, and place the highest specimens of it in the situations of greatest trust. Responsibility to an authority which has gone through none of the labor, acquired none of the capacity, and for the most part is not even aware that either, in any peculiar degree, is required, can not be regarded as a very effectual expedient for accomplishing these ends.

The government of a people by itself has a meaning and a reality, but such a thing as government of one people by another does not and can not exist. One people may keep another as a warren or preserve for its own use, a place to make money in, a human cattle-farm to be worked for the profit of its own inhabitants; but if the good of the governed is the proper business of a government, it is utterly impossible that a people should directly attend to it. The utmost they can do is to give some of their best men a commission to look after it, to whom the opinion of their own country can neither be much of a guide in

the performance of their duty, nor a competent judge
of the mode in which it has been performed. Let
any one consider how the English themselves would
be governed if they knew and cared no more about
their own affairs than they know and care about the
affairs of the Hindoos. Even this comparison gives
no adequate idea of the state of the case; for a people
thus indifferent to politics altogether would probably
be simply acquiescent, and let the government alone;
whereas in the case of India, a politically active people like the English, amid habitual acquiescence, are
every now and then interfering, and almost always in
the wrong place. The real causes which determine
the prosperity or wretchedness, the improvement or
deterioration of the Hindoos, are too far off to be
within their ken. They have not the knowledge necessary for suspecting the existence of those causes,
much less for judging of their operation. The most
essential interests of the country may be well administered without obtaining any of their approbation, or mismanaged to almost any excess without at-
tracting their notice. The purposes for which they
are principally tempted to interfere, and control the
proceedings of their delegates, are of two kinds. One
is, to force English ideas down the throats of the natives; for instance, by measures of proselytism, or acts
intentionally or unintentionally offensive to the religious feelings of the people. This misdirection of opinion in the ruling country is instructively exemplified
(the more so, because nothing is meant but justice and
fairness, and as much impartiality as can be expected

from persons really convinced) by the demand now so
general in England for having the Bible taught, at
the option of pupils or their parents, in the government schools. From the European point of view
nothing can wear a fairer aspect, or seem less open to
objection on the score of religious freedom. To Asiatic eyes it is quite another thing. No Asiatic people ever believes that a government puts its paid officers and official machinery into motion unless it is
bent upon an object; and when bent on an object, no
Asiatic believes that any government, except a feeble
and contemptible one, pursues it by halves. If government schools and schoolmasters taught Christianity, whatever pledges might be given of teaching it
only to those who spontaneously sought it, no amount
of evidence would ever persuade the parents that improper means were not used to make their children
Christians, or, at all events, outcasts from Hindooism.
If they could, in the end, be convinced of the contrary,
it would only be by the entire failure of the schools,
so conducted, to make any converts. If the teaching
had the smallest effect in promoting its object, it would
compromise not only the utility and even existence
of the government education, but perhaps the safety
of the government itself. An English Protestant
would not be easily induced, by disclaimers of proselytism, to place his children in a Roman Catholic sem-
inary; Irish Catholics will not send their children to
schools in which they can be made Protestants; and
we expect that Hindoos, who believe that the privileges of Hindooism can be forfeited by a merely phys-

ical act, will expose theirs to the danger of being made Christians!

Such is one of the modes in which the opinion of the dominant country tends to act more injuriously than beneficially on the conduct of its deputed governors.   In other respects, its interference is likely to be oftenest exercised where it will be most pertinaciously demanded, and that is, on behalf of some interest of the English settlers.   English settlers have friends at home, have organs, have access to the public; they have a common language, and common ideas with their countrymen; any complaint by an Englishman is more sympathetically heard, even if no unjust preference is intentionally accorded to it.   Now if there be a fact to which all experience testifies, it is that, when a country holds another in subjection, the individuals of the ruling people who resort to the foreign country to make their fortunes are of all others those who most need to be held under powerful restraint.   They are always one of the chief difficulties of the government.   Armed with the *prestige* and filled with the scornful overbearingness of the conquering nation, they have the feelings inspired by absolute power without its sense of responsibility. Among a people like that of India, the utmost efforts of the public authorities are not enough for the effectual protection of the weak against the strong; and of all the strong, the European settlers are the strongest.   Wherever the demoralizing effect of the situation is not in a most remarkable degree corrected by the personal character of the individual, they think the people of the country mere dirt under their feet: it seems to them monstrous that any rights of the natives should stand in the way of their smallest pretensions; the simplest act of protection to the inhabitants against any act of power on their part which they may consider useful to their commercial objects they denounce, and sincerely regard as an injury. So natural is this state of feeling in a situation like theirs, that, even under the discouragement which it has hitherto met with from the ruling authorities, it is impossible that more or less of the spirit should not perpetually break out. The government, itself free from this spirit, is never able sufficiently to keep it down in the young and raw even of its own civil and military officers, over whom it has so much more control than over the independent residents. As it is with the English in India, so, according to trustworthy testimony, it is with the French in Algiers; so with the Americans in the countries conquered from Mexico; so it seems to be with the Europeans in China, and already even in Japan: there is no necessity to recall how it was with the Spaniards in South America. In all these cases, the government to which these private adventurers are subject is better than they, and does the most it can to protect the natives against them. Even the Spanish government did this, sincerely and earnestly, though ineffectually, as is known to every reader of Mr. Helps' instructive history. Had the Spanish government been directly accountable to Spanish opinion, we may question if it would have made the attempt, for the Spaniards, doubtless, would have taken part with their Christian friends and relations rather than with pagans. The settlers, not the natives, have the ear of the public at home; it is they whose representations are likely to pass for truth, because they alone have both the means and the motive to press them perseveringly upon the inattentive and uninterested public mind. The distrustful criticism with which Englishmen, more than any other people, are in the habit of scanning the conduct of their country toward foreigners, they usually reserve for the proceedings of the public authorities. In all questions between a government and an individual, the presumption in every Englishman's mind is that the government is in the wrong. And when the resident English bring the batteries of English political action to bear upon any of the bulwarks erected to protect the natives against their encroachments, the executive, with their real but faint velleities of something better, generally find it safer to their Parliamentary interest, and, at any rate, less troublesome, to give up the disputed position than to defend it.

What makes matters worse is that, when the public mind is invoked (as, to its credit, the English mind is extremely open to be) in the name of justice and philanthropy in behalf of the subject community or race, there is the same probability of its missing the mark; for in the subject community also there are oppressors and oppressed—powerful individuals or classes, and slaves prostrate before them; and it is the former, not the latter, who have the means of access to the English public. A tyrant or sensualist who has been deprived of the power he had abused, and, instead of punishment, is supported in as great wealth and splendor as he ever enjoyed; a knot of privileged landholders, who demand that the state should relinquish to them its reserved right to a rent from their lands, or who resent as a wrong any attempt to protect the masses from their extortion—these have no difficulty in procuring interested or sentimental advocacy in the British Parliament and press. The silent myriads obtain none.

The preceding observations exemplify the operation of a principle—which might be called an obvious one, were it not that scarcely any body seems to be aware of it—that, while responsibility to the governed is the greatest of all securities for good government, responsibility to somebody else not only has no such tendency, but is as likely to produce evil as good. The responsibility of the British rulers of India to the British nation is chiefly useful because, when any acts of the government are called in question, it insures publicity and discussion; the utility of which does not require that the public at large should comprehend the point at issue, provided there are any individuals among them who do; for a merely moral responsibility not being responsibility to the collective people, but to every separate person among them who forms a judgment, opinions may be weighed as well as counted, and the approbation or disapprobation of one person well versed in the subject may outweigh that of thousands who know nothing about it at all.

It is doubtless a useful restraint upon the immediate rulers that they can be put upon their defense, and that one or two of the jury will form an opinion worth having about their conduct, though that of the remainder will probably be several degrees worse than none. Such as it is, this is the amount of benefit to India from the control exercised over the Indian government by the British Parliament and people.

It is not by attempting to rule directly a country like India, but by giving it good rulers, that the English people can do their duty to that country; and they can scarcely give it a worse one than an English cabinet minister, who is thinking of English, not Indian politics; who does not remain long enough in office to acquire an intelligent interest in so complicated a subject; upon whom the factitious public opinion got up in Parliament, consisting of two or three fluent speakers, acts with as much force as if it were genuine; while he is under none of the influences of training and position which would lead or qualify him to form an honest opinion of his own. A free country which attempts to govern a distant dependency, inhabited by a dissimilar people, by means of a branch of its own executive, will almost inevitably fail. The only mode which has any chance of tolerable success is to govern through a delegated body of a comparatively permanent character, allowing only a right of inspection and a negative voice to the changeable administration of the state. Such a body did exist in the case of India; and I fear that both India and England will pay a severe penalty for

the shortsighted policy by which this intermediate instrument of government was done away with.

It is of no avail to say that such a delegated body
can not have all the requisites of good government;
above all, can not have that complete and over-opera-
tive identity of interest with the governed which it is
so difficult to obtain even where the people to be ruled
are in some degree qualified to look after their own
affairs. Real good government is not compatible with
the conditions of the case. There is but a choice of
imperfections. The problem is, so to construct the
governing body that, under the difficulties of the position, it shall have as much interest as possible in
good government, and as little in bad. Now these
conditions are best found in an intermediate body. A
delegated administration has always this advantage
over a direct one, that it has, at all events, no duties
to perform except to the governed. It has no interests to consider except theirs. Its own power of deriving profit from misgovernment may be reduced—
in the latest Constitution of the East India Company
it was reduced—to a singularly small amount; and it
can be kept entirely clear of bias from the individual
or class interests of any one else. When the home
government and Parliament are swayed by such partial influences in the exercise of the power reserved
to them in the last resort, the intermediate body is the
certain advocate and champion of the dependency before the imperial tribunal. The intermediate body,
moreover, is, in the natural course of things, chiefly
composed of persons who have acquired professional

knowledge of this part of their country's concerns; who have been trained to it in the place itself, and have made its administration the main occupation of their lives. Furnished with these qualifications, and not being liable to lose their office from the accidents of home politics, they identify their character and consideration with their special trust, and have a much more permanent interest in the success of their administration, and in the prosperity of the country which they administer, than a member of a cabinet under a representative constitution can possibly have in the good government of any country except the one which he serves. So far as the choice of those who carry on the management on the spot devolves upon this body, their appointment is kept out of the vortex of party and Parliamentary jobbing, and freed from the influence of those motives to the abuse of patronage for the reward of adherents, or to buy off those who would otherwise be opponents, which are always stronger with statesmen of average honesty than a conscientious sense of the duty of appointing the fittest man. To put this one class of appointments as far as possible out of harm's way is of more consequence than the worst which can happen to all other offices in the state; for, in every other department, if the officer is unqualified, the general opinion of the community directs him in a certain degree what to do; but in the position of the administrators of a dependency where the people are not fit to have the control in their own hands, the character of the government entirely depends on the qualifications, moral and intellectual, of the individual functionaries.

It can not be too often repeated that, in a country like India, every thing depends on the personal qualities and capacities of the agents of government. This truth is the cardinal principle of Indian administration. The day when it comes to be thought that the appointment of persons to situations of trust from motives of convenience, already so criminal in England, can be practiced with impunity in India, will be the beginning of the decline and fall of our empire there. Even with a sincere intention of preferring the best candidate, it will not do to rely on chance for supplying fit persons. The system must be calculated to form them. It has done this hitherto; and because it has done so, our rule in India has lasted, and been one of constant, if not very rapid improvement in prosperity and good administration. As much bitterness is now manifested against this system, and as much eagerness displayed to overthrow it, as if educating and training the officers of government for their work were a thing utterly unreasonable and indefensible, an unjustifiable interference with the rights of ignorance and inexperience. There is a tacit conspiracy between those who would like to job in first-rate Indian offices for their connections here, and those who, being already in India, claim to be promoted from the indigo factory or the attorney's office to administer justice or fix the payments due to government from millions of people. The "monopoly" of the civil service, so much inveighed against, is like the monopoly of judicial offices by the bar; and its abolition would be like opening the bench in Westminster Hall to the first comer whose friends certify that he has now and then look- ed into Blackstone. Were the course ever adopted of sending men from this country, or encouraging them in going out, to get themselves put into high appointments without having learned their business by passing through the lower ones, the most important offices would be thrown to Scotch cousins and adven- turers, connected by no professional feeling with the country or the work, held to no previous knowledge, and eager only to make money rapidly and return home. The safety of the country is, that those by whom it is administered are sent out in youth, as can- didates only, to begin at the bottom of the ladder, and ascend higher or not, as, after a proper interval, they are proved qualified. The defect of the East India Company's system was that, though the best men were carefully sought out for the most important posts, yet, if an officer remained in the service, pro- motion, though it might be delayed, came at last in some shape or other, to the least as well as to the most competent. Even the inferior in qualifications among such a corps of functionaries consisted, it must be re- membered, of men who had been brought up to their duties, and had fulfilled them for many years, at low- est without disgrace, under the eye and authority of a superior. But, though this diminished the evil, it was nevertheless considerable. A man who never becomes fit for more than an assistant's duty should remain an assistant all his life, and his juniors should be promoted over him. With this exception, I am

аոt aware of any real defect in the old system of Indian appointments. It had already received the greatest other improvement it was susceptible of, the choice
of the original candidates by competitive examination, which, besides the advantage of recruiting from
a higher grade of industry and capacity, has the rec-
ommendation that under it, unless by accident, there
are no personal ties between the candidates for offices and those who have a voice in conferring them.

It is in no way unjust that public officers thus selected and trained should be exclusively eligible to
offices which require specially Indian knowledge and
experience. If any door to the higher appointments,
without passing through the lower, be opened even
for occasional use, there will be such incessant knocking at it by persons of influence that it will be impossible ever to keep it closed. The only excepted appointment should be the highest one of all. The
Viceroy of British India should be a person selected
from all Englishmen for his great general capacity for
government. If he have this, he will be able to distinguish in others, and turn to his own use, that special knowledge and judgment in local affairs which
he has not himself had the opportunity of acquiring.
There are good reasons why the viceroy should not
be a member of the regular service. All services
have, more or less, their class prejudices, from which
the supreme ruler ought to be exempt. Neither are
men, however able and experienced, who have passed
their lives in Asia, so likely to possess the most advanced European ideas in general statesmanship, which

the chief ruler should carry out with him, and blend
with the results of Indian experience. Again, being
of a different class, and especially if chosen by a different authority, he will seldom have any personal
partialities to warp his appointments to office. This
great security for honest bestowal of patronage existed in rare perfection under the mixed government of
the crown and the East India Company. The supreme dispensers of office—the governor general and
governors—were appointed, in fact though not formally, by the crown, that is, by the general government,
not by the intermediate body, and a great officer of the
crown probably had not a single personal or political
connection in the local service, while the delegated
body, most of whom had themselves served in the
country, had, and were likely to have, such connections. This guaranty for impartiality would be much
impaired if the civil servants of government, even
though sent out in boyhood as mere candidates for
employment, should come to be furnished, in any considerable proportion, by the class of society which
supplies viceroys and governors. Even the initiatory competitive examination would then be an insufficient security. It would exclude mere ignorance and
incapacity; it would compel youths of family to start
in the race with the same amount of instruction and
ability as other people; the stupidest son could not
be put into the Indian service, as he can be into the
Church; but there would be nothing to prevent undue preference afterward. No longer, all equally unknown and unheard of by the arbiter of their lot, a

portion of the service would be personally, and a still greater number politically, in close relation with him. Members of certain families, and of the higher classes and influential connections generally, would rise more rapidly than their competitors, and be often kept in situations for which they were unfit, or placed in those for which others were fitter. The same influences would be brought into play which affect promotions in the army; and those alone, if such miracles of simplicity there be, who believe that these are impartial, would expect impartiality in those of India. This evil is, I fear, irremediable by any general measures which can be taken under the present system. No such will afford a degree of security comparable to that which once flowed spontaneously from the so-called double government.

What is accounted so great an advantage in the case of the English system of government at home has been its misfortune in India—that it grew up of itself, not from preconceived design, but by successive expedients, and by the adaptation of machinery originally created for a different purpose. As the country on which its maintenance depended was not the one out of whose necessities it grew, its practical benefits did not come home to the mind of that country, and it would have required theoretic recommendations to render it acceptable. Unfortunately, these were exactly what it seemed to be destitute of; and undoubtedly the common theories of government did not furnish it with such, framed as those theories have been for states of circumstances differing in all the most important features from the case concerned. But in government as in other departments of human agency, almost all principles which have been durable were first suggested by observation of some particular case, in which the general laws of nature acted in some new or previously unnoticed combination of circumstances. The institutions of Great Britain, and those of the United States, have had the distinction of suggesting most of the theories of government which, through good and evil fortune, are now, in the course of generations, reawakening political life in the nations of Europe. It has been the destiny of the government of the East India Company to suggest the true theory of the government of a semi-barbarous dependency by a civilized country, and after having done this, to perish. It would be a singular fortune if, at the end of two or three more generations, this speculative result should be the only remaining fruit of our ascendency in India; if posterity should say of us that, having stumbled accidentally upon better arrangements than our wisdom would ever have devised, the first use we made of our awakened reason was to destroy them, and allow the good which had been in course of being realized to fall through and be lost from ignorance of the principles on which it depended. *Di meliora ;* but if a fate so disgraceful to England and to civilization can be averted, it must be through far wider political conceptions than merely English or European practice can supply, and through a much more profound study of Indian experience and of the conditions of Indian government than either English politicians, or those who supply the English public with opinions, have hitherto shown any willingness to undertake.

THE END.

ORDER FORM

GREAT BOOKS IN PHILOSOPHY PAPERBACK SERIES

ETHICS

Aristotle—*The Nicomachean Ethics*	$7.95
Jeremy Bentham—*The Principles of Morals and Legislation*	7.95
Immanuel Kant—*The Fundamental Principles of the Metaphysic of Morals*	4.95
John Stuart Mill—*Utilitarianism*	4.95
George Edward Moore—*Principia Ethica*	7.95
Friedrich Nietzsche—*Beyond Good and Evil*	6.95
Bertrand Russell—*On Ethics, Sex, and Marriage* (edited by Al Seckel)	16.95
Benedict de Spinoza—*Ethics* and *The Improvement of the Understanding*	8.95

SOCIAL AND POLITICAL PHILOSOPHY

Aristotle—*The Politics*	6.95
Edmund Burke—*Reflections on the Revolution in France*	6.95
John Dewey—*Freedom and Culture*	9.95
G.W.F. Hegel—*The Philosophy of History*	8.95
Thomas Hobbes—*The Leviathan*	6.95
Sidney Hook—*Paradoxes of Freedom*	8.95
Sidney Hook—*Reason, Social Myths, and Democracy*	10.95
John Locke—*Second Treatise on Civil Government*	4.95
Niccolo Machiavelli—*The Prince*	4.95
Karl Marx/Frederick Engels—*The Economic and Philosophic Manuscripts of 1844* and *The Communist Manifesto*	5.95
John Stuart Mill—*Considerations on Representative Government*	6.95
John Stuart Mill—*On Liberty*	4.95
John Stuart Mill—*On Socialism*	6.95
John Stuart Mill—*The Subjection of Women*	4.95
Thomas Paine—*Rights of Man*	6.95
Plato—*The Republic*	7.95
Plato on Homosexuality: Lysis, Phaedrus, and *Symposium*	5.95
Jean-Jacques Rousseau—*The Social Contract*	5.95
Mary Wollstonecraft—*A Vindication of the Rights of Women*	5.95

METAPHYSICS/EPISTEMOLOGY

Aristotle—*De Anima*	5.95
Aristotle—*The Metaphysics*	8.95
George Berkeley—*Three Dialogues Between Hylas and Philonous*	4.95
René Descartes—*Discourse on Method* and *The Meditations*	5.95
David Hume—*An Enquiry Concerning Human Understanding*	4.95
William James—*Pragmatism*	6.95
Immanuel Kant—*Critique of Pure Reason*	7.95
Plato—*The Euthyphro, Apology, Crito,* and *Phaedo*	4.95
Bertrand Russell—*The Problems of Philosophy*	7.95
Sextus Empiricus—*Outlines of Pyrrhonism*	7.95

PHILOSOPHY OF RELIGION

Ludwig Feuerbach—*The Essence of Christianity*	7.95
David Hume—*Dialogues Concerning Natural Religion*	4.95
John Locke—*A Letter Concerning Toleration*	3.95
Thomas Paine—*The Age of Reason*	12.95
Bertrand Russell—*On God and Religion* (edited by Al Seckel)	16.95

GREAT MINDS PAPERBACK SERIES

Charles Darwin—*The Origin of Species*	9.95
Edward Gibbon—*On Christianity*	8.95

SPECIAL—For your library . . . the entire collection of 42 "Great Books in Philosophy" available at a savings of more than 15%. Only $250.00 (plus $9.00 postage and handling). Please indicate "Great Books—Complete Set" on your order form.

The books listed can be obtained from your book dealer or directly from Prometheus Books. Please indicate the appropriate books. Remittance must accompany all orders from individuals. Please include $3.00 postage and handling for the first book and $1.50 for each additional title (maximum $9.00. NYS residents please add applicable sales tax.) **Prices subject to change without notice.**

Send to _____
                    Please type or print clearly)

Address _____

City _____ State _____ Zip _____

                                    Amount enclosed _____

Charge my   ☐ **VISA**   ☐ **MasterCard**

Account # ☐☐☐☐☐☐☐☐☐☐☐☐☐☐☐☐☐☐

Exp. Date _____/_____ Tel.# _____

Signature _____

Prometheus Books Editorial Offices
700 E. Amherst St., Buffalo, New York 14215

Distribution Facilities
59 John Glenn Drive, Amherst, New York 14228

Phone Orders call toll free: (800) 421-0351
FAX: (716) 691-0137
Please allow 3-6 weeks for delivery